Our COMMONWEALTH

PEOPLE & PLACES OF VIRGINIA

Our COMMONWEALTH

PEOPLE & PLACES OF VIRGINIA

Andrew Talkov

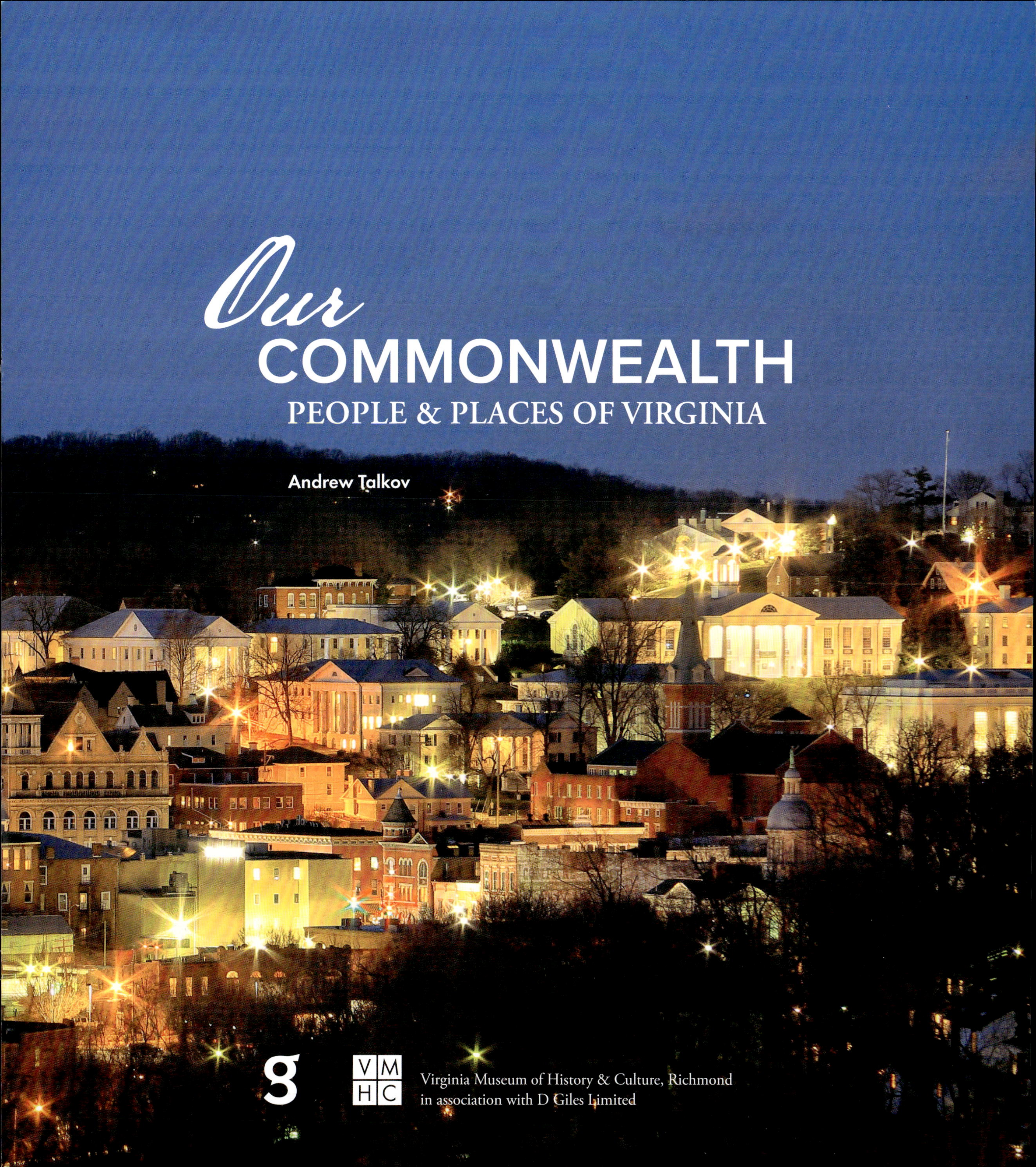

Virginia Museum of History & Culture, Richmond
in association with D Giles Limited

***Winter Wonder*, 2022**
Sharon Fisher (photographer)
Courtesy of Scenic Virginia

First published jointly in 2024 by GILES
An imprint of D Giles Limited
66 High Street,
Lewes, BN7 1XG, UK
gilesltd.com

ISBN: 978-1-913875-34-3

For D Giles Limited:
Copy-edited and proofread by Jenny Wilson
Designed by Ocky Murray
Printed and bound in China

Front cover: (top) Virginia State Capitol, Joe Daniel Price / Getty Images; (bottom, left to right) Ella Fitzgerald, VMHC Collection; George Washington, after 1787, James Peale (artist), VMHC Collection; Chief Anne Richardson, 2013, Rod Lamkey (photographer); Just Veliz Valdez, 2010, Glen McClure (photographer), Courtesy of Glen McClure; Adèle Clark, 1915, VMHC Collection

Back cover: Sunlight streaming through clouds over the Shenandoah Valley, 2013, Nick Roush / Cavan Images; Assateague Island at sunset, 2017, Cyndi Monaghan / Getty Images

Frontispiece: Staunton skyline, 2019, Pat & Chuck Blackley / Alamy Stock Photo

CONTENTS

FOREWORD

The Virginia Museum of History & Culture was founded in 1831 as the Virginia Historical Society. Older than the Smithsonian Institution and half the states of our nation, this organization has devoted nearly two centuries to collecting and preserving the artifacts and archives of the Commonwealth's past to share its own extensive, consequential story as well as its far-reaching and outsized influence on our American journey.

What began as a modest and traditional history organization—one of the first of its kind—has blossomed into a national leader in the museum field, a vast resource that informs an ever-growing body of original research in Virginia history, and a source of pride and learning for many Virginians. The VMHC's headquarters building in the state capital now covers nearly a quarter-million square feet, housing an historical collection of more than nine million items and welcoming hundreds of thousands of guests.

The core preservation and education mission of this special place has changed little over the years. However, its vision and values have grown and adapted considerably. In the past decade, its growth and progress have been largely empowered by a sincere and strategic focus on public engagement and an entirely new level of institutional vibrancy and activity.

Following the most extensive renovation and reimagination in the museum's history, the VMHC has emerged as not only a home for compelling history, but a place of convening. Buoyed by new and developing relationships in its community and across the Commonwealth, the VMHC has embraced its responsibility to better welcome and represent the experiences of all Virginians. At its grand reopening in May of 2022, the VMHC looked different, in many ways, because it is different—a thoughtfully evolved version of itself that has carried forward its many strengths while adding profoundly to the ways it serves Virginians.

Our Commonwealth, one of the marquee exhibitions produced as part of this reimagination, is a genuine demonstration of the VMHC's desire to reflect the people of this unique state and to connect with them in a meaningful way. *Our Commonwealth*—a stirring, and often personal, story about people and the place they call home—shines a fresh light on what makes living in Virginia and its various regions so special. *Our Commonwealth* adds to the tapestry of the VMHC's storytelling and deeply enriches the experience of visiting this museum. We hope this companion book will similarly enrich your home, rekindle memories you cherish, and foster the Virginia stories you share.

Jamie O. Bosket
President & CEO, Virginia Museum of History & Culture

ACKNOWLEDGMENTS

This book is the product of a dedicated and talented community of people who came together to share these remarkable stories.

The desire to explore Virginia in a new and meaningful way via its distinct regions emerged from a three-year effort to reimagine the guest experience at the Virginia Museum of History & Culture and help people connect the past to the present. *Our Commonwealth* was the signature exhibition of that effort and is at the heart of this companion book. This long-term exhibition was presented by TowneBank. It was also generously sponsored by General & Mrs. John P. Jumper, The Mars Family, Mr. and Mrs. Gerald F. Smith, Jr., and Melanie Trent De Schutter and the Melanie Trent Family Foundation. Thoughtful support was also received from the American Electric Power Foundation, Mr. and Mrs. William C. Davis, Mr. and Mrs. W. Heywood Fralin, and Mr. and Mrs. William H. Fralin, Jr.

For more than two years, a remarkable team at the VMHC dedicated themselves to conceiving, researching, and writing *Our Commonwealth*. Many of the ideas and words in this volume are theirs. With gratitude, we recognize VMHC colleagues Maggie Creech, Director of Education; Hailey Fenner, Manager of Multimedia Production; Dale Kostelny, Manager of Exhibition Production; L. Paige Newman, Curator; Rebecca Rose, Director of Museum Collections; Adam Scher, Lisa & Bill Moore Vice President for Collections & Exhibitions; Dr. Karen Sherry, Sr. Curator; and our former colleagues Veronica Blanco, Exhibition Technician; Dr. William M.S. Rasmussen, Sr. Curator of Exhibitions and Lora M. Robins Curator of Art; and Catherine Stergar, Associate Curator.

To better understand the distinct culture of each region, we sought guidance from cultural institutions and museums across Virginia. They generously offered their expertise, their collections, and the relationships they have built with their communities to help us share their stories. Many thanks to the staff at the Blue Ridge Institute & Museum (Ferrum), the Eastern Shore of Virginia Historical Society (Onancock), the Fredericksburg Area Museum, the Lynchburg Museum, the Manassas Museum, The Mariners' Museum and Park (Newport News), the Museum of the Shenandoah Valley (Winchester), the Office of Historic Alexandria, the Rockbridge Historical Society, and the William King Museum of Art (Abingdon).

The organization, graphic design, and many of the stories included here were developed in partnership with the creative team at The PRD Group. They helped us transform *Our Commonwealth* from a one-page idea into an engaging exhibition that truly evokes the diverse histories, cultures, and beauty of Virginia. Thank you to Dan Murphy and Philip Brady, principals; Mary Marvell, graphic designer; and Ashley Hinkle, exhibition designer. We are particularly grateful to Kim Nelson, principal, whose coordination, research, creativity, and prose were essential to the success of this project.

Likewise, the team at Donna Lawrence Productions introduced us to many compelling stories and beautiful images from across the Commonwealth that were incorporated into audiovisual programs throughout the exhibition. Many of those found their way into this publication. We are lucky to have been able to work with Donna Lawrence, principal; Lynn Birkett, Studio Managing Producer and Senior Producer; Robert Cassetti, Creative Strategist; and Cindy Kittner, Senior Producer.

Many of our other VMHC colleagues contributed directly to this effort and include Heather Beattie, Collections Manager; Dr. James Brookes, Melanie Trent De Schutter Library Director; Bryan Condra, Exhibition Designer; Graham Dozier, Publications Managing Editor; Danni Flakes, Photographer & Digital Asset Specialist; Sam Florer, Manager of Public Programs; Andrew Foster, Collections Management Assistant; and Stacy Rusch, Senior Conservator. The beautiful maps in this volume were designed by Karen Polesky.

Transforming *Our Commonwealth* into this lasting work was a major undertaking. Although many of the themes and specific stories were identified in the exhibition-building process, the creation of a meaningful companion book required a much deeper dive. Andrew Talkov, Sr. Director of Curatorial Affairs, took on this work and, like everything he has done in his sixteen years at the museum, he demonstrated his immense historical knowledge, his talent as a writer, his dedication to the mission of the VMHC, and his great passion and humanity. He devoted months of effort to bringing this book together, which meant time distracted from his "day job" and his family. We sincerely offer our thanks to his wife, Sara, and his parents, Joan and Lenny, for their continuous support. We thank Andy for making this book possible, and for all his exceptional contributions to the growth and progress of the VMHC.

Lastly, we are truly grateful to the many Virginians who allowed us to include them in this book. We are honored to help share their stories and their meaningful contributions to our Commonwealth. Thank you.

Jamie O. Bosket
President & CEO, Virginia Museum of History & Culture

INTRODUCTION

What we know of as Virginia has evolved over centuries from the intersections of geography, people, and events. Its dramatic natural diversity—from seashore to mountains—has attracted and sustained an equally diverse population. Indigenous peoples; Anglo-European settlers; enslaved Africans, and their descendants; and subsequent waves of immigrants from around the globe have made Virginia home. Their stories and experiences have made Virginia, Virginia.

This book explores how the forces of people, place, and history have created five distinctive regions of the Commonwealth: Tidewater, Northern Virginia (NoVA), Central Virginia, the Shenandoah Valley, and Southwest Virginia.

Water defines the eastern boundaries of Virginia and shapes the lives of the people who live in the Tidewater region—where rivers and their tributaries rise and fall with the tides as they join the Chesapeake Bay and the Atlantic Ocean. These waterways connect Virginia to the interior of the continent and to the world beyond. Long the homeland of thriving Indigenous civilizations, Tidewater was where England established its first permanent colony in North America and forcibly brought the first enslaved West Africans to these shores. Although the interaction between European, Native, and African peoples was often marked by violence, their respective cultural traditions intermingled to create a unique American culture of foodways, music, trades, and other forms of expression. Water has also profoundly influenced the communities living along Tidewater's shores. Virginians in this region have long harvested, processed, and shared the bounty of marine life found in its waters. Maritime life influenced the development of specialized watercraft to navigate these waters and established Tidewater as a shipbuilding center for centuries, from early Indigenous canoes to modern aircraft carriers. Benefiting from easy access to the Atlantic Ocean (and beyond) has made Tidewater a strategic hub for international commerce and national military bases. Having always provided sustenance and work, the water has also been a source of recreation and artistic inspiration in the Tidewater region.

Northern Virginia is a region of extremes, where today the traffic congestion and suburban sprawl around Washington, D.C., give way to beautiful rolling hills in its more rural counties. It is proximity to the nation's capital that has defined life here. When the new United States established the District of Columbia in 1790, the surrounding area began its transformation from a rural, agrarian region to a metropolitan one. World War II was a major catalyst for this transformation as the growth of the military, government agencies and contractors, and later technology companies, brought an influx of workers and their families to the region. The demand for skilled labor and increased opportunities attract people from across the country and the globe—making Northern Virginia one of the most diverse parts of the Commonwealth, where more than a hundred languages can be heard along its streets. Throughout the region, old Virginia traditions—such as breeding horses—and cultural festivals from around the world are frequently shared and sometimes adapted into new traditions.

Central Virginia covers a large swathe of the state, from where Tidewater's coastal plain ends in the east to the Blue Ridge Mountains to the west. Here, the many rivers, fertile plains, and rolling hills—known also as the Piedmont—have long fostered agriculture and industry. The earliest Indigenous peoples planted corn, beans, and squash here. English colonists found the soil conducive to tobacco—a commodity that dominated Virginia's economy and fueled settlement across Central Virginia and the institutionalization of slavery. After the American Civil War, which ravaged the landscape of Central Virginia, new industries emerged and cities like Richmond, Fredericksburg, Lynchburg, and Danville expanded. Long an agricultural and economic powerhouse, this region also became Virginia's center of political influence after the state capital moved here from Williamsburg in 1782. Central Virginia has often been a gathering place where people can find like-minded individuals to celebrate their interests and cultures, or to rally together to have their voices heard.

Along Virginia's northwestern edge, the Shenandoah Valley region is bordered by the Blue Ridge Mountains to the east and the Allegheny Mountains to the west, with the fertile and beautiful valley in between. The Valley has long been a "highway" or conduit, first for Indigenous people and then for European settlers. Today's highways in the region continue along a similar path used by earlier travelers. The Valley has been a fertile land for agriculture and for cultural exchange. In the 1700s, English, German, and Scots-Irish people seeking new land and opportunities migrated into the region from more settled areas and brought their distinctive cultural traditions with them. Enslaved and free people of African descent also added to the region's cultural diversity. Today, immigrants from around the world continue to find a home in the Valley. In the heart of the Valley, Harrisonburg is among the most diverse communities in the state. For centuries, the natural beauty and bounty of the region have long drawn visitors and fueled a thriving tourism industry. People from all over come to enjoy breathtaking scenery, go hiking, explore caves, and relax at natural springs throughout the Shenandoah Valley.

The mountainous and rugged terrain of Southwest Virginia is connected to the larger Appalachian Mountain chain that extends from Canada to Alabama. Largely isolated until the railroads opened the region in the late 1800s, the people here have long been associated with self-sufficiency and resilience, as well as a distinctive Appalachian culture. The mountains and forests of the Southwest have driven its economy through the dangerous, though lucrative, extractive industries like coal and timber. As people settled here to work in the mines or the timber fields, European ballads blended with African American musical traditions to create a unique form of mountain music. Exported around the globe, "old time" music influenced the development of country music and continues to inspire musicians today. Perhaps the independent spirit of the people of Southwest Virginia is best illustrated by the region's famous resistance to Prohibition through the illegal production of moonshine and the rumrunners who started a car racing culture that evolved into NASCAR. Although the coal and timber industries have diminished, the region's rich culture, educational opportunities, and ecotourism attract people to the area.

The stories that follow exemplify some of the most distinctive characteristics of each of Virginia's unique and dynamic regions, which together form the rich cultural tapestry of our Commonwealth.

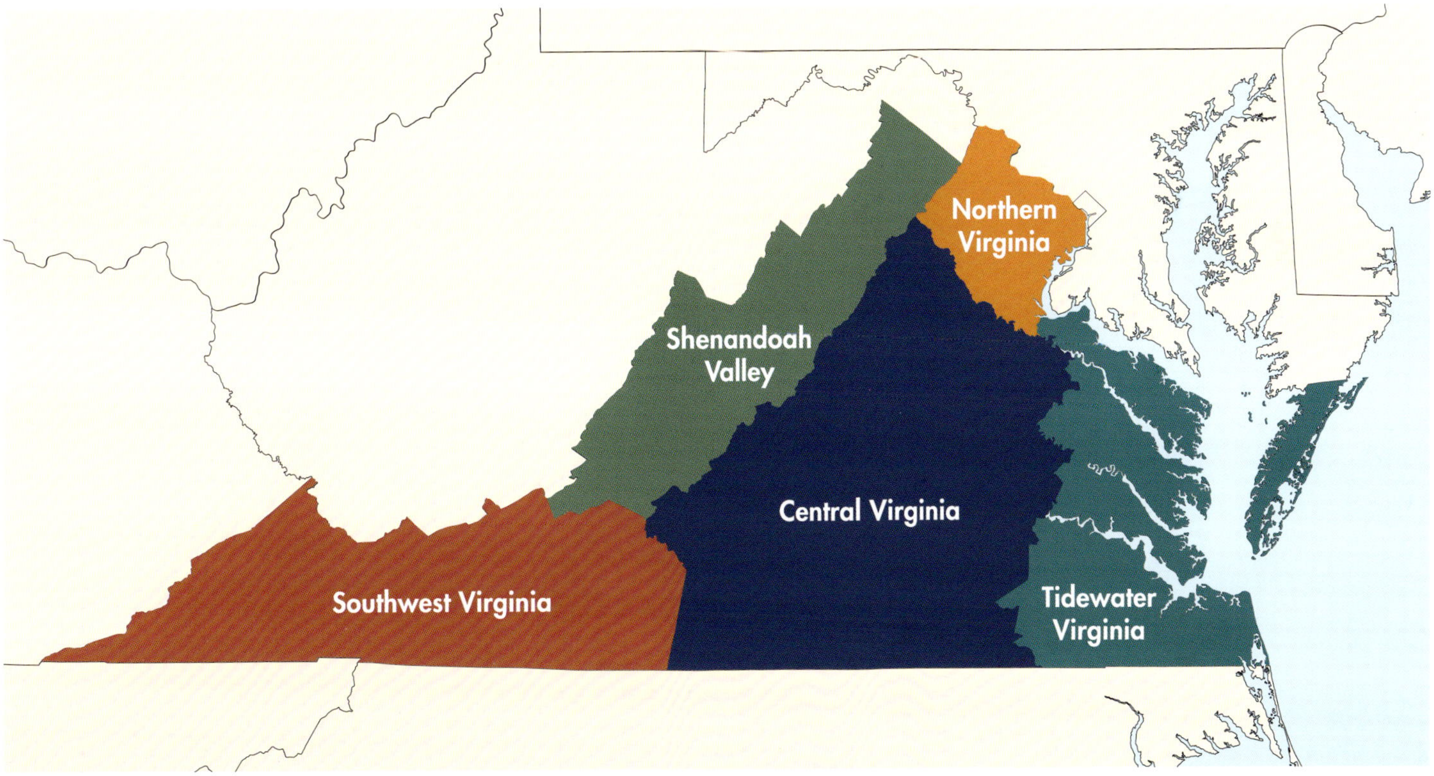

Tidewater VIRGINIA

Water defines the eastern parts of Virginia, known as the Tidewater. For centuries, Indigenous people lived and worked along the Atlantic coast, the Chesapeake Bay, and the region's many tidal creeks and rivers. By the early 1600s three cultures converged when English colonists established Jamestown in 1607, and enslaved Africans were forcibly brought there in 1619.

For more than 400 years, the same waterways have continued to provide opportunities for work, sustenance, and recreation. Communities have established regional traditions shaped by the offerings that these unique aquatic ecosystems provide.

Assateague Island at sunset, 2017
Cyndi Monaghan / Getty Images

Bald cypress in Lake Drummond, Great Dismal Swamp National Wildlife Refuge, 2006
Rebecca Wynn (photographer)
U.S. Fish & Wildlife Service

In 1732, while surveying the boundary line between Virginia and North Carolina, William Byrd II (1674–1744) described the one-million-acre swamp he encountered as a "vast body of mire and nastiness." For centuries, enslaved people came to the swamp, seeking freedom. For some, it was part of their journey northward, but others remained in hidden communities that existed until after the Civil War. Today, 113,000 acres of the swamp are preserved by the U.S. Fish and Wildlife Service.

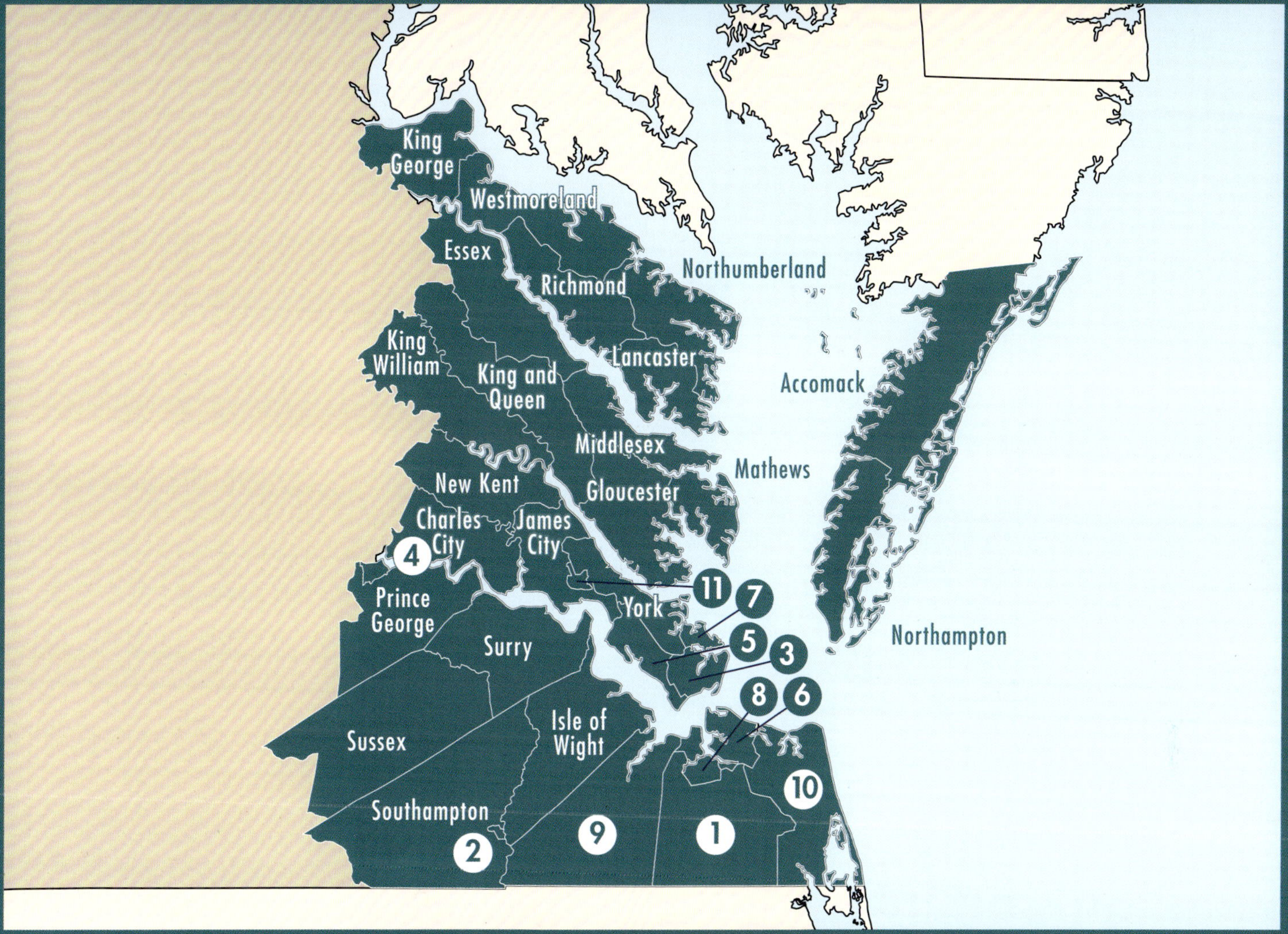

Tidewater Virginia Independent Cities

1. Chesapeake
2. Franklin
3. Hampton
4. Hopewell
5. Newport News
6. Norfolk
7. Poquoson
8. Portsmouth
9. Suffolk
10. Virginia Beach
11. Williamsburg

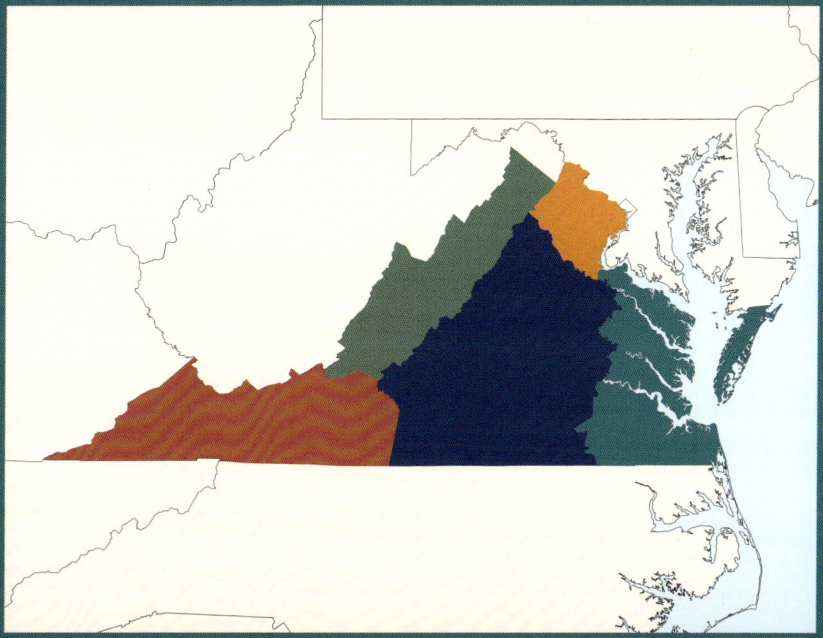

Virginia is the only state in the country in which incorporated cities are politically and administratively independent from their neighboring counties. This tradition began in 1722 with the incorporation of Williamsburg, Virginia's first city. Today there are thirty-eight incorporated cities in the Commonwealth.

BUILDING BOATS

Waterways have always provided critical travel routes in Tidewater, fostering the active adaptation of watercraft. Indigenous boatbuilders first hollowed out tree trunks for transportation and fishing. Over time, specialized boat designs have evolved to meet local commercial fishing needs and to navigate the regional waterways. Today, Tidewater's shores boast a mix of boat styles, from deadrises to kayaks, adapted to the region's many water-based jobs and activities.

***Lintrium conficiendorum ratio* (*A Method of Making Canoes*), about 1590**

Theodor de Bry (engraver) after John White (artist)

From the collection of The Mariners' Museum and Park, Newport News, Virginia

Dugout canoes, made from a single log, were the primary watercraft used by the dozens of Indigenous tribes living in the region. Indigenous boatbuilders burned a slow fire on a log and repeatedly scraped out the resulting charcoal to create the canoe's shape. Well-adapted to Tidewater's rocky rivers and narrow streams, the dugout canoe was soon adopted by English colonists.

"Their boates are made of one tree, either of Pine, or of Pitch. . . . They have no edge tooles to make them . . . they sette fire into it, and when it hath burnt it hollowe, they cutte out the coale with their shels . . . and by this meanes they fashion very fine boates, and such as will transport twentie men."

Arthur Barlowe, member of Sir Walter Raleigh's expedition to Virginia, describing Indigenous boatbuilding, 1584

A Typical Crab Dock at Sunnybank, Va., about 1940

Harriet Frye (artist)

From the collection of The Mariners' Museum and Park, Newport News, Virginia

Author and illustrator Harriet Frye (1914–2013) lived in the Northern Neck and later Hampton with her family. Her images for children's books often depicted landscapes and fishing scenes in the area. In the background of this watercolor, a soft-crabbing skiff is being used to catch crabs that have shed their shells—considered a delicacy. Flat-bottomed skiffs were often made locally and can easily be maneuvered through shallow waters. They are typically powered by pushing the boat with a pole or the long handle of a net along the bottom of the water.

Patricia Ann deadrise model, about 1998

Curt E. Shields (maker)

From the collection of The Mariners' Museum and Park, Newport News, Virginia

One of the primary vessels used by watermen throughout the region, the Chesapeake deadrise (a term describing the underwater shape of the hull) can be rigged with nets, dredges, or pots for different types of fishing. This model represents a setup for dredging clams. Its high, sharp bow cleaves through choppy waters, and its flat bottom provides greater stability on the Chesapeake Bay and its rivers. The Chesapeake deadrise is the official state boat of Virginia.

George M. Butler in his Reedville boat shop, 2006

Morgan Miller / Virginia Humanities

Reedville—a commercial fishing town on Virginia's Northern Neck—boasts a proud history of boatbuilders. From the 1920s, the Butler family owned and operated the Reedville Marine Railway. George M. Butler (b. 1952) inherited the business in 1976, and for fifty years enhanced an institution started by his grandfather. Butler retired and sold the Railway in 2021 but vowed not to give up working on boats.

***Amber Leigh* and *Elizabeth Ashby* dredging for oysters near Tangier Island, 2018**

Jay Fleming (photographer)

Photograph by Jay Fleming

WORKING ON THE WATER

Many aquatic species abound in Tidewater's surf, estuaries, and rivers. Generations of watermen and women have harvested oysters, crabs, shad, duck, trout, and bass for their own tables and customers around the world. It is often dangerous and challenging work. Modern fishing focuses on sustainability to ensure that Tidewater species will be available for years to come.

Members of the Pamunkey Indian Tribe curing shad, 1941

Courtesy of *Richmond Times-Dispatch*

Shad has been a staple food of the Pamunkey Indian Tribe for centuries. Believing that if you take fish from the water, you should put some back, the Pamunkey established an indoor hatchery in 1918. During a few weeks every spring, shad eggs hatched in tanks and the young fish, known as fry, were allowed to grow for a few days before being released into the river. In the 21st century, commercial fishing, pollution, and dams blocking shad from their spawning grounds have threatened the shad population.

"[T]he thing that I grew up knowing and hearing about my whole life: shad, shad, shad, shad. . . . [We have an annual fish fry to] celebrate the end of the shad run [and] the fishermen and what they caught and how well our hatchery has done. So, shad has definitely been the biggest part of my life, [as] a part of this community."

Ashley Atkins Spivey, member of the Pamunkey Indian Tribe, 2018

Women picking crabs at the Samuel S. Coston Company, 1907
C.E. Cheyne (photographer)
From the collection of the Hampton History Museum, Cheyne Studio Collection

The Samuel S. Coston Company plant in Hampton could process three hundred bushels of crabs each day and started transporting fresh crab meat to as far away as Salt Lake City and Chicago in 1899. The crabmeat was meticulously picked from the shells by dozens of workers—most of whom were Black women.

Just Veliz Valdez at Graham & Rollins Seafood Co., 2010
Glen McClure (photographer)
Glen McClure

Valdez (b. 1983), his wife, and mother worked at Graham & Rollins Seafood Co. in Hampton. He handled steamer baskets full of crabs destined for pressure cookers on the wharf, and his wife and mother picked crabs. The family, originally from Mexico, are part of an industrywide trend that began in the late 1980s in which companies have hired increasing numbers of immigrant workers.

A waterman checks on a crab pot along the Chesapeake Bay, 2019
Aileen Devlin (photographer)
Virginia Sea Grant

BLUE CRABS

Blue crabs range from Nova Scotia to Argentina, but are often associated with the Chesapeake Bay. These crustaceans thrive in the brackish estuaries and salt marshes of Tidewater Virginia. Bay watermen and women trap blue crabs from late spring to early winter and take their catch to processing houses where workers pick the tender meat from the shells. Chesapeake blue crabs have a distinctively sweet, delicate flavor. They can be boiled or steamed, fried as soft shells (right after the crab molts), or made into cakes, soups, and dips.

"Mine Oyster—Dredging Boats in the Chesapeake," *Harper's Weekly*, 1872
William Ludwell Sheppard (artist);
John Dalziel (engraver)

VMHC Collection

This engraving shows how oysters were harvested in the late 1800s. The sail-powered dredging boat remains in place as oysters are scooped from the bottom of the Bay using tongs. The two boys (center) use hammers to split apart the oysters attached to rocks or one another.

Set of oyster tongs, about 1950–80
Unknown manufacturer

From the collection of The Mariners' Museum and Park, Newport News, Virginia, Gift of United Leasing Corporation

Hand tonging for oysters was once a way of life for thousands of watermen on the Chesapeake Bay. Known as "tongers," these fishermen dropped their tongs down to the river bottom and listened for the distinctive sound of metal against shell. Opening then closing the handles, they used the teeth to help break oysters loose from the reef. A muddy mass of oysters was then dumped into the boat and sorted. More efficient means of gathering oysters have since replaced hand tonging.

Capt. Fisher Oysters can, about 1970
Lance G. Fisher
Oyster Company

VMHC Collection

OYSTERS

Virginia's Indigenous people relied on oysters for sustenance, and this shellfish quickly became a staple of colonists' diets. Tidewater Virginia's unique mix of ocean and freshwater habitats yields oysters that are variably sweet, creamy, and salty. Beginning in the mid-1800s, canning allowed Virginia oysters to be packaged and transported to distant markets. Once on the brink of collapse, Virginia's oyster beds are rebounding thanks to conservation efforts by watermen, scientists, and environmentalists. In 2023, Virginia was the leading oyster producer on the East Coast.

Deborah Pratt (foreground) and Clementine Macon Boyd compete in oyster shucking competition, 2019
Pat Jarrett / Virginia Humanities

Sisters Deborah Pratt and Clementine Macon Boyd grew up in Middlesex County, where the oyster industry dominated the economy until the 1990s. Able to shuck two dozen oysters in less than three minutes, the sisters dominated oyster shucking contests from Virginia to Galway, Ireland. In 2021, they hung up their shucking knives to enjoy a well-earned retirement.

"Virginia and Maryland are the only two states that I can think of that open oysters from the lip. Most states further south always open from the hinge. A hinge shucker doesn't shuck a very beautiful oyster . . . shucking from the lip of the oyster has a beautiful clean-cut oyster."

Deborah Pratt, champion oyster shucker, 2013

Dudley Biddlecomb seeds the bottom of the Great Wicomico River with oyster shells, 2012
Pat Jarrett / Virginia Humanities

"Oysters help to purify the water, and the water quality is the key to everything we're doing, so the more oysters you have, the more water they can filter. And the more water you filter, the cleaner the bay and the rivers will be, and in my case, the more oysters will grow. So it's ecology and economy."

Dudley Biddlecomb, oysterman and ecologist, 2013

Miles Hancock carving duck decoys, 1960s
VMHC Collection, Gift of Hamilton Bryson

Miles Hancock (1887–1974) was a renowned Eastern Shore carver of decoys, which hunters place in the water to attract waterfowl. Inexpensive and serviceable, his decoys are distinguished by their broad, flat-bottomed body and flat, paddle-shaped tail.

"I am seventy years old and met Miles Hancock when I was about twelve. He was my friend and mentor. From the time I was a boy, I always wanted to be a decoy carver and hunting guide. I achieved that dream, in a large part thanks to him. I tried to pass on the things he taught me to anyone who wanted to learn. It is my way of repaying him."

Grayson Chesser, decoy carver and hunting guide in Accomack County, 2017

Mallard drake decoy, 2016
Grayson Chesser (maker)
From the collection of Parke Atkinson

Scaup or bluebill hen decoy, 1962–74
Miles Hancock (maker)
From the collection of the Eastern Shore of Virginia Historical Society

SHIPPING THROUGH PORTS

The rivers running to the Chesapeake Bay and the Atlantic Ocean connect Virginia to the world. For more than 400 years, Virginia's goods have shipped in and out of Tidewater ports. Early colonists traded tobacco, corn, wheat, pork, deer hides, and lumber across the ocean. Today, large container ports at Newport News, Portsmouth, and Norfolk—part of a maritime "superhighway" known as Hampton Roads—export raw materials like coal and grains and import items like coffee, cars, and electronics for Virginia and the country.

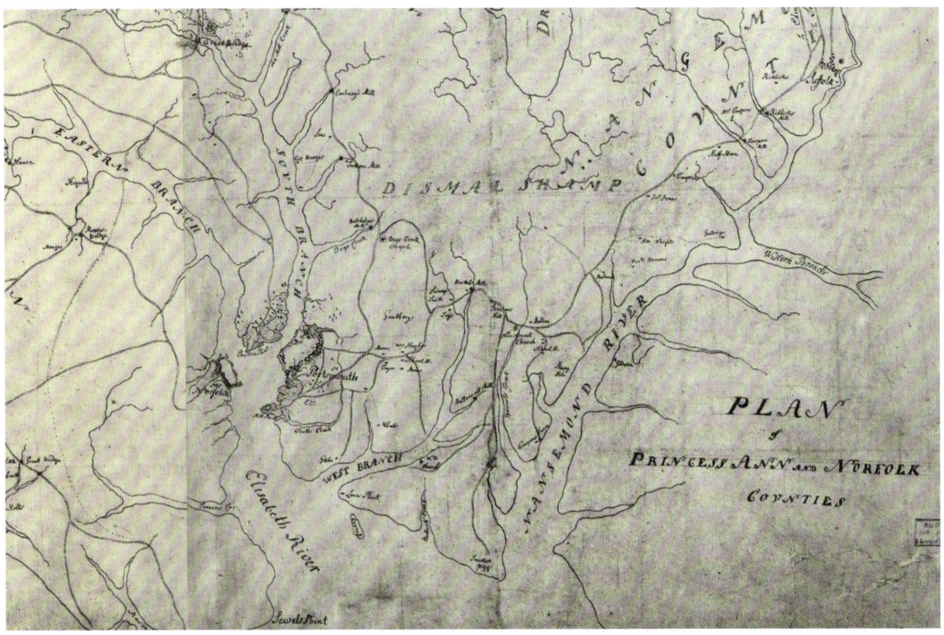

***Plan of Princess Ann and Norfolk Counties* (detail), about 1780**

Library of Congress, Geography and Map Division

In this map, the port of Norfolk is on the left bank of the Elizabeth River, and Portsmouth is on the right. The Norfolk Naval Shipyard (in Portsmouth) is the oldest naval shipyard in the United States. Known as the Gosport Shipyard when it was established in 1767, it served as the nucleus of the largest naval base in the world.

Cotton bales ready for shipment from Norfolk, early 1900s

H.C. Mann (photographer)

VMHC Collection, Gift of the Pennsylvania Historical Museum Commission

In February 1866, two railcar loads of cotton arrived in Norfolk from Georgia. In the following decades, Norfolk's port grew with the addition of new rail connections. By the early 1890s the cotton trade in Norfolk was booming and the city established itself as a major outlet for the nation's cotton belt.

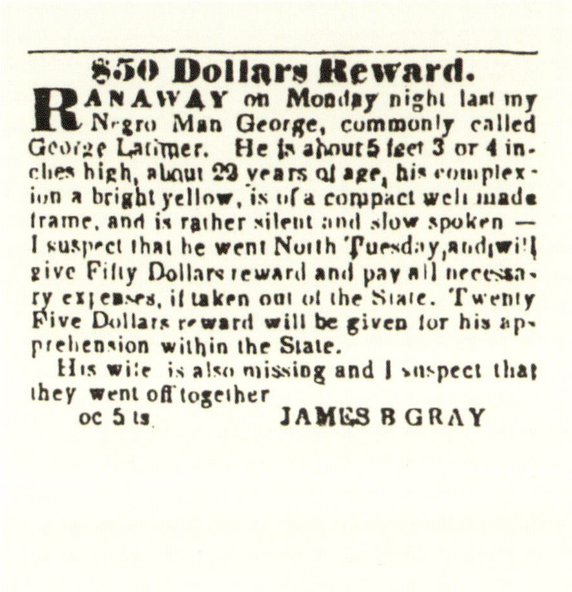

$50 Dollars Reward.

RANAWAY on Monday night last my Negro Man George, commonly called George Latimer. He is about 5 feet 3 or 4 inches high, about 22 years of age, his complexion a bright yellow, is of a compact well made frame, and is rather silent and slow spoken — I suspect that he went North Tuesday, and will give Fifty Dollars reward and pay all necessary expenses, if taken out of the State. Twenty Five Dollars reward will be given for his apprehension within the State.

His wife is also missing and I suspect that they went off together

oc 5 ts JAMES B GRAY

Advertisement from *The American Beacon* offering rewards for George and Rebecca Latimer, 1842

Courtesy of the Queens Borough Public Library, Archives, Lewis H. Latimer Papers

With its heavy shipping traffic and large workforce of Black seamen, the Hampton Roads region was an important hub on the maritime underground railroad. In 1842, George (1820–1896) and Rebecca Latimer (1822–1910) escaped slavery by stowing away on a ship docked in Norfolk. George was identified and arrested when they reached Massachusetts. A court battle ensued that fired up key abolitionists and helped solidify a Massachusetts law that protected self-emancipated people from being returned to slavery. Funds were raised to emancipate him.

"With my wife, also a slave, I secreted myself under the fore-peak of the vessel, we lying on stone ballast in the darkness for nine weary hours. As we lay concealed in the darkness we could peek through the cracks of the partition into the bar-room of the vessel, where men who would have gladly captured us were drinking."

George Latimer, self-emancipated enslaved person and abolitionist, 1894

CMA CGM *Marco Polo* departing from the Virginia International Gateway, 2021

Aerophoto America (photographer)

Virginia Port Authority

After World War II, the cities of Newport News, Portsmouth, and Norfolk each built a shipping terminal and competed for business. By the 1960s, new containers required expensive investments in cranes and the redesign of land-based facilities. The Virginia Port Authority acquired the three terminals and advertised a consolidated Port of Virginia. In 2022, the Port of Virginia was the sixth-largest port in the United States and handled 65,476,000 tons of cargo.

LAUNCHING THE FLEET

Since the 1700s, the sounds of shipbuilding have thumped along the Tidewater's shores. The region's forests and swamps provided ideal resources—oak, pitch, and tar—for ship construction. Shipbuilding in Britain had dwindled because of deforestation, so overseas merchants ordered Virginia-made ships stocked with local goods to sell. Skilled European shipwrights and carpenters immigrated to the region to fill the demand. World Wars I and II launched the transformation of the Newport News area into a powerhouse for turning out Navy troopships, cruisers, aircraft carriers, and submarines.

***Battle between the Monitor and the Merrimack*, about 1880**
Xanthus Smith (artist)
VMHC Collection, Purchased with funds provided by Lora M. Robins

As they evacuated Norfolk in April 1861, United States forces scuttled the USS *Merrimack*—then under repair at the Gosport Navy Yard. Recovered by the Confederates, it was converted into an ironclad ship. Renamed the CSS *Virginia* (far left), it destroyed two wooden-hulled U.S. warships at Hampton Roads in March 1862. The next day the United States' first ironclad, the USS *Monitor* (center), arrived and fought the *Virginia* to a draw. The battle revolutionized naval warfare by proving that wooden vessels were obsolete against ironclads.

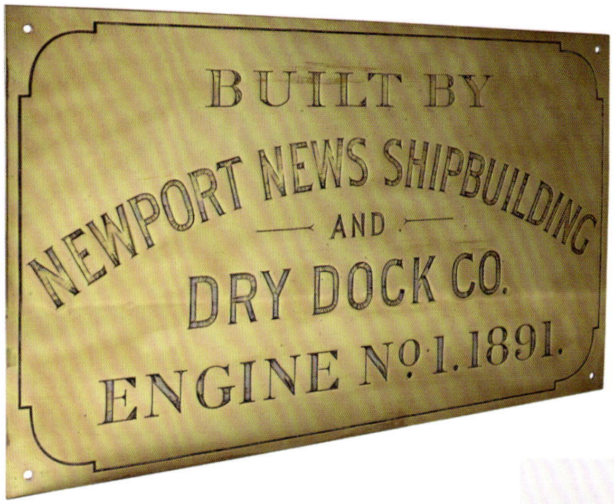

Builder's plate, 1891
Newport News Shipbuilding and Dry Dock Co.
From the collection of The Mariners' Museum and Park, Newport News, Virginia

The tugboat *Dorothy*, launched in 1891, was the first vessel constructed at Newport News Shipbuilding and Dry Dock Co. She was reputedly named in honor of the four-year-old daughter of William C. Whitney, Secretary of the Navy between 1885 and 1889.

Tugboat *Dorothy* at Newport News Shipbuilding and Dry Dock, undated
From the collection of The Mariners' Museum and Park, Newport News, Virginia

The USS *Delaware* secured in Drydock No. 1 at the Gosport Navy Yard, 1833–5
Joseph Goldsborough (artist); Childs & Mann (lithographer)
From the collection of The Mariners' Museum and Park, Newport News, Virginia

In 1833, when the USS *Delaware* entered the stone-lined drydock at Portsmouth's Gosport Navy Yard, it marked the first time a large ship was drydocked in the United States. Until that time, ships needed to undergo the difficult and time-consuming process of being turned onto their sides for repair. After nearly 200 years, Drydock No. 1 is still in use.

Propeller from the SS *United States*, 1957
Baldwin-Lima-Hamilton Corporation (manufacturer); Amanda Shields (photographer)
From the collection of The Mariners' Museum and Park, Newport News, Virginia

Built by Newport News Shipbuilding and Dry Dock Co. in 1950–2, the SS *United States* was the largest ocean liner constructed solely in the United States and the fastest ocean liner ever built. It was driven by four eighteen-foot-diameter propellers, each weighing over 63,000 pounds. Although it was popular for transatlantic travel—making the trip from New York to England in a record-breaking three-and-a-half days—the *United States* could also be converted into a troopship in times of war.

Riveting air hammer, about 1920
William H. Keller, Inc. (manufacturer)
From the collection of The Mariners' Museum and Park, Newport News, Virginia, Gift of Newport News Shipbuilding

Trying or jointer plane, about 1849–78
Thomas Ibbotson & Co. (blade manufacturer); D. Malloch (body manufacturer)
From the collection of The Mariners' Museum and Park, Newport News, Virginia, Gift of David Dick

Broad axe, about 1853–8
Horton & Arnold (manufacturer)
From the collection of The Mariners' Museum and Park, Newport News, Virginia, Gift of David Dick

Robert Murray Dick (1860–1941), an employee at Newport News Shipbuilding for a time, used this axe and trying plane in his work as a ship's carpenter.

Thelma Bendler Stern Neubauer, about 1942

VMHC Collection, Gift of Thelma S. Neubauer

Thelma Neubauer (1923–2015) was the first woman allowed to go aboard U.S. Navy ships as part of her official responsibilities. As a draftsman at the Norfolk Naval Shipyard during World War II, her job included taking measurements of ship features for use in engineering upgrades. Up to that time, work rules, male prerogatives, and superstition kept women on land. She worked on 229 ships before she was released from her job in 1946.

"At first it was difficult for a nineteen-year-old girl to convince those 'Old Salts' that I knew what I was doing. With help from the Navy Yard Officers, the reluctance was overcome. The Damage Control people were soon convinced [that] women could draw blue prints and do the job. . . ."

Thelma Bendler Stern Neubauer, U.S. Navy draftsman, 1991

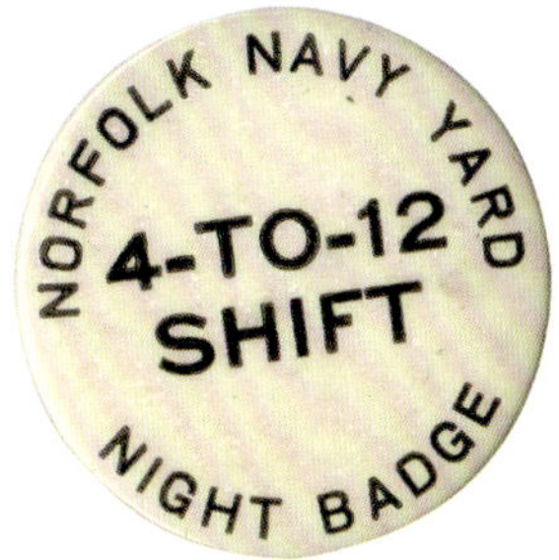

Pin belonging to Thelma Neubauer, about 1942

VMHC Collection, Gift of Thelma S. Neubauer

USS *Enterprise* (CT-6) and USS *Yorktown* (CT-5) at Newport News Shipbuilding, 1930s

From the collection of the Naval History and Heritage Command

The carrier *Yorktown* (right) was the first of the new Yorktown class of aircraft carriers developed before World War II. Construction began in August 1934 and lasted two years. Work on the *Enterprise* (left) also began that summer and she was launched in October 1936. The *Yorktown* sank during the Battle of Midway (June 4–7, 1942) and *Enterprise* became the most decorated warship of World War II.

Heather Johnson at Newport News Shipbuilding, 2015

Joe Fudge / *Daily Press* / TCA

Welders at the shipyard often work at great heights, in tight spaces, and in extreme cold and heat. Nevertheless, Heather Johnson fell in love with the trade when she started at Newport News Shipbuilding in 2004. Eleven years later, she became the first woman in the shipyard's history to perform the honor of burning the initials of a ship's sponsor onto a plate affixed to the ship's keel. Approximately 9 percent of the shipyard's welders are women.

View of Newport News Shipbuilding, 2021

Ashley Cowan (photographer)

Courtesy of Newport News Shipbuilding

Newport News Shipbuilding is the only shipyard designing and building U.S. Navy aircraft carriers, and one of two designing and building nuclear submarines. In 2021—one of the busiest times in four decades—shipbuilders were working on 37 aircraft carriers, including the USS *Gerald R. Ford* (CTN 78, far right) and the second *John F. Kennedy* (CTN 79).

GOVERNING THE PEOPLE

In 1619, British colonists in Jamestown established the General Assembly with representatives from settled areas. This was the first legislative assembly in North America and established a model of representational government that influenced the development of democracy in the United States. As the Virginia colony expanded westward, its seat of government moved first to Williamsburg (1699) and then to Richmond (1780).

Before European settlement, Tsenacommacah's (Tidewater's) thirty or more Indigenous tribes representing more than 22,000 people had their own forms of government. Yet, only two tribes, the Pamunkey and Mattaponi, still govern the same lands they lived on when the English colonists arrived in the 1600s.

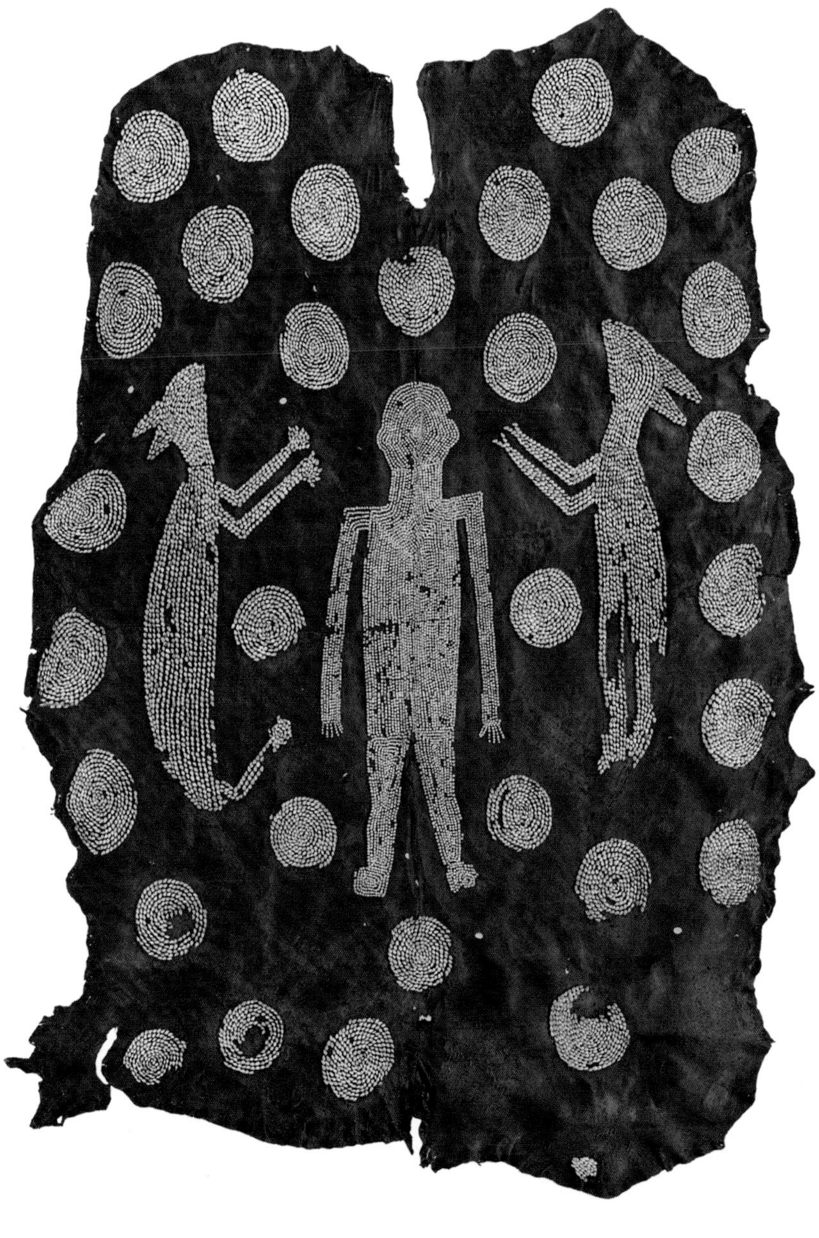

Powhatan's Mantle, about 1600–38

From the collection of the Ashmolean Museum, University of Oxford

The extraordinary effort and skill to create this cloak or wall hanging from deer hide and shells speak to the importance of its owner. The central figure may represent paramount chief Wahunsunacock (Powhatan, about 1550–1618). By the late 1500s, Wahunsunacock established a chiefdom that influenced over thirty Algonquian-speaking communities in the Tidewater region. Among them were the ancestors of contemporary Virginia tribes, including the Pamunkey, Mattaponi, Upper Mattaponi, and likely the Nansemond and Rappahannock.

Illustration of Werowocomoco, showing the settlement in the late 1500s, 2015
Rob Wood (artist)
National Park Service

The village of Werowocomoco rested along the north bank of Pamunke River (renamed the York River by English colonists). It was from this cultural and religious center that Wahunsunacock (Powhatan) controlled the territory his people called Tsenacommacah, meaning "densely inhabited place." The site is in present-day Gloucester County.

Site of the Powhatan village of Werowocomoco, 2017
Matt Rath (photographer)
National Park Service

Increasing conflict with English settlers led Wahunsunacock (Powhatan) to abandon Werowocomoco and move farther inland in 1609. For centuries, the site's identity as a native place was unappreciated until its location along the York River was rediscovered in 2001. Archaeological fieldwork revealed much about the long history of this important and sacred site. Today, Werowocomoco is stewarded by the National Park Service in cooperation with Virginia Indian tribes.

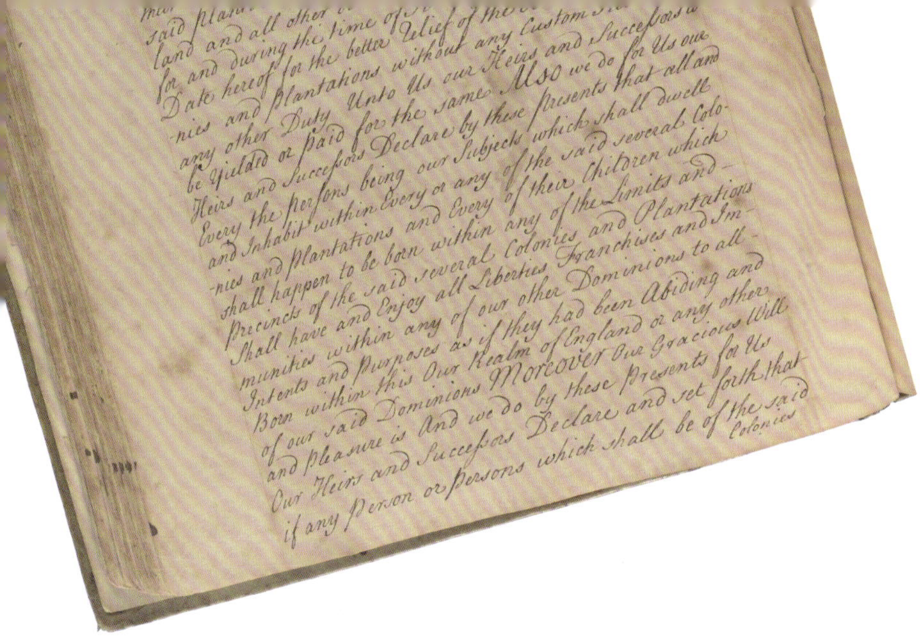
said Plan...
land and all other ...
for and during the time of ... Relief of the ...
Date hereof for the better ... any Custom ...
-nies and Plantations without any Custom ...
any other Duty Unto Us our Heirs and Successors
be yielded or paid for the same Also we do for Us our
Heirs and Successors Declare by these Presents that all and
Every the persons being our Subjects which shall dwell
and Inhabit within Every or any of the said several Colo-
-nies and Plantations and Every of their Children which
shall happen to be born within any of the Limits and
Precincts of the said several Colonies and Plantations
Shall have and Enjoy all Liberties Franchises and Im-
munities within any of our other Dominions to all
Intents and Purposes as if they had been Abiding and
Born within this Our Realm of England or any other
of our said Dominions Moreover Our Gracious Will
and Pleasure is And we do by these Presents for Us
Our Heirs and Successors Declare and set forth that
if any Person or Persons which shall be of the said Colonies

"The Virginia Charter of 1606," a passage from the Records of the Virginia Company of London, 1619 Copy made in 1700s, bearing bookplate of John Randolph of Roanoke

VMHC Collection, Gift of William Leigh

Jamestown was established by the Virginia Company of London, a stock company granted a royal charter by James I. There the king made promises that Virginians would remember in 1776: all in Virginia "and every of their children shall have and enjoy all Liberties, Franchises, and Immunities as if they had been abiding and born within this our Realm of England." Virginians who launched the American Revolution would complain that they were disenfranchised—denied the right to vote—resulting in taxation without representation.

***The Portraictuer of Captayne John Smith*, 1624**

Unidentified artist after Simon van de Passe

VMHC Collection

Soldier, explorer, and author, Smith (1580–1631) fought in the Netherlands and Hungary, toured France, Italy, the Mediterranean, Russia, Central Europe, and North Africa, and was enslaved in Turkey and Russia—all before landing at Jamestown in 1607. In Virginia he showed brashness and bravery that garnered both the respect of the Powhatan Indians and disdain from a number of English colleagues. Largely through his bold leadership in 1607–9 the Jamestown settlement survived.

***Pocahontas*, 1616**

Simon van de Passe (engraver)

VMHC Collection

This is the only portrait of Pocahontas taken from life. In rigid Jacobean attire, twenty-one-year-old Pocahontas (about 1596–1617) seems uncomfortable, but the costume probably hid tattooing and certainly provided the chaste image wanted by the Virginia Company. That organization sponsored the Virginia settlement and Pocahontas's trip to England, and it probably commissioned this print for publicity, to celebrate the conversion of an "Indian princess" to English and Christian ways.

Virginia Discovered and Discribed by Captayn John Smith, 1624

VMHC Collection, Bequest of Paul Mellon

Smith traveled throughout the region and gathered information from the Indigenous peoples he encountered. The map he helped to create is the first detailed map of the Chesapeake region and was referenced by settlers for decades. It continues to be used by researchers—particularly those interested in the locations of many Indian settlements, including Werowocomoco which can be seen in the detail at right.

First Legislative Assembly in the New World, 1969

Jack Clifton (artist)

Courtesy of the Library of Virginia

In 1618, the Virginia Company of London, which ran the Virginia colony under a royal charter, abolished martial law and ordered that a legislative assembly be formed. Elected by the free white male inhabitants of each town, 22 burgesses met in the church at Jamestown on July 30, 1619. It was the first representative governing body to meet in North America and continues to meet as the Virginia General Assembly today.

". . . our intente is to establish one equal and uniforme kinde of government over all Virginia &c."

John Pory, "A Reporte of the Manner of Proceeding in the General Assembly Convented at James City," 1619

Wrist shackles, 1600s–1700s

VMHC Collection

The first enslaved people in British North America arrived at Point Comfort, Virginia, in 1619. Gradually, race-based slavery became entrenched in Virginia and throughout the American South, and would dramatically shape history for the next four centuries. Between 1619 and 1807, twelve-and-a-half million Africans were enslaved and transported from Africa to North and South America and the Caribbean, against their will and in chains—128,000 were brought to the Chesapeake Bay region.

Wren Building at William & Mary, 2013

Stephen Salpukas / William & Mary

Chartered in 1693—six years before Williamsburg became Virginia's capital—the College of William & Mary is the nation's second-oldest college, after Harvard. The Wren Building, completed in 1699, is the oldest building still standing. From 1700 to 1778, the college also included the Brafferton Indian School, intended to Anglicize and Christianize Virginia's Indigenous people. Alumni of W&M have played important roles in shaping the United States, including President Thomas Jefferson and Chief Justice of the U.S. Supreme Court John Marshall.

***Peyton Randolph*, about 1755–8**
John Wollaston (artist)
VMHC Collection

Part of a wealthy Williamsburg family, Randolph (1721–1775) served as Speaker of the Virginia House of Burgesses, President of the Virginia Conventions that established an independent Virginia and its constitution, and President of both the First and Second Continental Congresses.

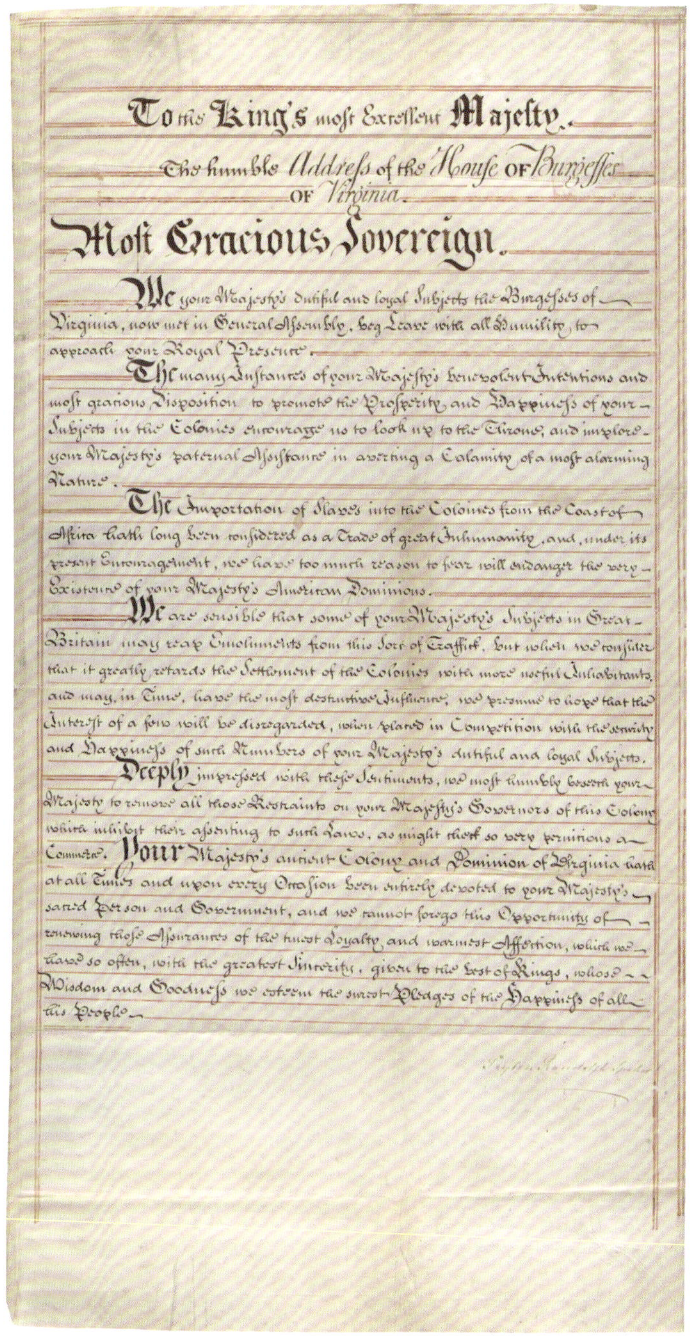

To the King's most Excellent Majesty.

The humble Address of the House of Burgesses of Virginia.

Most Gracious Sovereign.

We your Majesty's dutiful and loyal Subjects the Burgesses of Virginia, now met in General Assembly, beg Leave with all Humility, to approach your Royal Presence.

The many Instances of your Majesty's benevolent Intentions and most gracious Disposition to promote the Prosperity and Happiness of your Subjects in the Colonies encourage us to look up to the Throne, and implore your Majesty's paternal Assistance in averting a Calamity of a most alarming Nature.

The Importation of Slaves into the Colonies from the Coast of Africa hath long been considered as a Trade of great Inhumanity, and, under its present Encouragement, we have too much reason to fear will endanger the very Existence of your Majesty's American Dominions.

We are sensible that some of your Majesty's Subjects in Great Britain may reap Emoluments from this Sort of Traffick, but when we consider that it greatly retards the Settlement of the Colonies with more useful Inhabitants, and may, in Time, have the most destructive Influence, we presume to hope that the Interest of a few will be disregarded, when placed in Competition with the Security and Happiness of such Numbers of your Majesty's dutiful and loyal Subjects.

Deeply impressed with these Sentiments, we most humbly beseech your Majesty to remove all those Restraints on your Majesty's Governors of this Colony which inhibit their assenting to such Laws, as might check so very pernicious a Commerce. Your Majesty's antient Colony and Dominion of Virginia hath at all Times and upon every Occasion been entirely devoted to your Majesty's sacred Person and Government, and we cannot forego this Opportunity of renewing those Assurances of the truest Loyalty and warmest Affection, which we have so often, with the greatest Sincerity, given to the best of Kings, whose Wisdom and Goodness we esteem the surest Pledges of the Happiness of all his People.

Petition to King George III to end the slave trade, 1772
Virginia House of Burgesses
VMHC Collection, Bequest of Paul Mellon

Economic motives, not humanitarian feelings for the enslaved, led the Virginia House of Burgesses to petition King George III. In the 1760s and 1770s, a century of poor farming practices, a shift from growing tobacco to wheat, and the natural increase of the enslaved population resulted in a surplus of enslaved people in Virginia. Enslavers brutally calculated that the values of the enslaved would rise if importation of Africans was banned. The petition was rejected in London.

Chair used by the speaker of the House of Burgesses, about 1735

Hans Lorenz (photographer)

Commonwealth of Virginia, photo courtesy of The Colonial Williamsburg Foundation

From this seat, the Speaker of the Virginia House of Burgesses presided over the legislature in Williamsburg. It was here in 1774 that Speaker Peyton Randolph condemned the British response to the Boston Tea Party, which had occurred the previous December. In response to the protestations of Virginia burgesses, the royal governor dissolved the House—which continued to meet extralegally until 1776. Leaders established the independent Commonwealth of Virginia with a General Assembly made up of a Senate and House of Delegates. The chair continued to be used when the capital moved to Richmond in 1780.

A Declaration of Rights made by the representatives of the good people of Virginia, assembled in full and free Convention. . ., 1776

George Mason (author)

VMHC Collection

Written by planter and politician George Mason (1725–1792), the Declaration was part of the Virginia state constitution adopted when Virginia claimed independence from Britain. Mason argued that we the people have God-given rights, including life, liberty, and freedom of religion and the press. These ideas later became well known through Thomas Jefferson's Declaration of Independence and James Madison's Bill of Rights added to the Constitution. Although he and other Founding Fathers championed liberty and human rights, many of them were slaveholders.

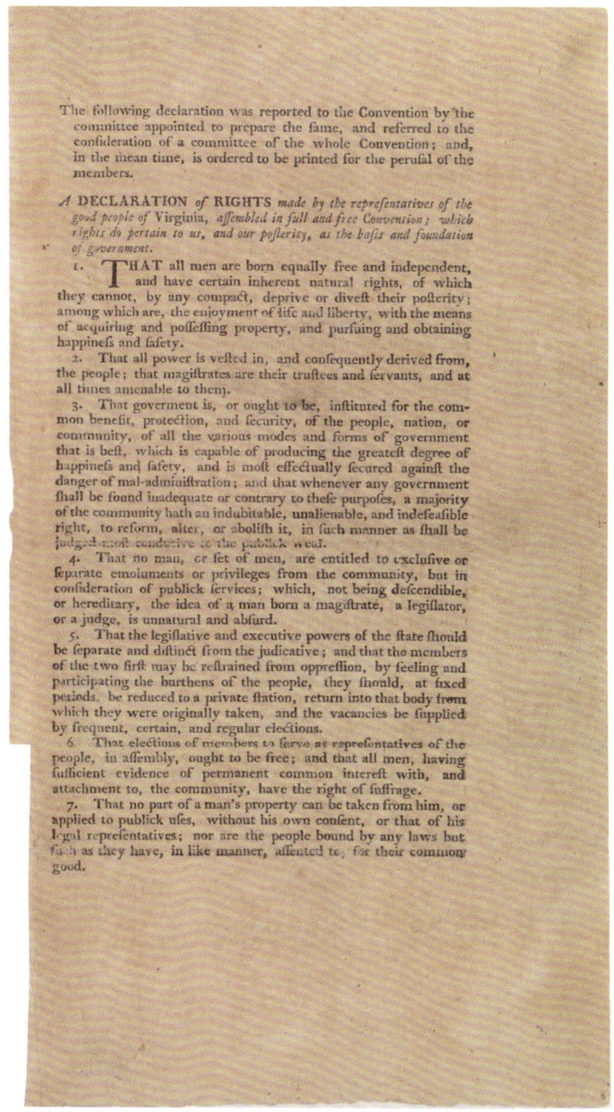

The following declaration was reported to the Convention by the committee appointed to prepare the ſame, and referred to the conſideration of a committee of the whole Convention; and, in the mean time, is ordered to be printed for the peruſal of the members.

A DECLARATION *of* RIGHTS *made by the repreſentatives of the good people of* Virginia, *aſſembled in full and free Convention; which rights do pertain to us, and our poſterity, as the baſis and foundation of government.*

1. THAT all men are born equally free and independent, and have certain inherent natural rights, of which they cannot, by any compact, deprive or diveſt their poſterity; among which are, the enjoyment of life and liberty, with the means of acquiring and poſſeſſing property, and purſuing and obtaining happineſs and ſafety.

2. That all power is veſted in, and conſequently derived from, the people; that magiſtrates are their truſtees and ſervants, and at all times amenable to them.

3. That goverment is, or ought to be, inſtituted for the common benefit, protection, and ſecurity, of the people, nation, or community, of all the various modes and forms of government that is beſt, which is capable of producing the greateſt degree of happineſs and ſafety, and is moſt effectually ſecured againſt the danger of mal-adminiſtration; and that whenever any government ſhall be found inadequate or contrary to theſe purpoſes, a majority of the community hath an indubitable, unalienable, and indefeaſible right, to reform, alter, or aboliſh it, in ſuch manner as ſhall be judged moſt conducive to the publick weal.

4. That no man, or ſet of men, are entitled to excluſive or ſeparate emoluments or privileges from the community, but in conſideration of publick ſervices; which, not being deſcendible, or hereditary, the idea of a man born a magiſtrate, a legiſlator, or a judge, is unnatural and abſurd.

5. That the legiſlative and executive powers of the ſtate ſhould be ſeparate and diſtinct from the judicative; and that the members of the two firſt may be reſtrained from oppreſſion, by feeling and participating the burthens of the people, they ſhould, at fixed periods, be reduced to a private ſtation, return into that body from which they were originally taken, and the vacancies be ſupplied by frequent, certain, and regular elections.

6. That elections of members to ſerve as repreſentatives of the people, in aſſembly, ought to be free; and that all men, having ſufficient evidence of permanent common intereſt with, and attachment to, the community, have the right of ſuffrage.

7. That no part of a man's property can be taken from him, or applied to publick uſes, without his own conſent, or that of his legal repreſentatives; nor are the people bound by any laws but ſuch as they have, in like manner, aſſented to, for their common good.

***John Murray, Fourth Earl of Dunmore*, 1920s**

Charles X. Harris (artist) after original by Sir Joshua Reynolds

VMHC Collection, Bequest of Mr. and Mrs. Alexander Wilbourne Weddell

John Murray, fourth Earl of Dunmore (1732–1809), was Virginia's last royal governor. When the American Revolution began in April 1775, he seized the colony's ammunition stores, and seven months later declared martial law and issued a proclamation that promised freedom to enslaved people who would fight for the king. As many as 800 enslaved Virginians reached the governor and raised widespread fear of a slave rebellion. Dunmore took the offensive at the Battle of Great Bridge (December 9, 1775) but was so soundly defeated that he burned nearby Norfolk and fled.

This is to certify that the Bearer by the Name of James
Has done Essential Services to Me While I Had the Honour to
Command in this State. His Intelligence from the Enemy's
Camp were Industriously Collected and More faithfully Delivered
He perfectly Acquitted Himself with Some important Commissions
I gave him and Appears to me Entitled to Every Reward his
Situation Can Admit of. Done Under My Hand, Richmond
November 21st 1784
Lafayette

Engraving of James Lafayette, after 1824

Unknown engraver after painting by John B. Martin

VMHC Collection

Born into slavery in New Kent County, James (about 1760–1832) joined the Continental Army and served as a spy for the Marquis de Lafayette. Playing the role of a runaway slave, he gained access to British general Cornwallis's headquarters and provided intelligence that contributed to the decisive victory at Yorktown. Only after Lafayette interceded in 1787 did James receive his manumission. He turned to a life of farming and assumed Lafayette's name as a gesture of respect for his wartime comrade.

***Storming a Redoubt at Yorktown*, 1840**
Eugène Louis Lami (artist)
From the collection of the Virginia State Capitol, Old Senate Chamber, Gift of William Corcoran

After conducting raids across Virginia during the spring and summer of 1781, British general Lord Charles Cornwallis entrenched his army at Yorktown. In September, American and French troops laid siege to the town. During a surprise attack on October 14, 1781, General Alexander Hamilton's 400 troops overran British Redoubt No. 10. Their success led to the British surrender five days later.

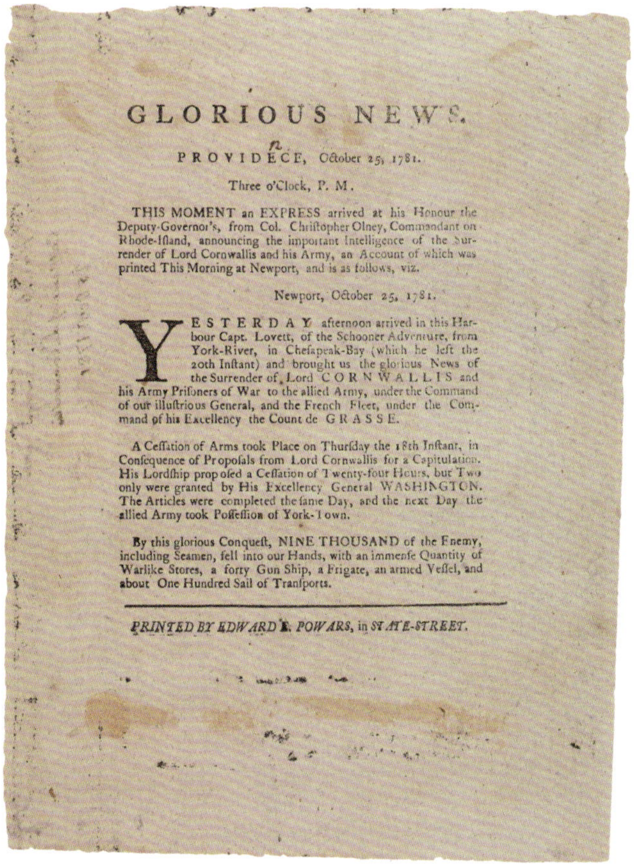

GLORIOUS NEWS.

PROVIDECE, October 25, 1781.

Three o'Clock, P. M.

THIS MOMENT an EXPRESS arrived at his Honour the Deputy-Governor's, from Col. Chriſtopher Olney, Commandant on Rhode-Iſland, announcing the important Intelligence of the Surrender of Lord Cornwallis and his Army, an Account of which was printed This Morning at Newport, and is as follows, viz.

Newport, October 25, 1781.

YESTERDAY afternoon arrived in this Harbour Capt. Lovett, of the Schooner Adventure, from York-River, in Cheſapeak-Bay (which he left the 20th Inſtant) and brought us the glorious News of the Surrender of Lord CORNWALLIS and his Army Priſoners of War to the allied Army, under the Command of our illuſtrious General, and the French Fleet, under the Command of his Excellency the Count de GRASSE.

A Ceſſation of Arms took Place on Thurſday the 18th Inſtant, in Conſequence of Propoſals from Lord Cornwallis for a Capitulation. His Lordſhip propoſed a Ceſſation of Twenty-four Hours, but Two only were granted by His Excellency General WASHINGTON. The Articles were completed the ſame Day, and the next Day the allied Army took Poſſeſſion of York-Town.

By this glorious Conqueſt, NINE THOUSAND of the Enemy, including Seamen, fell into our Hands, with an immenſe Quantity of Warlike Stores, a forty Gun Ship, a Frigate, an armed Veſſel, and about One Hundred Sail of Tranſports.

PRINTED BY EDWARD E. POWARS, in STATE-STREET.

***Glorious News* broadside, 1781**
Edward E. Powars (printer)
VMHC Collection, Bequest of Paul Mellon

The news that British general Lord Cornwallis and his army had surrendered at Yorktown was carried to New England by a schooner that left the York River five days earlier. This broadside was printed in Providence, Rhode Island, to inform the public of this significant American victory. With Cornwallis's surrender, the British lost their resolve to continue fighting and the war ended in 1783. American nation building could then begin in earnest.

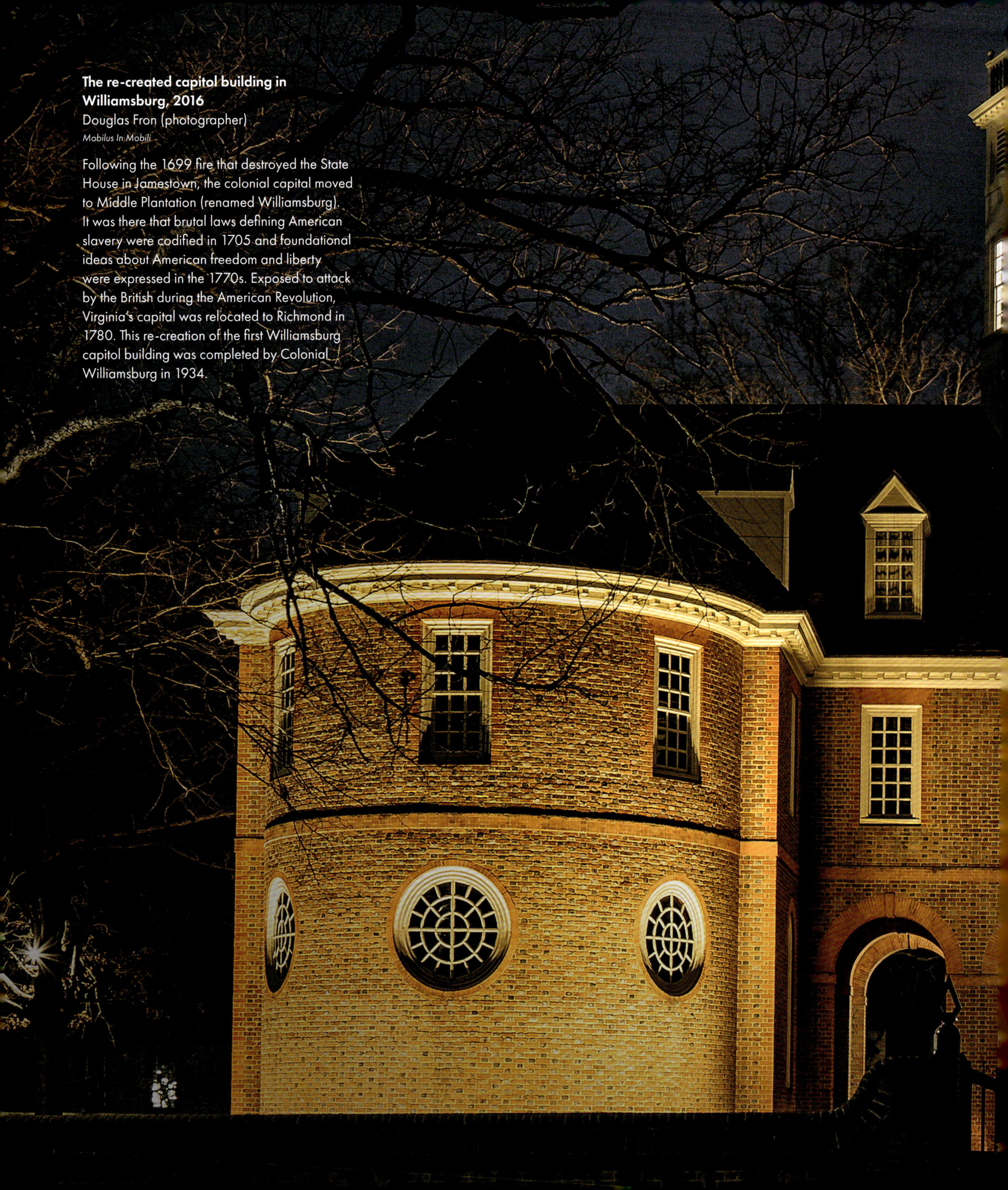

The re-created capitol building in Williamsburg, 2016
Douglas Fron (photographer)
Mobilus In Mobili

Following the 1699 fire that destroyed the State House in Jamestown, the colonial capital moved to Middle Plantation (renamed Williamsburg). It was there that brutal laws defining American slavery were codified in 1705 and foundational ideas about American freedom and liberty were expressed in the 1770s. Exposed to attack by the British during the American Revolution, Virginia's capital was relocated to Richmond in 1780. This re-creation of the first Williamsburg capitol building was completed by Colonial Williamsburg in 1934.

KEEPING TRADITIONS

The culture of Tidewater flows from enduring traditions. Folk songs, ancient dance steps, impactful communal stories, regional dialects, passed-down trades, and long-held celebrations all give the Tidewater region its unique character. They are often rooted in the experiences of living off the water and adapting to the region. These cultural ties reinforce the connections between Tidewater's people and where they come from.

Raven Brightwater Custalow performing the Eastern Blanket Dance, 2021
Brenda Williams (photographer)
Courtesy of Kindred

A member of the Mattaponi Indian Tribe, Custalow is a nurse practitioner who grew up on one of the oldest reservations in the country. She co-founded the Eastern Woodland Revitalization project to teach and share old and new ways of tribal life in collaboration with Virginia's eleven state-recognized tribes.

"[W]e needed something in our area where all our Tribal nations could come together and learn cultural practices that are specific to our own people. . . . We want to [grow and share them] with others so that people understand who we are as Virginia's first peoples."

Raven Brightwater Custalow, co-founder of Eastern Woodland Revitalization, 2021

Jar and stand made in Late Woodland archaeological style, 1980
Mildred Moore (maker)
From the collection of the National Museum of the American Indian, Smithsonian Institution (26/1864)

Members of the Pamunkey Indian Tribe have been making pottery for thousands of years. During the Great Depression, the government helped establish a school to teach Pamunkey women pottery-making for a souvenir market. Continuing into the 1970s, the Pamunkey Pottery Guild generated proceeds that helped to support the community and offered artists opportunities for self-expression. This jar, based on archaeological examples, represents a movement by Pamunkey potters, like Mildred Moore, to incorporate and teach historical techniques, forms, and patterns.

"Our culture isn't pow-wow. Our culture isn't . . . something that we wear on our bodies. It's something that we do, something that we live, or at least know about because that's the way that our grandparents lived or our great-grandparents lived, and that we grew up learning about."

Ashley Atkins Spivey, member of the Pamunkey Indian Tribe, 2018

Allyson Gray (citizen of Pamunkey Indian Tribe) smooths the side of a clay pot with a sturgeon scute, 2023

Photo by National Museum of the American Indian staff

Allyson Gray's (b. 1988) great-grandmother was a member of the Pamunkey Pottery Guild. Today, she continues to use many traditional techniques to create new forms of artistic expression.

"With each piece I create and each person I teach, I feel I am doing my part to ensure that our traditions carry on to future generations. The same traditions and resilience that my great-grandmother and many other ancestors have strived to preserve will continue to live through me."

Allyson Gray, Pamunkey potter, 2024

Tangier Island, 2017

Will Parson (photographer)

Chesapeake Bay Program

Many of Tangier Island's 437 (in 2023) residents are still descended from the Cornish families that settled the island in 1686. Their relative isolation—separated from mainland Virginia by 12 miles—has resulted in the islanders having a unique accent and speech patterns. Only accessible by boat or plane, their 300-year-old community faces the major threat of rising waters and erosion.

TANGIER TALK

Residents of Tangier Island use expressions only understood by islanders and they speak in a manner they call "talking backwards." With the advent of television and the internet, young people's speech sounds more like standard American English, but the older generations proudly carry on the dialect.

Here are some colorful Tangier Island expressions:

"punched tar" = flat tire

"ain't hard favored" = an unattractive person

"came nigh as peas" = useful phrase for when you almost fell off a boat

"iggy" = going to

"hucky" = dirty

"a fuzzy cod" = a storm is coming

"you get the cheese" = "what a liar you are"

"red lead" = ketchup

"eyewinkers" = eyelashes

"solid circus" = screamingly funny

From *Tangier Talk: A Collection of Over 300 of the Colorful Expressions and Terms Used and Understood Only by Islanders*, compiled by Bruce Gordy (2007)

82nd Annual Chincoteague Pony Swim, 2007
Jason O. Watson (photographer)
Jason O. Watson Photography

Assateague Island is home to about 300 wild ponies whose ancestors arrived in the 1600s. Since 1924, the Virginia herd has annually been rounded up and swum to the nearby town of Chincoteague for veterinary care and an auction. A festival attended by tens of thousands of people marks the event. The "Chincoteague Pony" became the official state horse of Virginia in 2023.

***Misty of Chincoteague*, 1955**
Marguerite Henry (author); Wesley Dennis (illustrator)
VMHC Collection

Inspired by a real-life pony of the same name, Marguerite Henry's (1902–1997) popular children's book, and the 1961 film *Misty*, introduced the annual Pony Swim and Auction to audiences around the world. For generations, fans have come to visit the town and island where they can see Misty's (1946–1972) hoof prints in the sidewalk outside the Roxy Movie Theatre in Chincoteague.

Tattoo Man figurine, 1920–36
August "Cap" Coleman (artist);
Johan Börjeson (sculptor)
From the collection of The Mariners' Museum and Park, Newport News, Virginia

This plaster figure was on display in the window of Coleman's tattoo shop in Norfolk. All the designs are assumed to have been painted by him and showcase numerous examples of tattoos and his distinctive style, characterized by bold outlining, meticulous shading, and a limited color palette.

"Any good tattooer that's worth anything will look up to and respect [Coleman and Rogers]. Those guys definitely paved the way for modern-day tattooing. They were doing the best tattoos. They were creating the best artwork."

Mike Cann, tattoo artist in Norfolk, 2013

August "Cap" Coleman in his Norfolk tattoo shop, 1936
William T. Radcliffe (photographer)
From the collection of The Mariners' Museum and Park, Newport News, Virginia

Many sailors marked their passage through Norfolk—as a thriving seaport—in ink. Eccentric and gruff, pioneering tattoo artist August "Cap" Coleman (about 1884–1973) opened his tattoo parlor in 1918. He also mentored tattooist Franklin Paul Rogers (1905–1990). Regarded by many as forefathers of the traditional American tattoo style, Coleman and Rogers continue to influence and inspire tattoo artists in the Tidewater region and around the world.

Bertha Winborne Edwards (left) and her assistant Charlotte Driver Foulk at the Portsmouth Community Library, 1945
From the collection of the Portsmouth Public Library

Edwards (1920–2009) was a driving force behind the creation of the Portsmouth Community Library, the only public library accessible to Black residents during segregation. As its first librarian from 1945 to 1963, she created an archive of local Black history that is still treasured by the community and scholars.

"I had a section of books by and about Negroes. . . . I started collecting history of the churches and then I thought about writing the history of the different neighborhoods in Portsmouth. And I interviewed a lot of older people here in Portsmouth. I found out people who were the first Blacks to do this [and other firsts]."

Bertha Winborne Edwards, librarian and archivist, about 1980

HONORING LANDMARKS

Leaders of English settlement, captains Christopher Newport (1561–1617) and John Smith (1580–1631) recognized the strategic importance of a spit of land on the Chesapeake they called Point Comfort (today part of Hampton). Since then, Hampton has played other pivotal roles in Virginia and U.S. history. In 1619, the first enslaved Africans disembarked from their torturous ocean journey at the site. At the height of the Civil War, Fort Monroe—completed in 1834—became a haven for those escaping slavery behind Union lines. Outside its walls they built a vibrant Black community and established a tradition of education under a nearby oak tree that continues at Hampton University.

Mary Peake, about 1862

Courtesy of Hampton University Archives

A free woman of color, Mary Peake (1823–1862) secretly taught Black children and adults in Norfolk and then Hampton, defying state laws restricting the education of enslaved and free Black students. During the Civil War, she held classes under an oak tree outside the walls of Fort Monroe that later became the site of the first Southern reading of the Emancipation Proclamation in 1863. The "Emancipation Oak" still stands on the campus of Hampton University.

The Emancipation Oak at Hampton University, 2019

Jerry Gammon (photographer)

Courtesy of Jerry Gammon

Planted in 1831, the Emancipation Oak stands near the entrance of the Hampton University campus. It is a National Historic Landmark, one of the National Geographic Society's "10 Great Trees of the World," and an enduring symbol of freedom and perseverance.

"[W]e had in her a teacher of the choicest spirit. . . . Her school numbered at first only about half a dozen [students], but in a few days she had between fifty and sixty. . . . While Mrs. Peake attached prime importance to the training of the rising generation, she felt that great improvement might be made among the adults [and established] an evening school [for them too.]"

Rev. Lewis C. Lockwood of the American Missionary Association, discussing the schools that Mary Peake started in 1861 at Fort Monroe, 1863

Black and Indigenous students in chemistry lab at Hampton Institute, 1899

Science History Images / Alamy Stock Photo

Established in 1868 as a teacher training school for formerly enslaved people, the Hampton Normal and Agricultural Institute expanded to offer instruction in trades and industry. After attending Hampton, educator Booker T. Washington (1856–1915) went on to create the Tuskegee Institute (1881) in Alabama. In 1917, the school received accreditation as a four-year college. Today, Hampton University has more than 5,500 students and is among the top Historically Black Colleges and Universities (HBCUs) in the world.

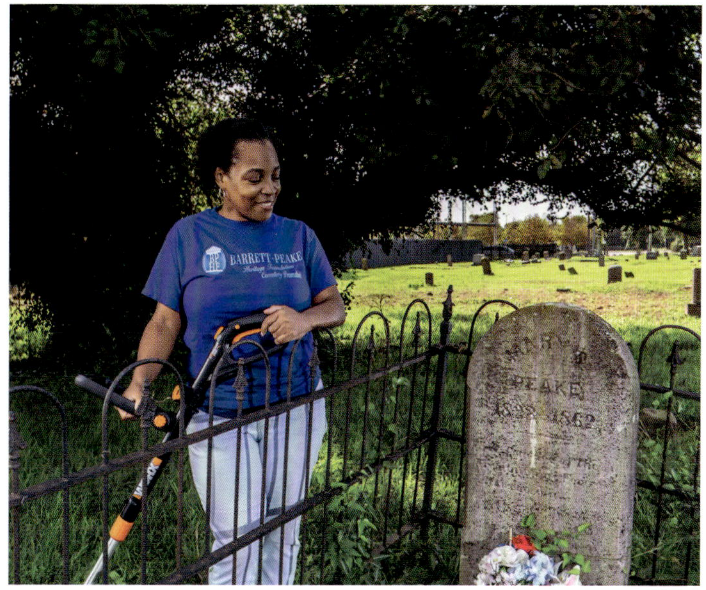

Ghana Smith, a volunteer with the Barrett-Peake Heritage Foundation, maintains Mary Peake's grave at Hampton's Elmerton Cemetery, 2020

Jim Agnew / William & Mary

"[Mary Peake's] remains are in Elmerton Cemetery [and had become overgrown]. . . . I could see us taking beautiful flowers and making that place so beautiful, and that's why we started the cleanup."

Dr. Mary T. Christian, co-founder of the Barrett-Peake Heritage Foundation, 2018

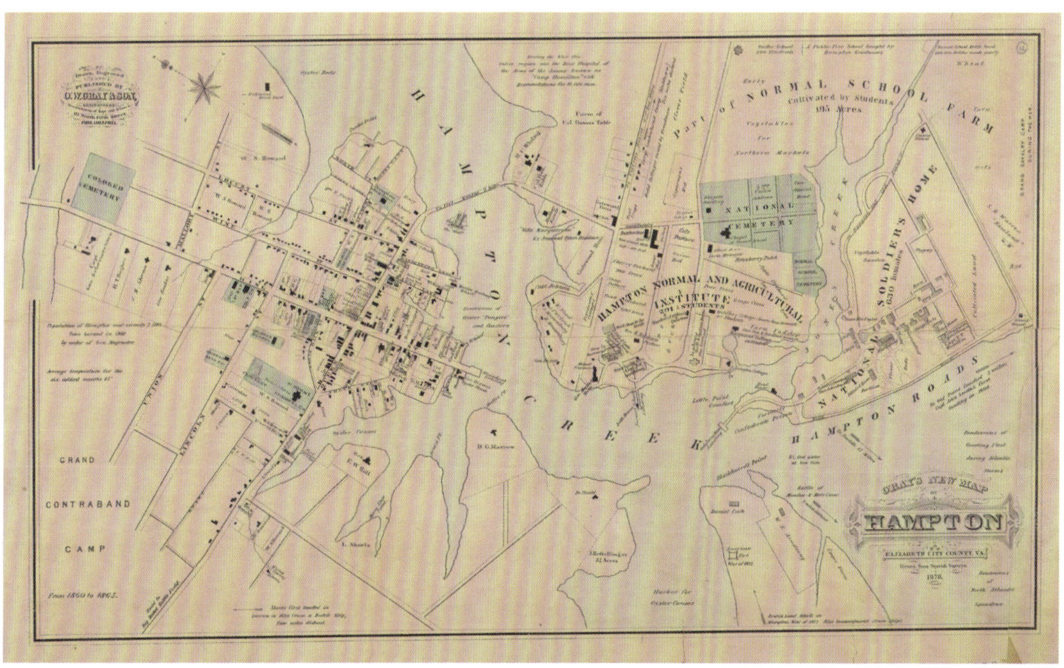

***Gray's New Map of Hampton, Elizabeth City County, Va.*, 1878**

O.W. Gray & Son (draftsman)

Lionel Pincus and Princess Firyal Map Division, The New York Public Library

The campus of the Hampton Normal and Agricultural Institute (now Hampton University) can be seen to the right of Hampton Creek.

The Freedmen's Village, Hampton, 1864
Alexander Gardner (photographer)
Library of Congress, Prints and Photographs Division

Near Fort Monroe, freedpersons established the Grand Contraband Camp, erecting homes and buildings from slabs of wood and salvaged materials. They nicknamed the new community "Slabtown." At the end of the war, many of the formerly enslaved settled the area once occupied by the camp. It was later incorporated into the City of Hampton.

"Hampton is now peopled chiefly by freedmen, who number about four thousand, most of whom occupy the interesting little village known as Slabtown. . . . There is a general uniformity both in the material and style of the architecture, the dwellings being built of rough barrel-staves, or slabs split out with the axe."
Harper's Weekly, September 30, 1865

***Plan of Fortress Munroe, Va.*, 1862**
Robert Knox Sneden (cartographer)
VMHC Collection, Purchased with funds provided by Mr. and Mrs. Floyd D. Gottwald, Jr.

During the Civil War, thousands of enslaved people self-emancipated and sought refuge at Fort Monroe, which remained in the control of the U.S. Army. To deny Confederates a vital workforce, the army declared that formerly enslaved people would be considered "contraband of war" and would not be returned to slavery. The fort lies very near to Point Comfort, where the first enslaved Africans arrived in Virginia in 1619.

Friden SW-10 Calculating Machine, 1945
Friden Calculating Machine Company
National Museum of American History, Smithsonian Institution

Beginning in the 1940s, hundreds of human "Computers"—almost exclusively women—used calculators like this one to complete complex mathematical equations necessary to the work being done at NASA Langley Research Center. With the arrival of electronic computers at Langley in 1946, many of those women became pioneers in computer programming or joined engineering groups working on everything from the space program to supersonic flight.

Dr. Christine Darden conducting a sonic boom test, 1990
Sandie Gibbs (photographer)
NASA

A graduate of Hampton University, Darden (b. 1942) joined NASA Langley as a data analyst and computer programmer in 1967. She was promoted to aerospace engineer in 1973, at a time when few women were employed as engineers at NASA. During her 40-year career she became a world-renowned leader in high-speed aerodynamics research and supersonic noise analysis and reduction.

Landing and Impact Research Facility (the "gantry"), 2012
Sean Smith (photographer)
NASA / Langley Research Center

Since 1917, the groundbreaking work done at NASA Langley Research Center (Hampton) has advanced our understanding of human flight. Their researchers improved airplane design, made it possible to break the sound barrier, helped us reach the edge of space, and paved the way to explore the Moon and beyond. Built in 1965 to help prepare Apollo astronauts for their final descent to the lunar surface, today the 240-foot-high, 400-foot-long "gantry" provides a site for full-scale crash and impact tests.

GOING TO THE BEACH

Generations of vacationers have flocked to Virginia's beaches along the Chesapeake Bay and the Atlantic Ocean. Beginning in the late 1800s, railways and later highways brought throngs of tourists to the shore and fueled the development of resorts, hotels, restaurants, amusement parks, and other attractions.

People fishing from the Lynnhaven Fishing Pier, 1986

The Virginian-Pilot Archive Photo / TCA

Extending 650 feet into the Atlantic, the all-wooden Lynnhaven Fishing Pier was the longest on the East Coast and attracted beachgoers from 1957 to 2017. The site ultimately included a tackle shop, restaurant, and gift shops. Built and managed by three generations of the Lachman family, the Pier was closed because of rising repair costs.

"[I] grew up in Virginia Beach, and my dad used to bring me out here and hold me between his knees. I used to fish between the rails. . . . I caught a flounder that was like maybe the size of my palm when I was like four or five."

Fisherman at Virginia Beach Fishing Pier, 2015

Bay Shore Hotel, Buckroe Beach, Hampton, Va., 1910–20

C.E. Cheyne (publisher)

From the collection of the Buckroe Historical Society

Throughout the Jim Crow era, Bay Shore Beach in Hampton was a popular vacation destination for Black residents and tourists. The beach was separated from the adjacent all-white Buckroe Beach by a fence that extended into the water. By the 1920s, Bay Shore featured a three-story, 70-room hotel. Destroyed in a 1933 hurricane, it was rebuilt to include an amusement park and midway that supported many Black-owned businesses.

Cora Mae Reid (center) and her family posing at Bay Shore Beach, Hampton, 1930s

Zeal Harris, LA visual artist raised in Phoebus (Hampton, VA)

"I remember [Bay Shore] from the 1960s as a young child. [We would] make the trip with my sisters, brother and cousins in the summertime maybe twice in the season. . . . [Today] I go . . . maybe once or twice a summer. . . . My grandkids are getting to know the place now. . . . We really like it when we meet people at the beach and tell them about the Black side. When it was finally allowed, I remember walking to the White side passing the trailer houses to go on the rides."

Carrie Wall, 2010

Bathers at Buckroe Beach, 1910

Claude B. Wagoner (photographer)

From the collection of the Hampton History Museum, Cheyne Studio Collection

Modesty standards in the early 1900s required female bathers to wear full-length bathing gowns at the beach. Made from wool or flannel, the fabric would not be transparent when wet, and weighted hems prevented the gown from floating in the water.

Women's swimsuit, about 1921
Jantzen Knitting Mills (manufacturer)
From the collection of The Mariners' Museum and Park, Newport News, Virginia

In the early 1900s, California beaches had a reputation for tolerating lighter clothing than beaches on the East Coast. Sleeveless, short, and straight, this "California-style" wool bathing suit became the suit of choice during the 1920s, when swimming replaced wading as a popular beach activity.

Men's swimsuit, about 1920–5
Jantzen Knitting Mills (manufacturer)
From the collection of The Mariners' Museum and Park, Newport News, Virginia

Woolen one-piece suits with cut-off sleeves and legs, like this one, were common for men in the early 1900s. Swimsuit regulations at the time prohibited men from going bare-chested in public.

Riders enjoy "The Dips/The Roller Dips" at Buckroe Beach Amusement Park, 1960s
From the collection of the Hampton History Museum, Donald R. Taylor Collection

During its heyday in the 1950s, Buckroe Beach Amusement Park attracted tens of thousands of thrill seekers to Hampton each year. The park included a roller coaster, Ferris wheel, Tilt-A-Whirl, funhouse, miniature golf, bumper cars, and games. The popularity of Buckroe Beach declined when larger, more elaborate parks opened in Williamsburg and near Richmond in the 1970s, and the nearly 100-year-old amusement park closed in 1985.

Gene Vincent and His Blue Caps, 1956

Pictorial Press Ltd / Alamy Stock Photo

Norfolk native and Navy veteran Gene Vincent (born Vincent Eugene Craddock, 1935–1971) and his backup band, the Blue Caps (named in honor of the headgear worn by sailors), rose to stardom with their 1956 hit "Be-Bop-A-Lula." During the 1960s, Vincent made the black leather jacket and disheveled appearance an iconic rock and roll look. His music influenced The Beatles, The Rolling Stones, and many superstar rock acts that followed.

Teddy Riley at Track Record Studios, 2008

Brandon Peters (photographer)

Brandon Peters Photography

When A-List music producer Teddy Riley (b. 1967) moved from New York to Virginia Beach in 1990, his arrival electrified the area. Riley had already revolutionized hip-hop by creating New Jack Swing—a genre that combined sweet melodies and big beats. He soon built Future Recording Studios and started looking for local talent. Among his first discoveries were Pharrell Williams (b. 1973) and Chad Hugo (b. 1974), who performed with their group, "The Neptunes," at a local talent show.

Chad Hugo (left) and Pharrell Williams, 2005
Clay Patrick McBride (photographer)
Clay Patrick McBride

Williams and Hugo met at a summer camp for the School of the Gifted and Talented in Virginia Beach when they were twelve years old. While working with Teddy Riley, they established themselves as a singing, songwriting, and production duo called The Neptunes. By 2002, they were one of the hottest teams in the United States and produced chart toppers like Nelly's "Hot in Herre" (2002), Kelis's "Milkshake" (2003), Britney Spears's "I'm A Slave 4 U" (2001), Jay-Z's "I Just Wanna Love U" (2000), and Gwen Stefani's "Hollaback Girl" (2004).

"When we started out, we had this whole water theme. . . . We were looking at people like Earth, Wind, and Fire, they had the earth, wind and fire, and Wu-Tang Clan had their kung fu, and we were just on a water trip."
Chad Hugo, *Vibe X* article, 2004

Something in the Water festival poster signed by Pharrell Williams, 2019
Gabriel Alcala (artist)
VMHC Collection

In 2019, Williams chose his hometown of Virginia Beach as the location of a weekend-long event bringing together a star-studded lineup of musical performances to celebrate the diversity of that city. Among the performers were Virginia artists Missy Elliott, Pusha T, Dave Matthews Band, and DRAM. In the following years, the festival was interrupted by the COVID pandemic and a decision to move it to Washington, D.C., to protest police violence against Black people. The festival returned to Virginia Beach in 2023.

"Artists, architects, athletes, academics, when they read about all of those interesting, really talented people who come from here, they always say 'Man, there must be something in the water'. . . . Still to this day, my best verses come from my shower, or when I am swimming, or when I am next to water. . . . I never forget where I come from."
Pharrell Williams, rapper and producer, 2019

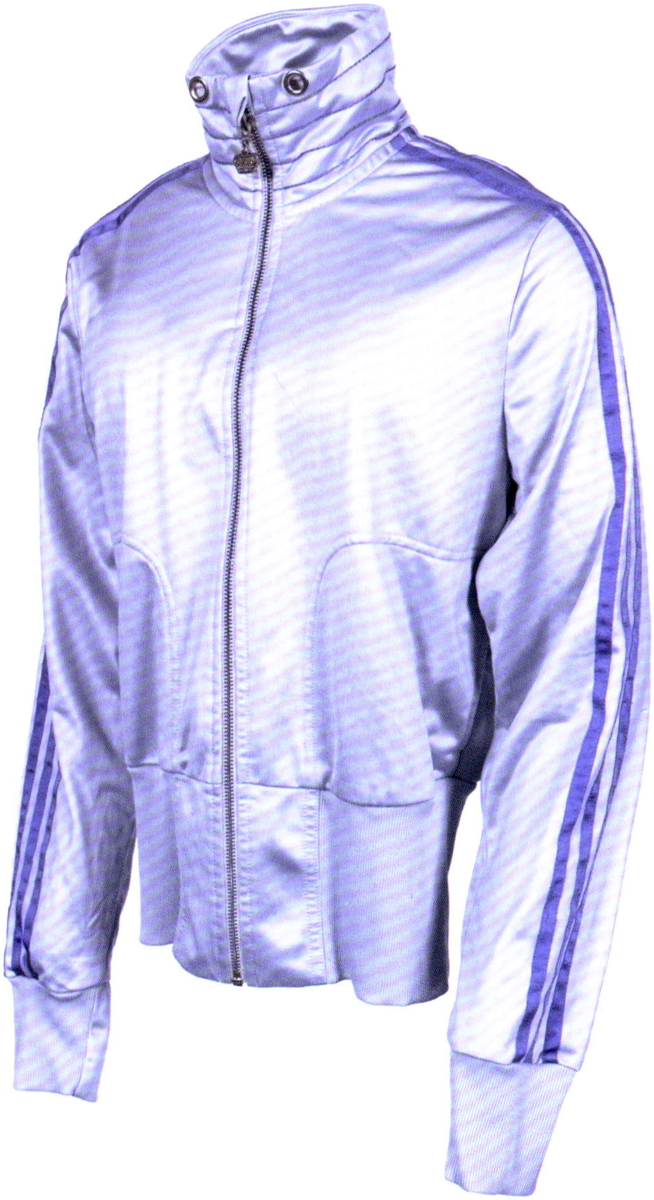

Tracksuit jacket from Missy Elliott's Respect M.E. clothing line, 2005
Adidas (manufacturer)
VMHC Collection, Purchased through the James H. Willcox, Jr. Fund

"Missy was a person who pushed me, who watched what I did, and turned around to make a masterpiece. . . . She makes something that's not the norm normal. . . . You will play her songs for twenty years; it will pass over generations. She's in that Sam Cooke, Miles Davis, Stevie Wonder [club]. She is the Aretha Franklin of hip-hop."

Timbaland, rapper and producer from Norfolk, discussing his work with Missy Elliott, 2019

Supa Dupa Fly **album, 1997**
Missy "Misdemeanor" Elliott
VMHC Education Collection

A Portsmouth native, Missy Elliott (b. 1971) has been revolutionizing the hip-hop genre since the early 1990s as a singer, songwriter, producer, and fashion icon. Her debut solo album *Supa Dupa Fly* (1997) catapulted her to the top of the charts and established her status as an original creative force. She presented a new vision of Black femininity in a genre that generally pigeonholed women as either aggressive or hyper-sexualized. Her work paved the way for other female superstars like Nicki Minaj and Beyoncé.

PEANUTS, POTATOES, AND PORK

Although Tidewater's economy and culture are shaped by water, the region also supports vibrant agriculture and foodways.

Farmhands or sharecroppers picking peanuts by hand in Virginia, late 1800s
VMHC Collection, Gift of the Pennsylvania Historical and Museum Commission

In Virginia, peanuts are planted in May and harvested in late September. Before the advent of mechanical harvesters, farmworkers plowed up the vines and stacked them into piles called shocks (like the ones seen at left and in the background of this photograph). After two to three weeks of curing, workers then picked the peanuts from the vines by hand.

Virginia farmers using a peanut picker, 1930s
Virginia New York World's Fair Commission (publisher)
Courtesy of the Library of Virginia

Benjamin Hicks (1847–1925), an Afro-Indigenous farmer and blacksmith from Southampton County, revolutionized peanut farming with his 1902 invention of a gas-powered machine that stemmed and cleaned peanuts.

PEANUTS

Peanuts came to Virginia with enslaved Africans and, until the late 1800s, were primarily used as food for livestock, the poor, and the enslaved. Although the first known commercial peanut crop was harvested in Sussex County (1842), it was not until the early 1900s—with the help of scientist George Washington Carver—that the popularity of the peanut transformed southeast Virginia. Consumers love the Virginia Peanut because of its large size, characteristic crunch, and rich flavor.

"Mr. P. Nut Planter, From Virginia," 1916
Antonio Gentile (artist)
Division of Work and Industry, National Museum of American History, Smithsonian Institution

In 1916, the Pennsylvania-based Planters Nut and Chocolate Company ran a contest for a new company trademark. Antonio "Tony" Gentile (1903–1939), a thirteen-year-old resident of Suffolk, Virginia, won. His drawings inspired one of the most famous brand icons, "Mr. Peanut." Amedeo Obici, the co-founder of Planters and a fellow Italian, took a personal interest in Tony and funded his education, including his medical degree.

Planters Pennant Peanuts pocket tin, after 1921
Planters (manufacturer)
Wm Morford Auctions / Morfauction.com

Virginia Peanuts grown at Belmont Peanuts, 2017
Ashley Johnson (photographer)
Belmont Peanuts

The Marks family, owners and operators of Belmont Peanuts of Southampton, have been in agribusiness for generations. These Virginia Peanuts are hand-roasted and seasoned at their family farm in Courtland.

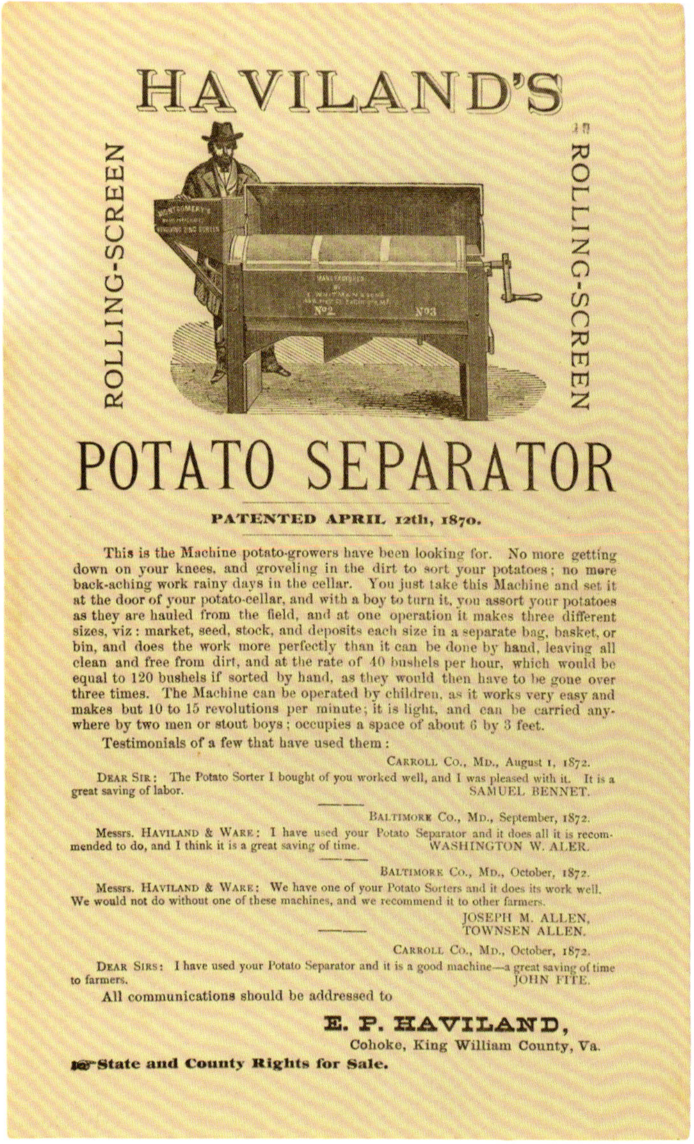

Haviland's Potato Separator advertisement, about 1872

VMHC Collection

Invented by E.P. Haviland of King William County, the potato separator allowed farmers to quickly sort potatoes into three different sizes—market, seed, and stock—three times faster than if done by hand. These hand-cranked machines could process 40 bushels each hour.

A farmhand or sharecropper sorting potatoes in Onley (Accomack County), 1927–1947

From the collection of the Eastern Shore of Virginia Historical Society

POTATOES

Potatoes arrived in the Commonwealth in 1621—a gift from the governor of Bermuda to the governor of Virginia. Large-scale potato farming "took root" on the Eastern Shore, where sandy, fertile soils and a temperate climate create an ideal environment for growing spuds. By the early 1900s, potato farming made Accomack County one of the wealthiest agricultural counties in the nation. Today, Virginia is the tenth-largest producer of early summer potatoes in the country and its farmers harvest over 200,000 pounds each year.

Potato processing in Thalia (now Virginia Beach), 1948

From the *Virginian-Pilot* Photograph Collection, Sergeant Memorial Collection, Norfolk Public Library

These potatoes are being processed and bagged for transport by train to markets worldwide.

Red Star brand label, 1900–55

From the collection of the Eastern Shore of Virginia Historical Society

Established in 1900, the Eastern Shore of Virginia Produce Exchange was a groundbreaking farmers' cooperative marketing organization that offered research, advertising, sales, and education for member farms. Its "Red Star" brand became synonymous with high-quality products, and the Exchange—which operated until the 1950s—served as a model for similar organizations that followed.

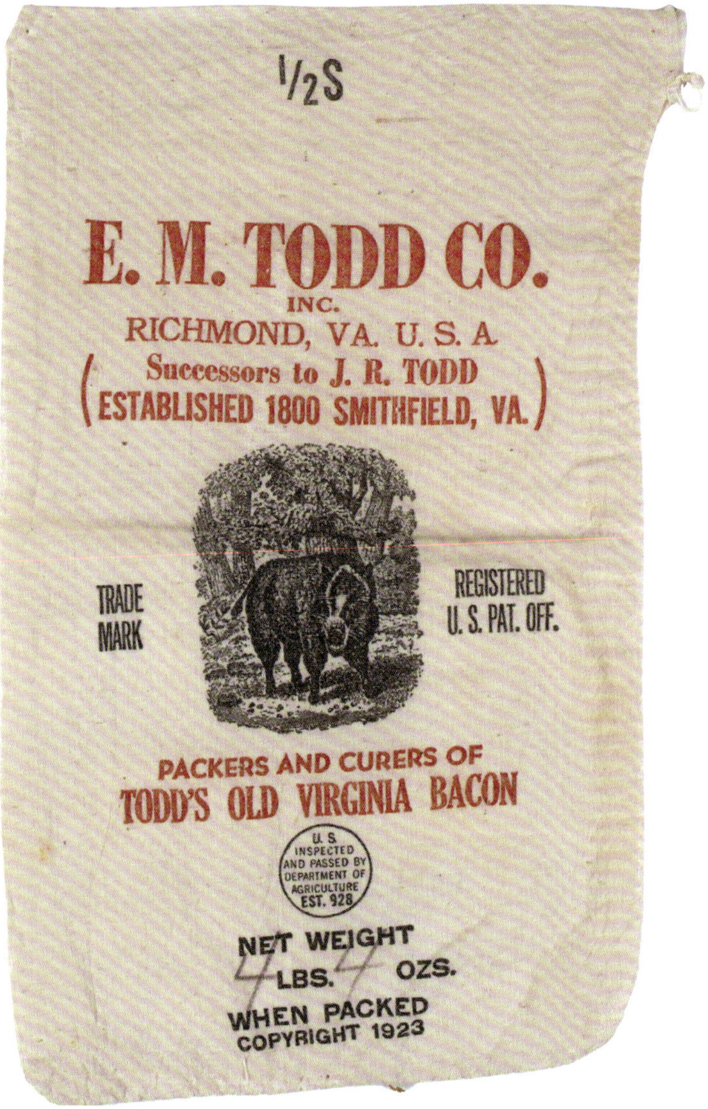

E.M. Todd Co. Inc. bacon bag, after 1923
VMHC Collection

Captain Mallory Todd (1742–1817), a Bermuda sea captain who settled in Isle of Wight County, is the earliest known producer and exporter of "Smithfield" hams (1779). His descendants, including Everard M. Todd (1827–1907), continued the business and helped establish "Smithfield hams" as a nationally recognized brand. From the 1920s until 1998, the Todd name was used by the Young family who established the E.M. Todd Co. headquarters in Richmond.

***Genuine Smithfield, Virginia, Hams come from Peanut Fed Hogs* postcard, early 1900s**
Tichnor Brothers, Inc. (publisher)
VMHC Collection

Traditionally, Virginia farmers let pigs roam their peanut fields after the harvest and eat what remained. It is believed that such a diet contributes to the sweet flavor and moistness of Virginia ham. According to Sam Edwards III (b. 1956), a third-generation curemaster based in Surry County, a diet comprised of 30% peanuts is ideal. Too many peanuts and the meat becomes flabby.

Smithfield Hams sign from J.P. Crowder's Delicatessen (Richmond), second half 1900s
Unknown manufacturer
VMHC Collection, Gift of Christine W. Banks

J.P. Crowder (about 1888–1972) opened his "Virginia and Smithfield" ham shop and delicatessen in 1919. In 1965, the business was purchased by longtime employee Christine Wilkins Banks (1929–2010), who ran the store until 2005. The deli was not only a fixture among downtown Richmond restaurants but also did a profitable mail order business, shipping Smithfield hams to customers nationwide.

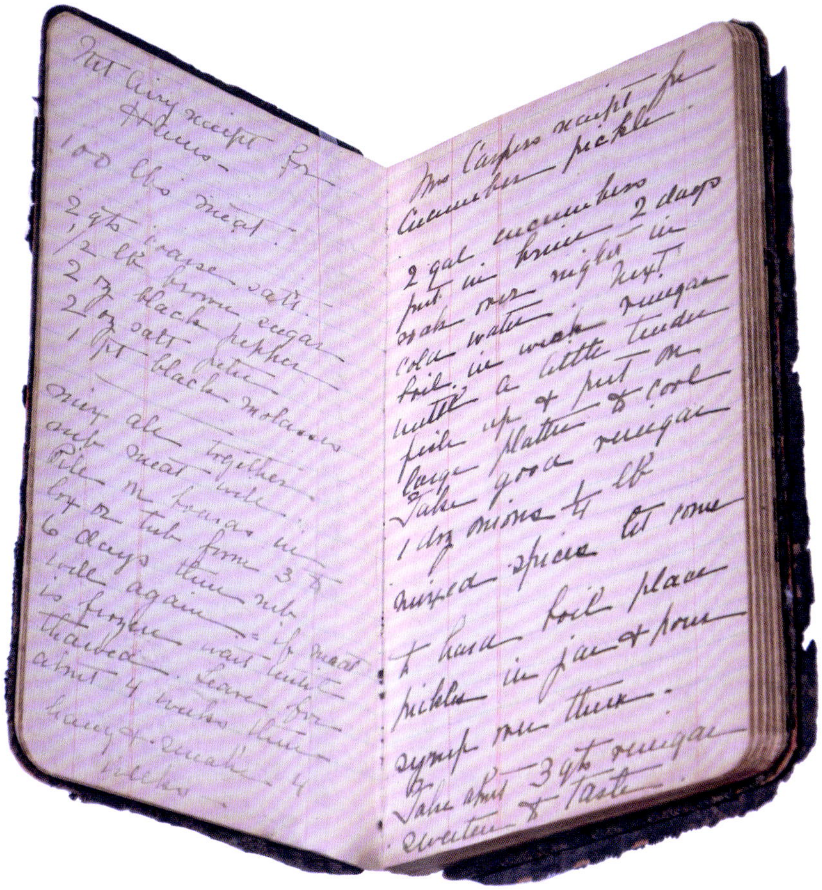

Commonplace book kept by Katharine Snyder, 1913–21

VMHC Collection, Gift of Sophie Burnham

Katharine Christine Parrish Snyder (1876–1965) of Fairfax County recorded her family's recipes for ketchup, apple butter, pickles, and cured hams in this commonplace book. The saltpeter (potassium nitrate) in this recipe helps to preserve the meat's pink color.

100 lbs meat
2 qts coarse salt
½ lb brown sugar
2 oz black pepper
2 oz salt petre [sic]
1 pt black molasses

Mix all together rub meat well. Pile on boards in box or tub from 3 to 6 days then rub well again if meat is frozen wait until thawed. Leave for about 4 weeks time. Hang and smoke 4 weeks.

"Mt. Airy receipt for Hams" from Katharine Snyder's commonplace book, 1913–21

PORK

Curing and aging meats is an ancient practice, but Virginians have long been recognized for their ham. For generations, farmers have butchered peanut-fed hogs, cured the meat with salts, added their favorite spice mix, and aged the hams in smokehouses for months. The process creates a uniquely dry, salty ham that generations of Virginians have paired with biscuits. Today, Virginia mandates that genuine Smithfield hams must be produced within the town's limits.

Mozelle Brown with her famous ham biscuits, 2013

Keith Lanpher (photographer)

Lanpher Productions Inc.

For more than fifty years, Mozelle Brown (1939–2021) worked at the Smithfield Inn and became renowned for her Smithfield ham biscuit—a secret family recipe she learned from her mother. Her biscuits were known to rise light and fluffy, and made the perfect complement to sweet, salty, wafer-thin slices of Smithfield ham.

Northern VIRGINIA

Life in Northern Virginia (NoVA) is largely influenced by its proximity to the nation's capital. Diverse neighborhoods grow and change with the pulse of world events. Commuters jam the region's highways and cram into trains as they travel to their federal and military jobs. Regional technology centers continue a long legacy of local industries built to support government operations.

Arlington skyline, 2020

Joe Daniel Price / Getty Images

Alexandria, Virginia, from the Potomac River, 2023
Steve Heap (photographer)
BackYardProduction

Northern Virginia Independent Cities

1. Alexandria
2. Fairfax City
3. Falls Church
4. Manassas
5. Manassas Park

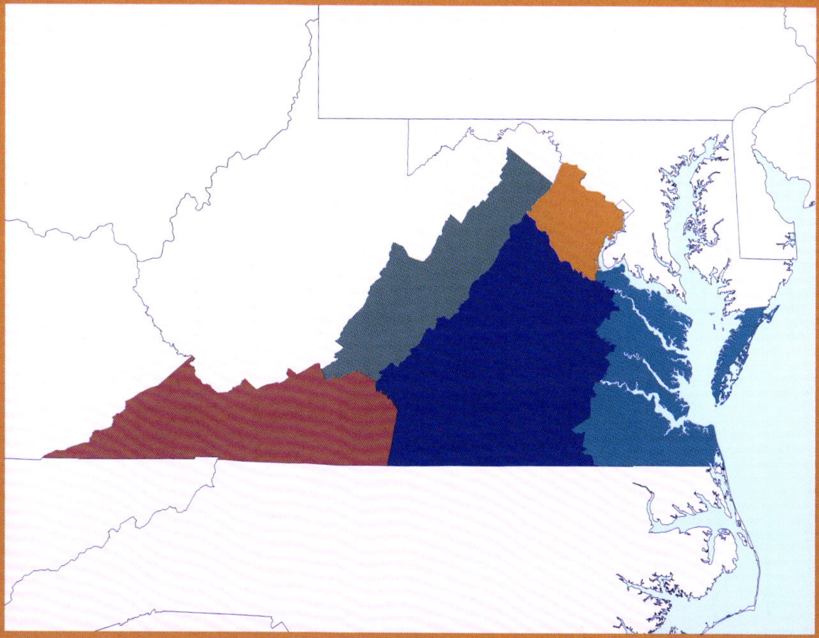

BEING PART OF WASHINGTON

In 1790, the U.S. Congress, after much debate, established the nation's permanent capital on a site along the Potomac River from land given by Maryland and Virginia. Its placement fundamentally changed the character of Northern Virginia. Almost 50 years later, the federal government returned the Virginia portion, which included parts of Alexandria and Arlington. Nevertheless, Washington has had lasting economic, historical, and social impact on NoVA that inextricably linked the region with U.S. government operations.

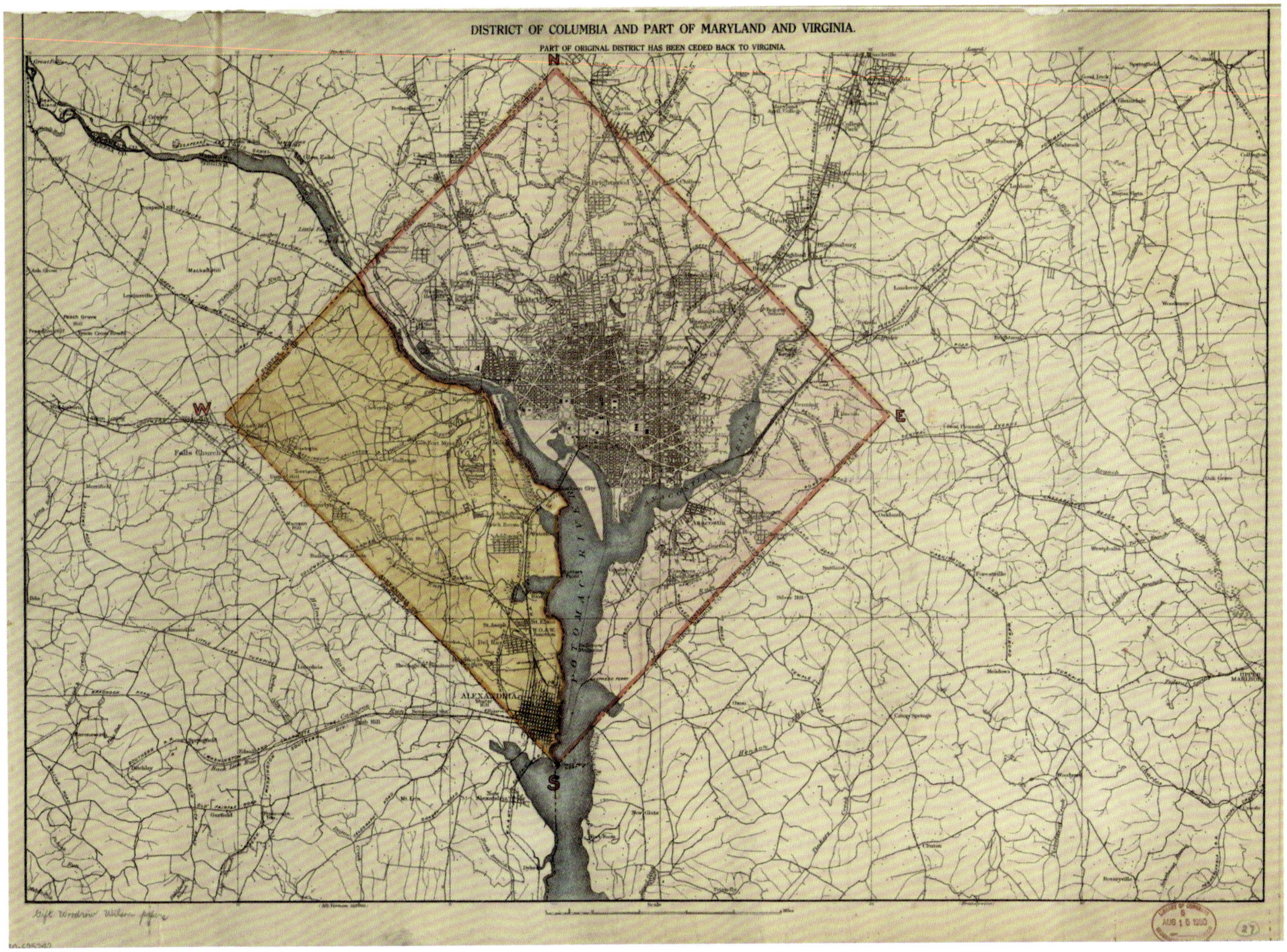

District of Columbia and Part of Maryland and Virginia, 1915

Library of Congress, Geography and Map Division

In 1791, Virginia gave 31 square miles along the Potomac (shown in yellow) to become part of the District of Columbia.

George Washington, after 1787
James Peale (artist), after or with Charles Willson Peale
VMHC Collection, Gift of R.B. Kennon

Passed by Congress in 1790, The Residence Act authorized the new nation's first president, George Washington (1731 – 1790), to select the site of the capital along the Potomac River. He included Alexandria—a well-developed port city five miles from his Mount Vernon home—in the hope that government activity would stimulate the local economy.

"[A] district of ten miles square, shall be found. . . . Running from the Court House in Alexandria in Virginia, due south west half a mile, and thence a due south East course, till it shall strike Hunting Creek, to fix the beginning of the . . . Experiment."

A Proclamation by George Washington, President of the United States of America, delineating the Virginia portion of the new Federal city, 1791

George Washington's Mount Vernon along the Potomac River, 2020
Cameron Davidson (photographer)
© Cameron Davidson

In 1674, John Washington secured a land grant along the Potomac River that became the core of his great-grandson's 8,000-acre estate. George Washington not only shipped and received goods via the river, but it also supplied him with vast quantities of fish that fed the free and enslaved residents of Mount Vernon and provided an important source of income.

Crock (detail), about 1830–50
Benedict Milburn for H.C. Smith (merchant)
From the collection of The Lyceum, City of Alexandria

Marked "Alex[andri]a, D.C.," this crock was made at a time when that city was still a part of the District of Columbia.

Storage jar, 1830
David Jarbour (maker); Hugh Smith (retailer)
From the William C. and Susan S. Mariner Southern Ceramics Collection at the Museum of Early Southern Decorative Arts

After becoming part of the nation's new capital, Alexandria's growing economy provided new opportunities for merchants and artisans. Although it had one of the nation's largest markets of enslaved people before the Civil War, it also had a thriving free Black community, including David Jarbour (about 1790–1841), a skilled potter. He worked at the Wilkes Street Pottery, a successful Alexandria stoneware manufactory owned for a time by Hugh Smith (1768–1852) and his sons.

Ewer, about 1830
William Alexander Williams (maker)
VMHC Collection, Gift of Betsy Gilmer Tremain

Originally from Baltimore, Williams (1784–1846) set up shop in Alexandria in 1811 and ran a flourishing business making clocks and luxury metal goods such as this elegant pitcher. Williams was also active in civic life as a member of the Masons, a theatrical organization, and the county militia.

Front of "slave pen," Alexandria, Va., 1861–5

Andrew J. Russell (photographer)

Library of Congress, Prints and Photographs Division

From 1828 to 1836, this complex of buildings served as the headquarters of Franklin and Armfield, the largest traders of enslaved African Americans in the United States. The company purchased more than 8,500 men, women, and children from Maryland and Virginia who were held in jail cells before their horrific journey to be sold in Louisiana and Mississippi. By 1858, the building was occupied by another slave trading firm, Price, Birch & Co.

View of a section of Alexandria with a slave ship receiving her cargo of slaves, 1836

American Anti-Slavery Society

Library of Congress, Rare Book and Special Collections Division

In 1846, the U.S. Congress returned land taken to create Washington, D.C.—including Alexandria—to Virginia. The "retrocession" had been lobbied for and was welcomed by many Alexandria residents who had lost their representation in Congress and were denied infrastructure improvements. The return of Alexandria would strengthen Virginia's proslavery legislature and protected the city's massive business in trading enslaved people, threatened by an anticipated ban of the slave trade in the District—which happened in 1850.

One abolitionist recorded what a group of Black Alexandrians wrote to him about the retrocession vote:

"Fancy, but for a moment, you could have seen [Black people] on the day of election. . . . Whilst the citizens of this city and county were voting . . . and, as the votes were announced every quarter of an hour, the suppressed wailings and lamentations of the people of color were constantly ascending to God for help and succor."

Gerrit Smith (1797–1874), abolitionist and social reformer, 1848

SUPPLYING THE CAPITAL

Dairy production was one of the first and most critical Northern Virginia industries to support the U.S. capital. Before refrigeration, city residents could only consume dairy products made regionally. NoVA's roads and rails helped local farmers transport supplies of milk, cheese, and butter to Washington residents. Some farms even had their own train platforms to load milk cans onto railroad cars. Although the dairy industry in Northern Virginia has decreased with regional development, many local farms still carry on the work. The long lines at ice cream farmstands prove that NoVA's cows are still a vital resource.

Dairy farmers waiting by the Herndon Depot, early 1900s

Herndon Historical Society, J. Berkley Green Photo Collection

In 1900, dairy farming was the most important industry in Fairfax County. The Washington and Old Dominion Railway ran trains every day to ship milk to Washington dairies for processing and distribution. By 1925, the majority of the county's residents lived in towns, but Fairfax County remained the state's leading producer of dairy products.

***Sadie the Cow*, early 1900s**

Fairfax County Public Library Photographic Archive

In 1923, Herndon dairyman Ben Middleton's cow Sadie was reportedly the best-known Holstein in the world. She produced over 30 tons of milk and one ton of butterfat in three years, when the average annual output for a Fairfax County cow was about four tons.

Lawrence Lee, Alta Lee, and an unidentified visitor inside the dairy barn, about 1955

Fairfax County Public Library Photographic Archive

In 1945, Lawrence and Gladys Lee left their higher-education teaching jobs in Washington, D.C., to buy a 120-acre dairy farm in Chantilly (Fairfax County). "The Alta Lee Farm" was named after their daughter. Until Lawrence's death in 1959, they shipped the milk they produced back to Washington.

Piedmont Virginia Dairy Festival program, 1932

From the collection of the Manassas Museum System

Nine counties and three cities in NoVA organized the Piedmont Dairy Festival to promote the region's dairy industry. This annual fair took place in Manassas from 1931 to 1936.

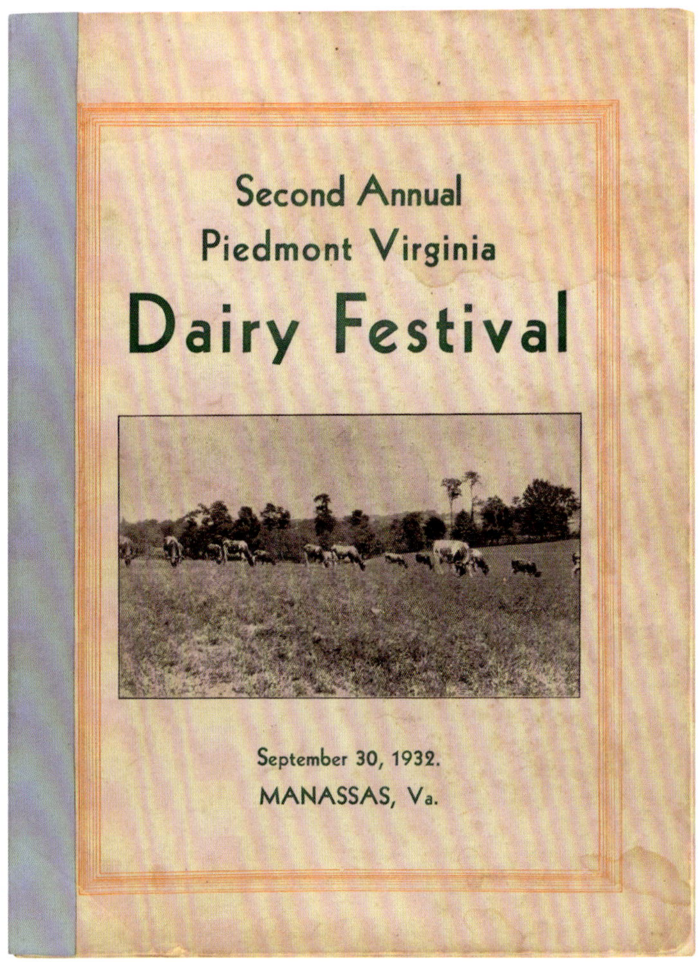

Second Annual
Piedmont Virginia
Dairy Festival

September 30, 1932.
MANASSAS, Va.

Piedmont Dairy Festival tiara, 1932

From the collection of the Manassas Museum System

Elizabeth Anne Davies (1913–2015) wore this rhinestone tiara at her coronation as Piedmont Dairy Festival Queen.

Clover Hill Farm, 1960s
Alton Marsh (photographer)
Courtesy of the Manassas Museum System

The Johnson family purchased Clover Hill Farm in 1770 and grew it into a dairy that produced about 30,000 gallons of milk per year by the late 1800s. In 1987, the Johnsons sold Clover Hill, the last operating farm in the City of Manassas, to developers for retail and housing units.

"What's affecting this farm is the development of the land around it. Farms within the limits of municipalities don't last very long. The future of this farm is not in our hands."
Bill Johnson, Clover Hill Farm, 1979

Alexandria Dairy Products Company milk bottle, mid-1900s
VMHC Collection

Before refrigeration, many households had perishable foods delivered daily. The Alexandria Dairy Products Company opened in June 1930 and could process more than 10,000 gallons of milk a day for families living in Alexandria, Arlington, and Fairfax County. By 1950, it had grown into one of the largest dairies in Virginia, serving more than 30,000 families with daily home deliveries.

Willowmere Farms (Fairfax) milk bottle, first half 1900s
VMHC Collection

BEING CONNECTED

With its proximity to Washington, D.C., Northern Virginia sits at the nexus of America's national and global influence. During the Cold War, new government agencies and "information" companies sprang up to supply intelligence for national security. As home to the first internet providers, NoVA has expanded its reach in the digital age.

Many national and global corporations have their headquarters here. In NoVA, these companies find a highly skilled workforce, cosmopolitan culture, and two international airports, as well as access to D.C.'s halls of power.

Equinix DC11 IBX Data Center in Ashburn, Virginia, 2021

Equinix

In 2022, Virginia was home to more than 300 data centers. Of those, 275 were concentrated in Loudoun, Fairfax, and Prince William counties.

". . . nearly 70% of all [the world's] Internet traffic flows through Northern Virginia."

Northern Virginia Chamber of Commerce, 2021

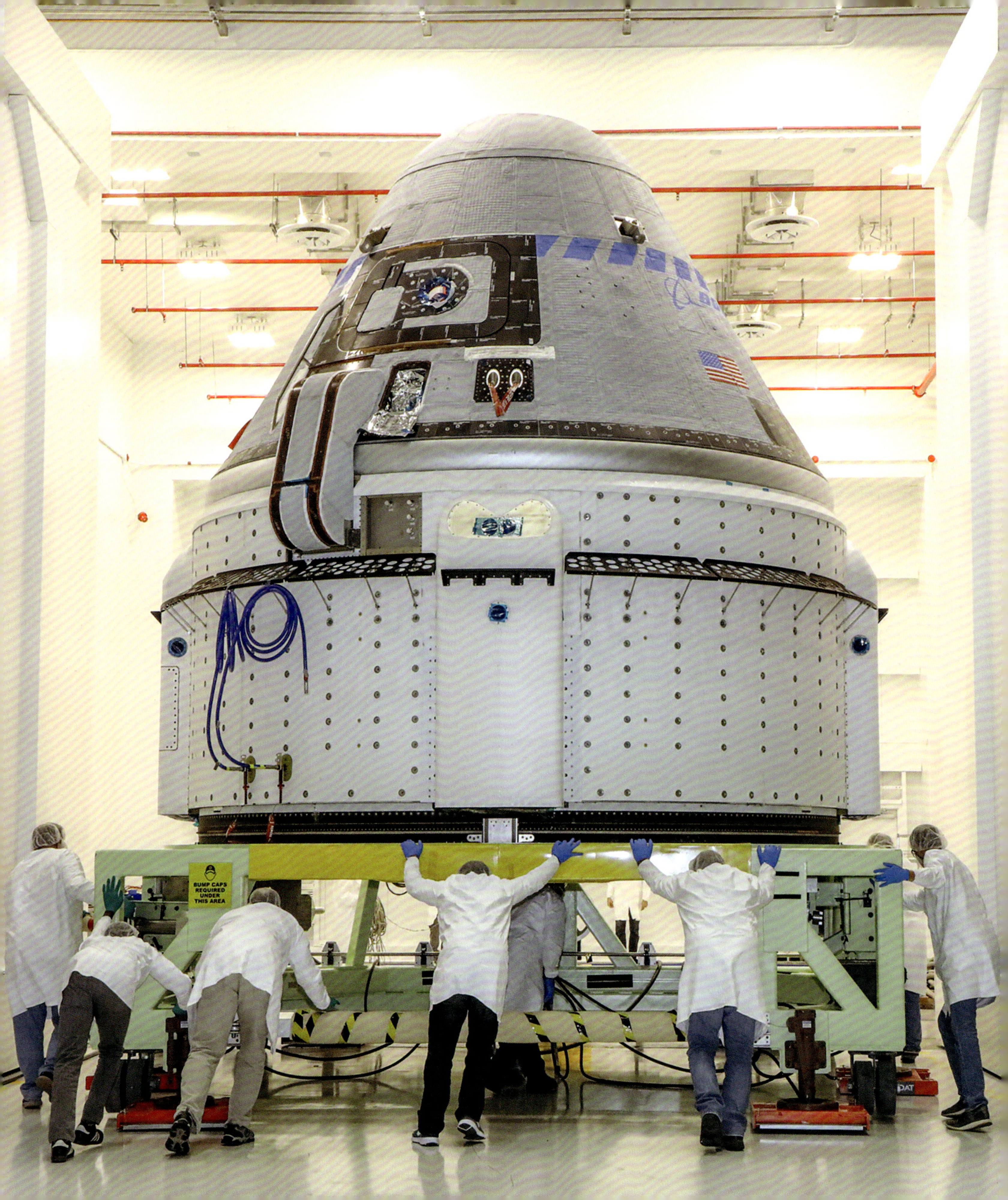
BUMP CAPS
REQUIRED
UNDER
THIS AREA

America Online Version 2.5 floppy disk, 1995
America Online (AOL)
VMHC Collection

In the mid-1990s, the pioneering internet provider America Online (AOL) helped establish Northern Virginia as a hub of technological innovation when it moved its headquarters to Fairfax County. AOL's "You've Got Mail" notification became a catchphrase of the early internet age.

M&M's dispenser, 1991
VMHC Collection

One of the largest food companies in the world, Mars, Inc. produces beloved brands including M&M's, Snickers, Wrigley, Iams, Whiskas, and Ben's Original. Working with food historians, their American Heritage Chocolate brand is inspired by historical recipes from the 1700s. Founded in 1911, the company moved its global headquarters to NoVA in 1984.

CST-100 Boeing Starliner, 2019
Boeing
NASA / Kennedy Space Center

Since 1916, Boeing has been a leader in aerospace innovation. The company introduced the first commercial jet airliner (1958) and developed portions of the Saturn V rocket that launched astronauts to the Moon (1969). Boeing is also well known for iconic military aircraft—including the B-17 Flying Fortress (1935) and the B-29 Superfortress (1942). Today, their reusable CST-100 Starliner is designed to transport crews to the International Space Station. Boeing moved their global headquarters to Arlington in 2023, to be closer to their customers and to have "access to world-class engineering and technical talent."

Fortune 500 Companies Headquartered in Northern Virginia

BOEING
MARS
DXC TECHNOLOGY
HILTON WORLDWIDE
Booz | Allen | Hamilton
Capital One
Raytheon Technologies
NORTHROP GRUMMAN
GENERAL DYNAMICS

CIA pilot Francis Gary Powers with a Lockheed U-2F at Van Nuys Airport, California, late 1950s

From the collection of Francis Gary Powers, Jr.

U-2 spy plane pilot suit, 1960

From the collection of Francis Gary Powers, Jr.

This pressurized suit was worn by Francis Gary Powers (1929–1977) of Pound, Virginia, a U.S. Air Force pilot who joined the CIA's U-2 program in 1956. On May 1, 1960, at the height of the Cold War, Powers's U-2 spy plane was shot down while flying a reconnaissance mission over the Soviet Union. He was captured and spent the next two years in a Soviet prison. Powers's release in 1962 garnered international attention and was the subject of the 2015 film *Bridge of Spies*.

Lobby of the Central Intelligence Agency Headquarters, 2010

Shutterstock

Completed in 1961, the CIA Headquarters were built in Fairfax County because of its proximity to Washington. Its iconic lobby includes the Office of Strategic Services Memorial and the William Donovan statue (left) and the Memorial Wall featuring 139 stars (as of 2022) representing agency officers who have died in the line of duty.

Dr. Gladys West (right) looking over GPS data, 1985

U.S. Navy / Wikipedia Commons

Born on a farm in rural Dinwiddie County, Gladys West (b. 1930) became a mathematician, and her work transformed modern life. She helped develop GPS technology during her 42-year career at the Naval Support Facility at Dahlgren, Virginia. Like other Black women in the defense and aerospace industries, West had to overcome racism and sexism. When she arrived at Dahlgren in 1956, she was one of only four Black professionals working in the lab.

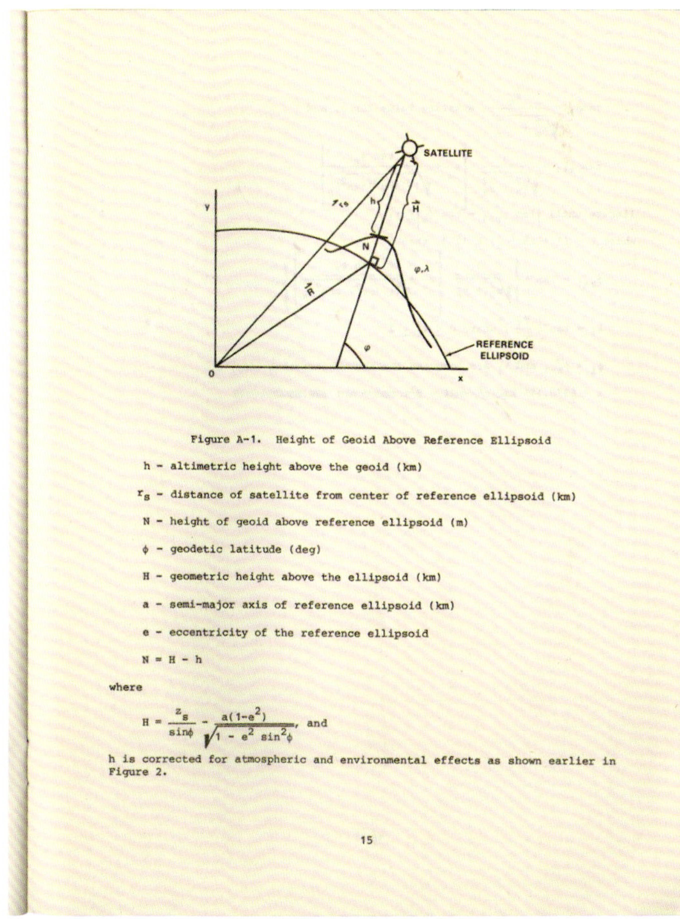

SATELLITE

REFERENCE ELLIPSOID

Figure A-1. Height of Geoid Above Reference Ellipsoid

h - altimetric height above the geoid (km)

r_s - distance of satellite from center of reference ellipsoid (km)

N - height of geoid above reference ellipsoid (m)

ϕ - geodetic latitude (deg)

H - geometric height above the ellipsoid (km)

a - semi-major axis of reference ellipsoid (km)

e - eccentricity of the reference ellipsoid

N = H - h

where

$$H = \frac{z_s}{\sin\phi} - \frac{a(1-e^2)}{\sqrt{1 - e^2 \sin^2\phi}}, \text{ and}$$

h is corrected for atmospheric and environmental effects as shown earlier in Figure 2.

15

"SEASAT Satellite Radar Altimetry Data Processing System," Naval Surface Weapons Center Report, 1981

Gladys West

VMHC Collection, Gift of Carolyn W. Oglesby

In her work on GPS technology and on the SEASAT project—the first satellite that could map oceans from space—West analyzed satellite measurements of the earth and developed algorithms for processing this data on some of the world's most powerful super-computers.

Sunrise over Arlington National Cemetery, 2014

Dennis Gavoni / Getty Images

American servicemen and women from every state are interred in Virginia's nineteen national cemeteries. The first military burial at Arlington—formerly the home of Confederate general Robert E. Lee—took place in May 1864. Still active, the 200-acre cemetery is the final resting place for more than 400,000 service members, veterans, and their families.

SERVICE TO THE NATION

Many Virginians have responded to calls to serve their country during times of conflict. In the late 1700s, George Mason wrote key documents rejecting British authority over the colonies from his home in Fairfax. During the Civil War, NoVA housed federal military installations which also became safe havens for Black Americans seeking freedom from slavery. In the mid-20th century, thousands of local men and women joined the growing government and defense industry workforce. They built a sprawling suburbia and supported a wide network of government and military agencies. The 9/11 attacks scorched NoVA's soil and activated local counterterrorism efforts that continue today.

U.S. Marine Corps War Memorial, 2014

Henk Meijer / Alamy Stock Photo

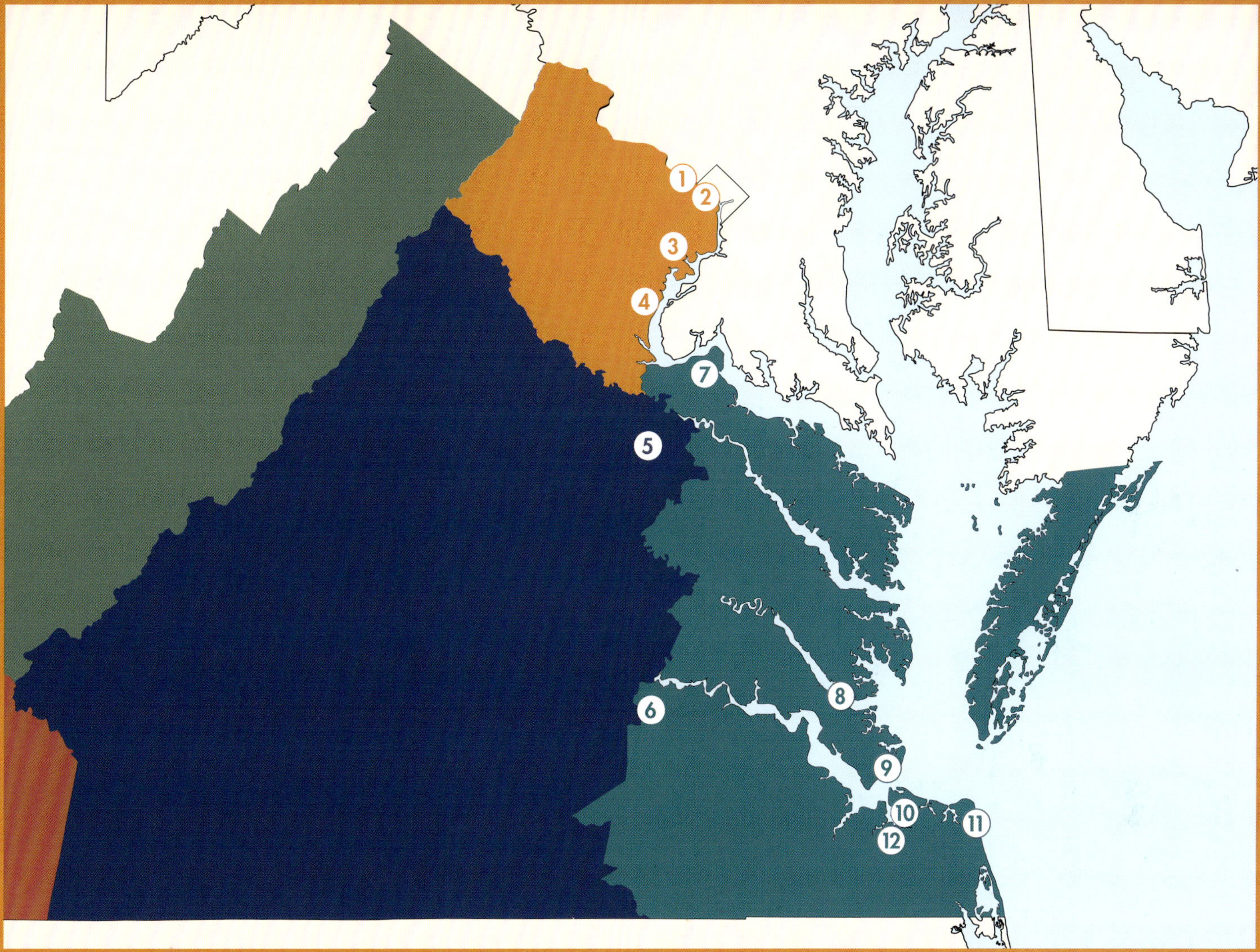

Major Military Installations in Virginia

Northern Virginia

1. Joint Base Myer-Henderson Hall, Arlington (U.S. Army)
2. The Pentagon, Arlington County
3. Fort Belvoir, Fairfax County (U.S. Army)
4. Marine Corps Base Quantico

Central Virginia

5. Fort Walker, Caroline County (U.S. Army)

Tidewater Virginia

6. Fort Gregg-Adams, Prince George County (U.S. Army)
7. Naval Support Facility Dahlgren, King George County (U.S. Navy)
8. Naval Weapons Station Yorktown (U.S. Navy)
9. Joint Base Langley-Eustis, Hampton (U.S. Air Force)
10. Naval Station Norfolk (U.S. Navy)
11. Naval Air Station Oceana, Virginia Beach (U.S. Navy)
12. Norfolk Naval Shipyard, Portsmouth (U.S. Navy)

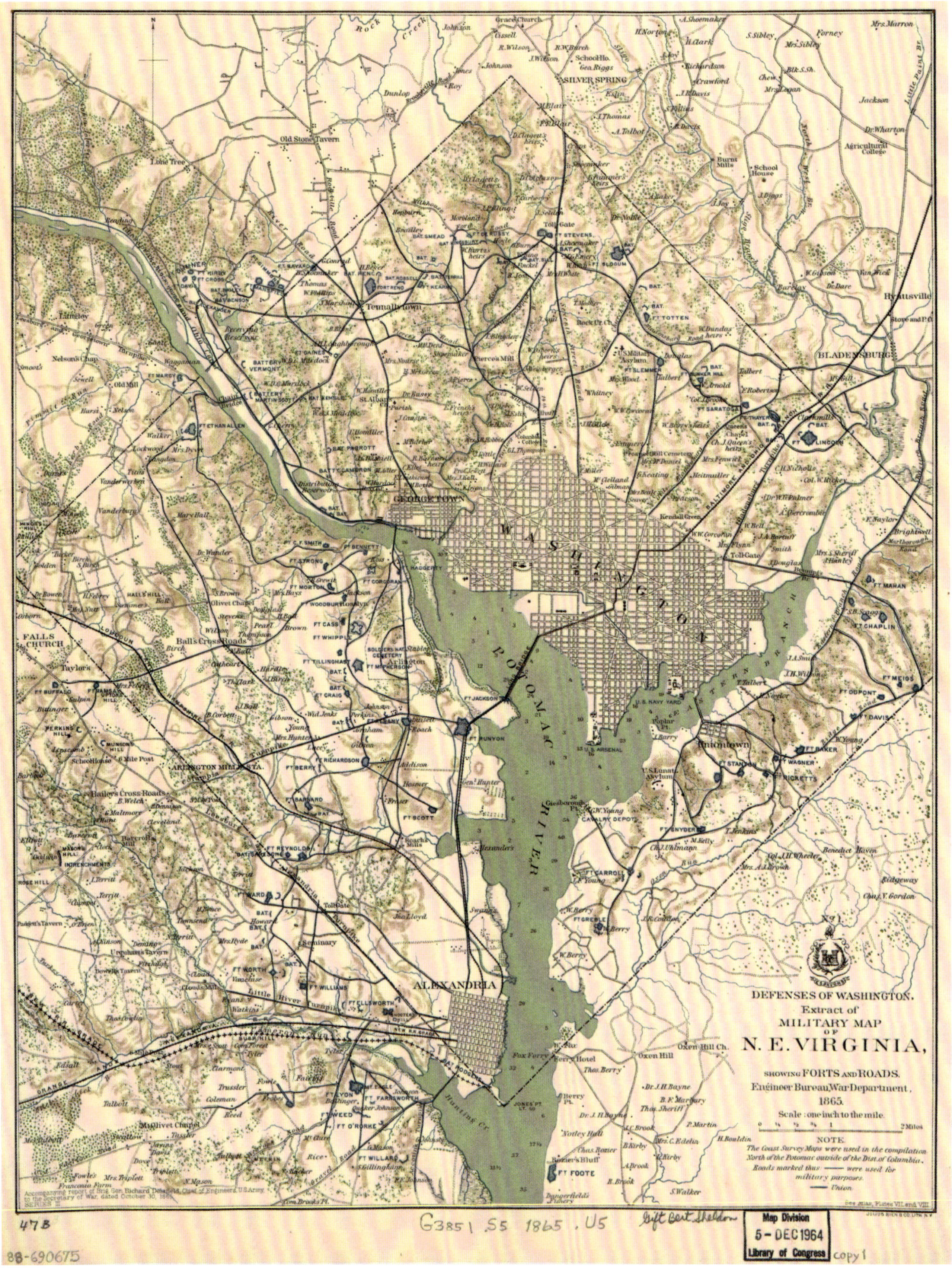
DEFENSES OF WASHINGTON.
Extract of
MILITARY MAP
OF
N. E. VIRGINIA,
SHOWING FORTS AND ROADS.
Engineer Bureau, War Department,
1865.
Scale : one inch to the mile.
NOTE.
The Coast Survey Maps were used in the compilation North of the Potomac outside of the Dist. of Columbia.
Roads marked thus —— were used for military purposes.
—— Union
WASHINGTON
GEORGETOWN
ALEXANDRIA
POTOMAC RIVER
BLADENSBURG
FALLS CHURCH
Map Division
5-DEC 1964
Library of Congress

View of the construction of the Pentagon, 1942

Department of Defense

In 1943, the War Department completed construction on a five-sided structure in Arlington to provide more office space. At the height of World War II, more than 33,000 people worked there. The Pentagon has become a symbol of strength and security across the world. Today, it is the location of the offices of the Secretary of Defense, the Joint Chiefs of Staff, and the highest levels of the Army, Navy, Marine Corps, and Air Force.

The west face of the Pentagon following the terrorist attack on 9/11, 2001

From the collection of the 9/11 Memorial & Museum, Gift of Special Agent Robert Walker

"I was in the office [at the Pentagon] when we felt the impact. We'd been . . . watching the events unfold on the World Trade Center. . . . I'm starting to think about THREATCON and things like that. . . . We heard the thud, the impact. . . . I said, 'It's time to go. Let's get out of here. We've got to evacuate.' . . . Got all of the Petty Officers together and just said, 'Move! Move! Move!'"

Captain Mary Jo Sweeney, U.S. Navy, Executive Assistant to Vice Admiral Patricia Tracey, on September 11, 2001

Defenses of Washington, 1865

Engineer Bureau, War Department (publisher)

Library of Congress, Geography and Map Division

During the American Civil War (1861–5), the U.S. Army constructed an imposing ring of forts and gun batteries (marked in blue) connected by more than 20 miles of fortifications around Washington to ensure its defense. Twenty-seven of these were built south of Potomac River in Virginia.

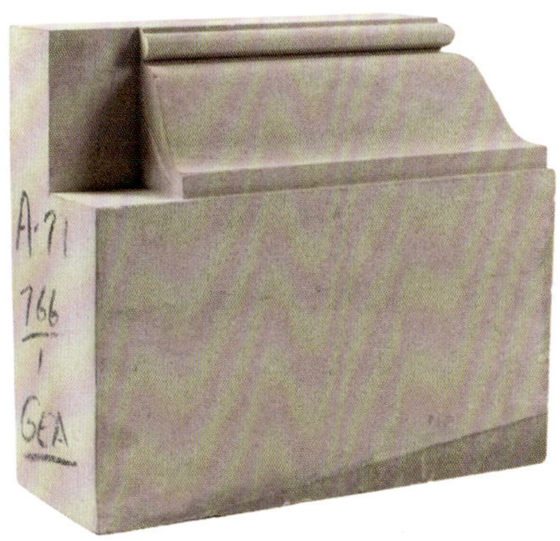

Limestone fragment from the Pentagon, 2001

VMHC Collection, Gift of United States Department of Defense

On September 11, 2001, American Airlines Flight 77 departed Washington Dulles International Airport. Islamic extremists enraged by U.S. involvement in the Middle East hijacked the plane and crashed into the Pentagon. All sixty-four people on board died, as did 125 people on the ground.

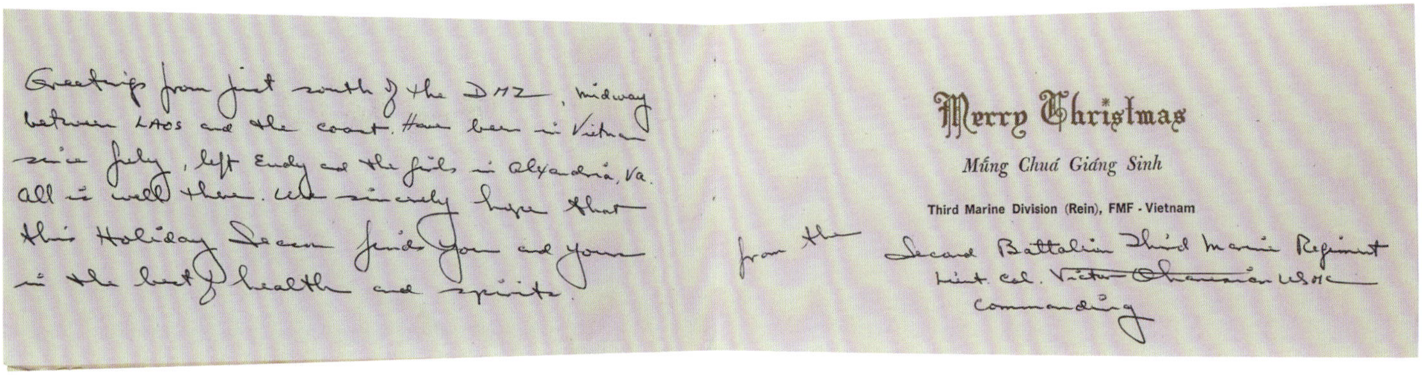

Greetings from just south of the DMZ, midway between LAOS and the coast. Have been in Vietnam since July, left Eudy and the girls in Alexandria, Va. All is well there. We sincerely hope that this Holiday Season finds you and yours in the best of health and spirits.

Merry Christmas

Mừng Chúa Giáng Sinh

Third Marine Division (Rein), FMF - Vietnam

from the Second Battalion Third Marine Regiment
Lieut. Col. Victor Ohanesian USMC
Commanding

Christmas card from Lt. Col. Victor Ohanesian, U.S. Marine Corps, to his family, 1966

VMHC Collection

Ohanesian (1926–1967) enlisted in the U.S. Marine Corps in 1944 and served in both World War II and Korea. When he was recalled to active duty in June 1966, he left his wife and daughters in Alexandria to fight in the Vietnam War. Mortally wounded by mortar fire in February 1967 while rescuing a fellow Marine, he is buried at Arlington National Cemetery.

"Greetings from just south of the DMZ [Demilitarized Zone], midway between Laos and the coast. Have been in Vietnam since July, left Eudy and the girls in Alexandria, Va. All is well there. We sincerely hope that this Holiday Season finds you and yours in the best of health and spirits."

Lt. Col. Victor Ohanesian, 1966

U.S. Naval Torpedo Station, Alexandria, about 1920

From the collection of George L. Dant, copyright the Naval History and Heritage Command

Plans to build the U.S. Naval Torpedo Station began during World War I, but construction did not begin until November 12, 1918—the day after the war ended. The first torpedo rolled off the production line in 1920. Closed three years later, it reopened during World War II and employed 6,000 people. Nearby Chinquapin Village was built to provide temporary housing for this influx of workers. The village no longer stands, and the torpedo factory building has been repurposed as an art center.

"[The Village] was a big family. Small town family. . . . When you walked down the street you could speak to everybody, because you knew everybody. Of course, there were 300 families, and you could easily have 1,500 people, with all the kids. . . ."

Jerry Sare, former Chinquapin Village resident, 2001

"Boonie" hat of John W. Listman, Jr., 1971–2

VMHC Collection, Gift of John W. Listman, Jr.

John W. Listman, Jr. (b. 1951) from Fairfax, wore this "Boonie" hat while serving in Vietnam. American soldiers purchased hats like this from Vietnamese vendors to keep the sun and rain off their necks. Listman personalized his hat with a patch referencing Vice President Spiro T. Agnew, who coined the phrase "silent majority," for the number of Americans he believed supported the war effort.

Marijke K. Verser receiving the Navy and Marine Corps Achievement Medal, 2010

From the collection of Marijke K. Verser

Verser joined the Navy in 2001. Her earliest days were served in the aftermath of the terrorist attacks on September 11, 2001. She was stationed in Norfolk and worked as a nuclear electronics technician, including operating the nuclear reactor powering aircraft carriers and supporting those on the front lines in the Persian Gulf.

U.S. Navy working uniform of Marijke K. Verser, about 2008–11

From the collection of The Mariners' Museum and Park, Newport News, Virginia, Gift of Marijke K. Verser

Sky Meadows State Park, 2006
Douglas Graham (photographer)
William Graham / Alamy Stock Photo

Within an hour's drive from Washington, D.C., the western counties of Northern Virginia are renowned for picturesque rolling hills, small villages, expansive horse farms, and wineries. Sky Meadows State Park (Loudoun County) officially opened in 1983 on land donated to the Commonwealth by philanthropist Paul Mellon. Mellon bred and trained thoroughbred racehorses at his farm in nearby Upperville (Fauquier County).

RIDING HORSES

Early Virginians used horses to travel, hunt, and transport goods. Some also raced them. Since the mid-1800s, thoroughbred horse breeding has been concentrated in Northern Virginia. Today, much of the land once used to support this industry has been subjected to real estate development, but the scenic rolling hillsides of towns like Middleburg and Upperville are still home to a vibrant equine culture. Shows, races, and polo matches are cherished annual traditions that continue to draw generations of enthusiasts.

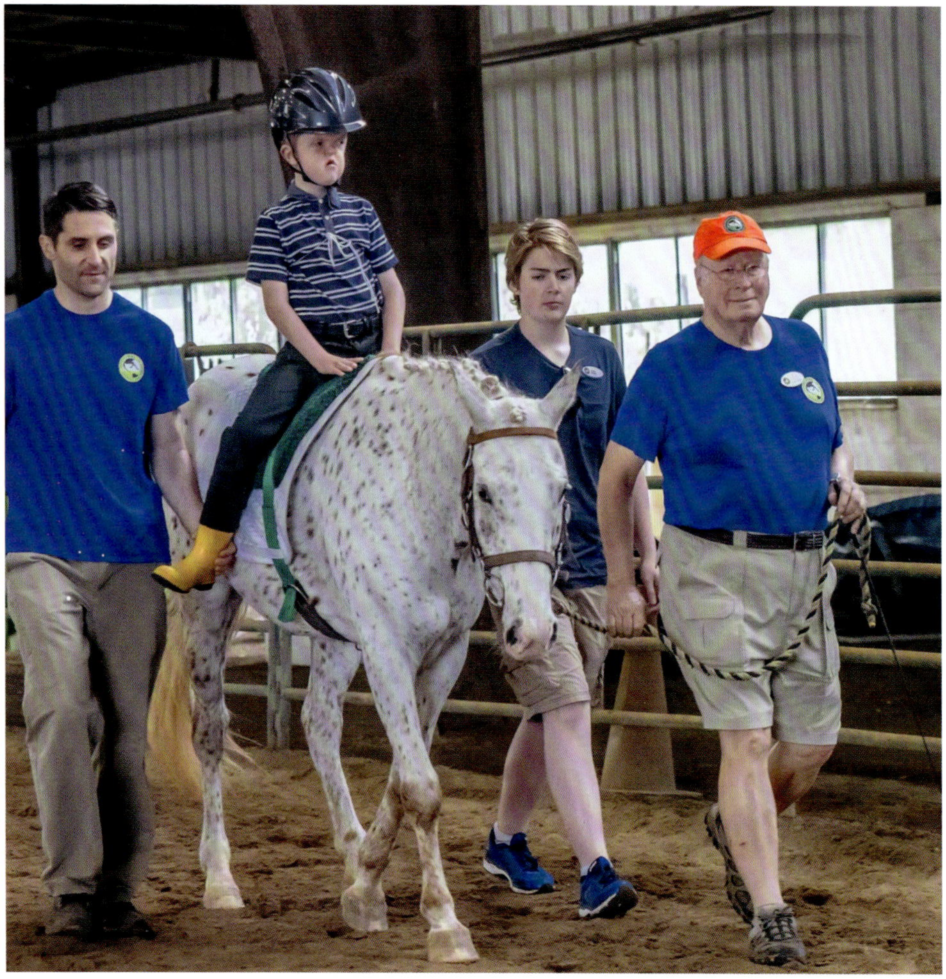

Ride to Thrive Horse Show, 2019

Sydney Sawyer / Northern Virginia Therapeutic Riding Program

Ride to Thrive Horse Show ribbon from the Northern Virginia Therapeutic Riding Program, 2021

From the collection of the Northern Virginia Therapeutic Riding Program

"We started the Ride to Thrive Horse Show so that local riders of all abilities would have the opportunity to compete in a horse show. It was the perfect way for NVTRP riders and riders from other local therapeutic riding programs to show off their skills in front of their friends and family!"

Northern Virginia Therapeutic Riding Program, 2005

A veteran works with one of the horses at the Project Horse Empowerment Center, 2021–2022

Courtesy of Project Horse

Beginning in 2008, counselors at Project Horse (Loudoun County) have used horses as part of non-riding therapy that helps people who have experienced trauma. The program moved to Colorado in 2023.

"The calming presence of horses. . . . Their keen ability to sense and respond to human emotion and intention provides an ideal environment for self-discovery, healing, and growth. . . . Horses facilitate healing for humans and teach us about connection and perseverance."

The Arc of Loudoun / Project Horse, 2022

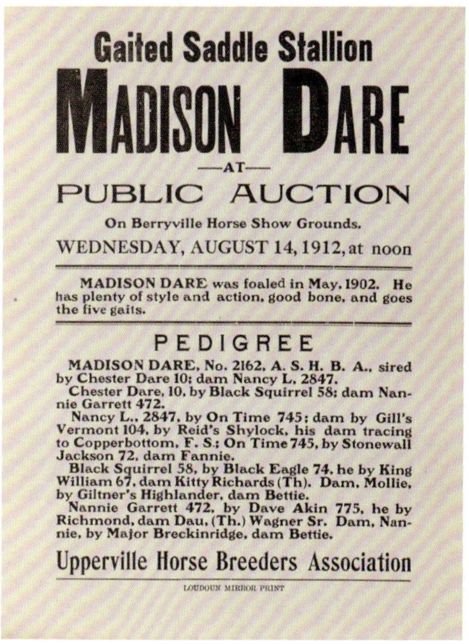

Gaited Saddle Stallion

MADISON DARE

—AT—

PUBLIC AUCTION

On Berryville Horse Show Grounds.

WEDNESDAY, AUGUST 14, 1912, at noon

MADISON DARE was foaled in May, 1902. He has plenty of style and action, good bone, and goes the five gaits.

PEDIGREE

MADISON DARE, No. 2162, A. S. H. B. A., sired by Chester Dare 10; dam Nancy L. 2847.

Chester Dare, 10, by Black Squirrel 58; dam Nannie Garrett 472.

Nancy L., 2847, by On Time 745; dam by Gill's Vermont 104, by Reid's Shylock, his dam tracing to Copperbottom, F. S.; On Time 745, by Stonewall Jackson 72, dam Fannie.

Black Squirrel 58, by Black Eagle 74, he by King William 67, dam Kitty Richards (Th). Dam, Mollie, by Giltner's Highlander, dam Bettie.

Nannie Garrett 472, by Dave Akin 775, he by Richmond, dam Dau, (Th.) Wagner Sr. Dam, Nannie, by Major Breckinridge, dam Bettie.

Upperville Horse Breeders Association

LOUDOUN MIRROR PRINT

Upperville Horse Breeders Association auction poster, 1912

VMHC Collection

This poster describes the stallion Madison Dare as having "plenty of style and action, good bone, and goes the five gaits." The five gaits referred to here are walk, trot, canter, slow gait, and rack (a specialized four beat gait).

Devon Sutherland (rider) and Dazzling Nocturne (owned by Nancy Winter) competing over fences at the Upperville Colt & Horse Show, 2023

Samantha Haynie (photographer)

Erin Gilmore Photography

Established in 1853, the Upperville Colt & Horse Show is the oldest horse show in America. Today, the show takes place over a full week each June, attracts tens of thousands of spectators, and includes nearly 2,000 horse and rider combinations.

"I've always been a horse-crazy kid. . . . My mother drove me out to Middleburg as many days as we could fight traffic from D.C. . . . Many people thought of the Upperville show as ranking next to Christmas in importance."

Miranda Scott, rider and trainer, 2019

May Amelia Muurling Maddux Belmont, early 1900s

VMHC Collection, Gift of Henrietta A. Laverge

Belmont (1880–1948), an immigrant to Northern Virginia from Holland, bred and raised thoroughbred horses, including the famous steeplechase champion Oracle II, in Warrenton (Fauquier County). Here she is shown jumping a fence while using a sidesaddle.

Sidesaddle, about 1935

Mayhew's (London, England)

From the collection of the Oak Spring Garden Foundation, Upperville, Virginia

Sidesaddle riding allows a rider in a skirt (usually female) to sit with both legs to one side of the horse. This practice dates to Europe in the Middle Ages. This example belonged to Rachel "Bunny" Lambert Mellon (1910–2014), a passionate horticulturist and art collector. She and her husband Paul raised thoroughbred horses at their Oak Spring estate in Fauquier County.

COMMUTING TO AND FROM

Washington, D.C., is just across the Potomac River from Northern Virginia and the traffic around the city is infamously congested. Over the years, a variety of options including trolleys, buses, light rail, subway lines, and high-occupancy carpool lanes have evolved to shuttle workers and visitors into and out of the city.

Travelers on I-66 in Fairfax County, 2019
Dave Dildine (photographer)
Courtesy of WTOP Radio

Mt. Vernon train at Potomac Park, 1907

LeRoy O. King, Sr. (photographer)

VMHC Collection

In the late 1800s and early 1900s, an extensive network of streetcar lines allowed workers without personal transportation to take jobs farther away from their homes. By 1896, the Washington, Alexandria, & Mount Vernon Railway moved people back and forth between NoVa and D.C. By the 1930s, improved roads led to increased use of automobiles and many of these commuter lines were abandoned.

Trolley fare box, about 1914

Johnson Fare Box Company

VMHC Collection, Gift of Nicholas F. Taubman

Beginning in the early 1900s, Johnson fare boxes could be found on many streetcars, trolleys, and buses. After a passenger inserted their fare into the box, the conductor cranked the handle to run the money through the counting mechanism. Today, such devices have been replaced by electronic and digital technologies.

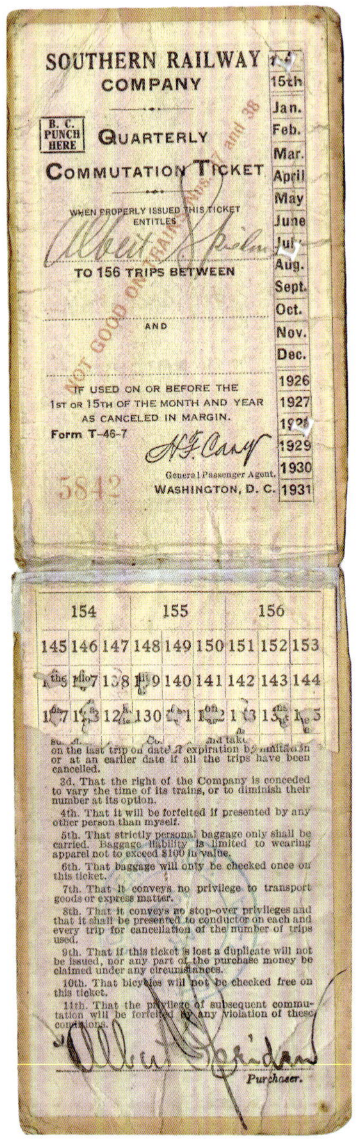

Albert Speiden's train pass for the Southern Railway Company, 1928

From the collection of the Manassas Museum System

Noted architect Albert Speiden (1868–1933) lived in Manassas and took a one-hour train trip each way to his office in Washington, D.C. In the late 1920s, he would have been accompanied by as many as 100 other commuters.

"My father commuted twenty-eight years back and forth on the train. . . . He could time it so that on a run he could leave [our home] when he heard the train blow, but he'd have to run for it."

Virginia Speiden Carper, reminiscing about her father's commuting lifestyle, about 1990

Virginia Railway Express at Manassas train station, 2019

Refrina / Shutterstock.com

Virginia Railway Express uniform, 2012

From the collection of the Manassas Museum System

Established in 1992, the Virginia Railway Express (VRE) runs two lines connecting Virginia commuters to Union Station in Washington, D.C.—one from Fredericksburg and the other from Manassas. In 2023, about 6,200 commuters used the VRE each day to reach jobs in and around Washington. The trip from Fredericksburg takes about 1 hour and 40 minutes.

Pentagon City Washington Metro station, 2011

Kumar Sriskandan / Alamy Stock Photo

Pentagon City is one of thirty-two Washington Metro (Metro) stations connecting Northern Virginia to the nation's capital. The Metro began operating in 1976 and reached Arlington the following year. The system later expanded to include the City of Alexandria as well as Fairfax and Loudoun counties. In September 2023, more than 400,000 riders used the Metro each weekday, making it the second-busiest rail rapid transit system in the United States.

SLUGGING

According to David LeBlanc, author of *Slugging: The Commuting Alternative for Washington DC*, there are some understood rules for passengers. Slugs do not:

Talk to the driver unless they speak first

Eat or drink

Fiddle with the radio

Roll down the window

Talk on a cell phone

Offer money, gifts, or tokens of appreciation

Northern Virginia commuters wait for a ride at Bob's Slug Lines in Springfield, 2018
Luz Lazo (photographer)
The Washington Post

"Slugging" is an informal carpooling system that has been a Northern Virginia tradition since the early 1970s. Passengers get a free ride from the suburbs into downtown Washington, and the driver gets to use the high occupancy "HOV" lanes reserved for vehicles with three or more people—cutting off about 30 minutes from their commute.

Terminal at Washington Dulles International Airport, 1968
Dean Conger (photographer)
Corbis Collection / Getty Images

The rapid increase in air traffic after World War II quickly outpaced the capacity at Washington National Airport (now Ronald Reagan Washington National Airport). Located 26 miles from the capital in Loudoun and Fairfax counties, Dulles International Airport (now Washington Dulles International Airport) began service in 1962. Together the airports served more than 45 million passengers in 2022. Travelers favor Reagan because of its proximity to Washington and Dulles for more flight options.

BUILDING COMMUNITY

This region of Virginia is the most diverse in the Commonwealth. Today, Black middle-class neighborhoods thrive not far from where Civil War Freedmen's camps once stood in Alexandria. Korean residents attend Annandale churches and worship in their native tongue. And chefs from a range of South American countries tempt diners with homeland treats in Manassas. People from all over the world have migrated to Northern Virginia for its opportunities. Small, established communities welcome others from their own cultural backgrounds, creating pockets of ethnic groups throughout this area.

Residents of the Freedman's Village (Arlington), 1861–5

Library of Congress, Prints and Photographs Division

Throughout the American Civil War, the U.S. Army maintained control of Arlington and Alexandria. Thousands of enslaved people in the area seized freedom by crossing Union lines. In 1863, to meet a growing need for housing, the federal government built Freedman's Village on part of the Arlington estate—once home to Confederate general Robert E. Lee. Having intended it as temporary housing, the government closed the village in 1900, despite the continued presence of a strong Black community.

Queen City (East Arlington), 1910

Center for Local History, Arlington Public Library

Before Arlington's Freedman's Village closed, Black residents built other communities in the eastern part of the county. Many of the men worked in nearby brickyards, women took in work (such as sewing), and children attended the Jefferson School. The federal government demolished the neighborhood and displaced this tight-knit community of 903 people in 1942, when it exercised eminent domain to build the Pentagon.

Mekong Center, late 1970s

Courtesy of Min Van Nguyen and Bach Luu Nguyen

Communities along the corridors of Wilson Boulevard and Columbia Pike in Arlington, and in Falls Church and Annandale, became home to thousands of Vietnamese people who immigrated to the D.C. area during and after the Vietnam War.

"[W]hen my parents opened our grocery store, Mekong Center . . . [it] was the fourth Vietnamese store opened on this strip. . . . I am proud of the fact that my family, along with other Vietnamese families, took part in building the legacy and bringing diversity to Arlington County."

Lieu Nguyen, a resident of "Little Saigon," 2016

Nhi Le at Hoi Nha Viet Nam, a Vietnamese cultural center in Falls Church, 2018

Pat Jarrett / Virginia Humanities

"I don't want the Vietnamese people to live without the culture. That's why it's very important for me to keep the Vietnamese culture. . . . Because I now have two countries—Vietnam and America. . . . I feel very lucky to have the chance to live in America. I talk to my children and say 'we live in America' . . . but we still have a homeland."

Nhi Le, founder of the Vietnamese Literary and Artistic Club in Northern Virginia, 2019

Sgt. Maj. Randall Woods reading with a first grader in Arlington, 2015
Damien Salas (photographer)
Joint Base Myer-Henderson Hall PAO

A primary goal of the Better Opportunities for Single Soldiers program at Joint Base Myer-Henderson Hall is to enhance the morale and welfare of single soldiers by connecting them with the community outside their base.

Families evacuated from Kabul, Afghanistan, arriving at Washington Dulles International Airport, 2021
Gemunu Amarasinghe / AP Photo

The U.S. government processed more than 45,000 Afghan evacuees through the Dulles area following the withdrawal of military forces from their country in September 2021. More than 6,000 evacuees hoped to find welcoming communities in Virginia, which has the second-largest Afghan population in the United States.

"My two sons and my husband, they served America for twenty-two years, they help[ed] them. Now I want a better, more peaceful life here for my kids and for myself."

Fauzia, refugee from Afghanistan whose sons and husband worked with the U.S. military in Kabul, 2021

Flory Jagoda (Vlasenica, Bosnia and Herzegovina), 2002
Tom Pich (photographer)
National Endowment for the Arts

A Sephardic Jew, Flory Jagoda (1923–2021) fled Nazi-occupied Yugoslavia for Italy, where she met an American soldier and her future husband Harry Jagoda. The couple later settled in Northern Virginia. In the 1970s, Flory started recording Sephardic music from her childhood and became an award-winning superstar of this tradition. Called the "Keeper of the Flame," she was a significant force in helping to revive the Sephardic language, Ladino.

"I went home and I wrote songs. I just threw myself into music. When I sing, my family is in my heart with me. So the trip had a purpose, as horrible as it was."

Flory Jagoda, reflecting on a trip to Bosnia and learning 42 family members were massacred during World War II

Owner/manager Befekadu Mosa (left), daughter Hawwi Mosa (center), and chef Hanan Mosa (right), 2015
Chester Simpson (photographer)
Rock-N-RollPhotos.com

"I was brought up in a large family, in a culture where a mastery of cooking is expected of one's daughter. At the age of twelve, I learned to make authentic Ethiopian foods from my late dear mother. People who have eaten my healthy and delicious food . . . gave me the warm approval and courage to start my own family restaurant. I am always curious to see how first-time customers respond to Ethiopian cuisine."

Ethiopian chef Hanan Mosa, Alexandria, 2022

Columbia Pike Documentary Project

To document life along the Pike, Arlington photography teacher Paula Endo created the Columbia Heights West Teen Photo Project with her students in 1996. The project was later joined by photographer Lloyd Wolf and renamed the Columbia Pike Documentary Project. The stories gathered by the CPDP—some of which are shared here—reveal the successes, challenges, and dreams of individuals and families building lives in a community in which diversity is valued.

Intersection of the Georgetown-Alexandria Road and Columbia Pike, about 1934

Center for Local History, Arlington Public Library

Constructed in 1810, the Columbia Pike began as a toll road connecting rural Virginia with the nation's capital. Today, the area around the Pike is home to historically significant Black American communities as well as immigrants from every continent. More than 100 languages can be heard along this three-mile-long corridor.

Janeth Valenzuela (Bolivia), 2019
Lloyd Wolf (photographer)
Columbia Pike Documentary Project

In 1998, Janeth Valenzuela, an aspiring journalist in Bolivia, wanted to cover the war in Nicaragua. To keep her away from the fighting, her father asked her to visit a friend who lived in Arlington. She ended up staying, marrying the woman's son, and raising a family. Valenzuela started parents' groups in her son's schools and helped found the Arlington Schools Hispanic Parents Association to be an independent voice for parents.

"They leave everything back home, so they have to start with nothing here. I said, 'I will help them navigate the education system, so their kids can have a better future.'"

Janeth Valenzuela, 2019

Aseel Elborno (Kuwait) and Omar Bassiouny (Alexandria, Egypt), 2019
Lloyd Wolf (photographer)
Columbia Pike Documentary Project

Aseel Elborno's Palestinian family was expelled from Kuwait in 1990 and immigrated to North Carolina. She met Omar Bassiouny on a trip to Egypt. After a three-year courtship, they married, and he came to the United States. They chose to live in Arlington because she had one of her first jobs there, and because it has a subsidized para-transit program for citizens with disabilities (Bassiouny is legally blind). Elborno works for Islamic Relief USA; Bassiouny worked in information technology. They have two sons.

". . . we can prove to the world that, 'Hey, you don't have to be homogenous to be harmonious.' You can be diverse and still coexist very peacefully, and not just peacefully, but actually appreciate the place that you live in."

Aseel Elborno, 2019

Delia Ngugi (Mombasa, Kenya), 2019
Lloyd Wolf (photographer)
Columbia Pike Documentary Project

Ngugi came to the United States by herself at age 26—she has extended family here, but she had never met them. "I believe in the American dream, and I believed I could better myself and have more choices to grow here," she says. She currently works for a Fairfax-based company supporting the construction of energy-efficient buildings. Raised in an entrepreneurial family, Ngugi studied business management in college and hopes to create businesses in her home country.

"This is going to sound weird, but sometimes I forget that I'm in America, it's so diverse here."

Delia Ngugi, 2019

Bolivian-American folk dance at the Prio Bangla Festival, 2018
Lara Ajami (photographer)
Columbia Pike Documentary Project

"Arlington is like a little Bolivia. You can find salteñas, typical Bolivian restaurants, stores, and businesses. . . . They celebrate all Bolivian holidays like Carnaval and Fiesta de Urkupiña. After a few went to Virginia [in the 1980s, as a result of a suffering Bolivian economy], their family members followed, and the population grew."

Patricia Zamora, native Bolivian and former Arlington resident, 2015

Bangladeshi-American celebrants at the Prio Bangla Festival, 2019
Lara Ajami (photographer)
Columbia Pike Documentary Project

"[We] organize five regular events throughout the year—Saraswati Puja, Poila Boisakh at Kali Bari, Summer Picnic, Kobi Jayanti, and Durga Puja. By engaging in such social, cultural, developmental, and fun activities, all the year round, we endeavor to create a caring, respectful, compassionate and socially cohesive community that embraces people of all cultural, ethnic, and spiritual backgrounds."

সবারে করি আহ্বান,
এসো উৎসুক চিত্ত, এসো আনন্দিত
প্রাণ।

Translation:
I urge everyone,
Come, curious heart,
come, happy soul.

Ruchir Ghosh, Northern Virginia Bengali Association President, Chantilly, 2020

Margaret Chung (Korea), 2018
Xang Mimi Ho (photographer)
Columbia Pike Documentary Project

Chung came to the United States from Korea at age 10, speaking "only a little" English. Today, she is the principal of Arlington Career Center. Her high school focuses on career and technical education, offering programs in subjects ranging from information technology to early childhood education. They also offer a High Intensity Language Training Institute serving recently arrived immigrant students and older students who "come with interrupted schooling."

"I think my experience as an immigrant helps me relate to the students. When you move to a country . . . and you're having to learn a new language, and customs, and you don't fit in, I know what that's like."

Margaret Chung, 2018

FINDING COMMON GROUND

Youth and professional soccer create a shared experience across the diverse residents of Northern Virginia. Players and spectators can rely on standard rules of the game to bridge their linguistic and cultural differences. Northern Virginians cheer goals and boo fouls on their turf. The words or dialects may be different, but the colors and logos of teams worn by their fans can overcome language barriers. A shared passion for sports unites the people of NoVA.

Arlington Soccer Association vs. Freedom Football Club during the Virginia Presidents Cup, 2018

Virginia Youth Soccer Association

Virginia United Football Club huddling up before their first game at the U.S. Open Cup, 2019
Courtesy of U.S. Soccer

"There are small communities out there with real talent and something to show. We are a Hispanic-based team from a Hispanic-based league and we're here to show them what we can do with a chance."

Jimmy Ramos, co-founder and player, Virginia United, Woodbridge, 2019

Manassas Soccer Club coach Karl Gibbons, about 2021
Courtesy of Manassas Soccer Club

"I grew up playing soccer on the beaches of Puerto Viejo, Costa Rica, and have played all over the world. In 2006, I moved to Virginia, where I continued my career as a soccer player and managed soccer programs. In 2016, I started the Manassas Soccer Club to provide academy training programs for local youth. My career demonstrates how the love of soccer can transform your life and the lives of so many others."

Karl Gibbons, player, coach, and founder and president of the Manassas Soccer Club, 2021

Manassas Soccer Club jersey, 2019–20
From the collection of the Manassas Soccer Club

Reflective of the cultural diversity of Northern Virginia, the Manassas Soccer Club includes young players representing 25 different countries.

Central VIRGINIA

Bordered on the west by the Blue Ridge Mountains and separated from Tidewater by rapids and waterfalls that prevent ocean-going ships from traveling inland by river, Central Virginia is the Commonwealth's largest region. Siouan-speaking people have called the area home for 1,000 years and have lived along many of its waterways. Several of Virginia's major cities grew up along the Fall Line as European colonists moved westward and harnessed water to power industry and establish inland ports. Political power moved into Central Virginia in 1780 when Virginia's capital moved from Williamsburg to Richmond. Eighty years later, the city became the capital of the Confederate States of America. Central Virginia was engulfed by the American Civil War, and the many battlefield parks and national cemeteries that exist today serve as reminders of that conflict. The growth of tobacco, textile, and other industries helped the region recover after the war, and Central Virginia has become a forum for civic discourse where diverse perspectives drive the region's intellectual, cultural, and economic creativity.

Richmond skyline reflecting in James River, 2020
Paul Hamilton (photographer)
Courtesy of Paul T. Hamilton

***Malvern Hill Battlefield*, 2009**
Tim Wilson (photographer)
Tom Wilson Photography

In July 1862, with the Confederate capital only fifteen miles away, more than 57,000 men fought to control the now quiet fields around Malvern Hill. One in ten were killed, captured, or wounded. The American Civil War (1861–5) engulfed Virginia. More military engagements occurred here than in any other state, and more than half the soldiers, U.S. and Confederate, who died during the war perished within 150 miles of Richmond.

Central Virginia Independent Cities

1. Charlottesville
2. Colonial Heights
3. Danville
4. Emporia
5. Fredericksburg
6. Lynchburg
7. Petersburg
8. Richmond

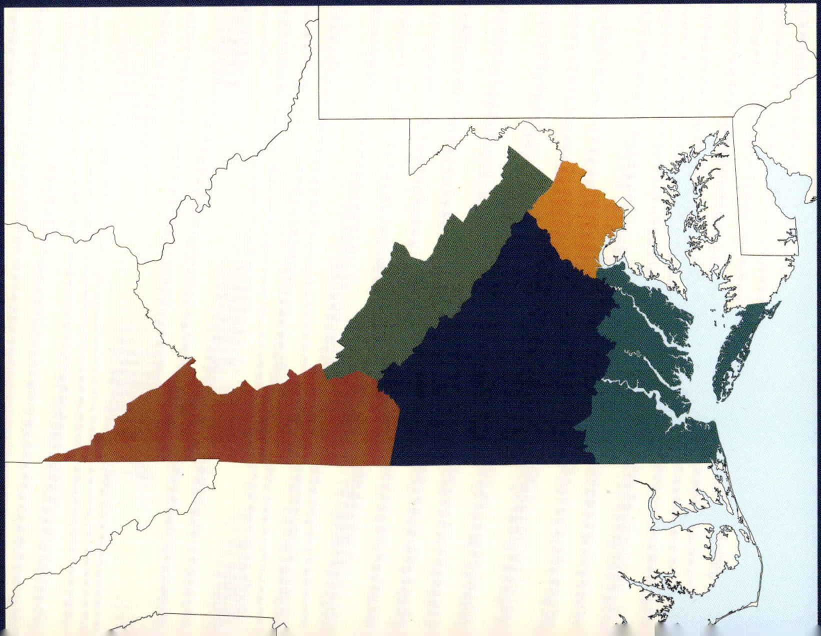

GROWING TOBACCO

Native tobacco played an important role in the social and religious lives of the Indigenous people living in what we call Virginia. European taste for a different strain of tobacco that was cultivated from Caribbean seeds and thrived in Central Virginia's climate fueled the expansion of English colonization and a demand for laborers to produce it.

Tobacco became Virginia's primary crop and, with it, a codified system of race-based slavery that became a model throughout British America. More than a century of tobacco cultivation in Tidewater exhausted the soil, and farmers expanded into Central Virginia. The tobacco industry—growing, processing, and selling tobacco products—continued to dominate Virginia's economy through the 1900s.

Health concerns raised in the late 20th century led to a downturn in the domestic tobacco market. Today, Central Virginia's tobacco farmers supply international markets. Across the region's rolling landscape, many of the farms and buildings that supported a booming industry have been lost to development. In some former tobacco towns—like Danville, Farmville, and Lynchburg—old warehouses are being adapted to other uses.

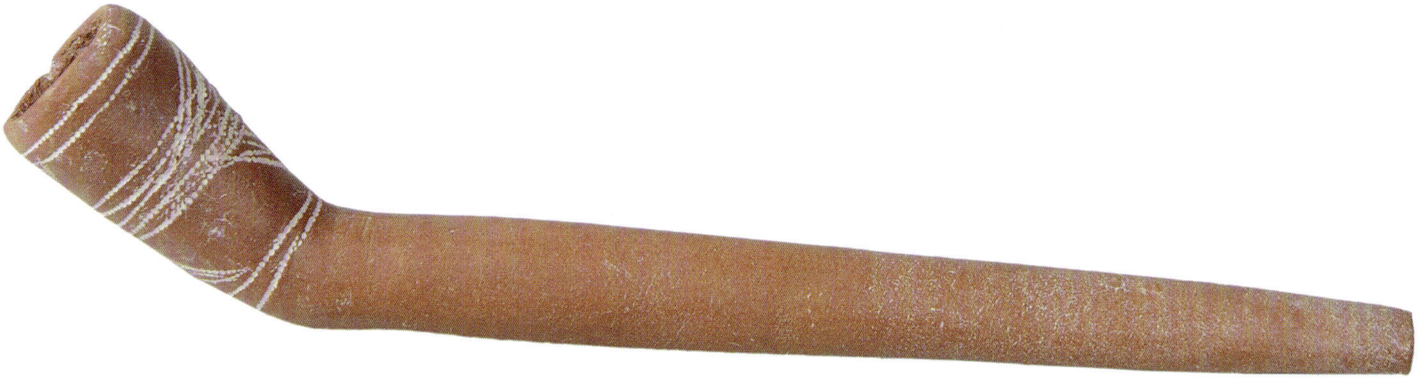

"The [Indigenous] people of the South-parts of Virginia esteeme [tobacco] exceedingly, and so doe the rest: they say that God in the creation did first make a woman, then a man, thirdly great maize or Indian wheat, and fourthly, Tobacco: They use it for the curing of wounds, and in smoke as we doe. . . . The Virginians [Indians] call Tobacco, Opoak . . . and it is everywhere, and in England itself, greater, according to the soyle."

An Advice How to Plant Tobacco in England, 1615

Pipe recovered from Jordan's Point (reproduction), 1620
Taft Kiser (maker) after an unknown Indigenous maker
Courtesy of the Virginia Department of Historic Resources

Indigenous people used tobacco as part of religious ceremonies, as a medicine, and for a variety of other purposes. The pipe recovered from Jordan's Point (Prince George County) is typical of pipes made by Algonquian communities for trade throughout Tidewater and parts of Central Virginia during the 1600s. Its size reflects the transformation of tobacco from a sacred herb to a secular pleasure. The patterns on the bowl are believed to represent a corn plant.

Twist of dried tobacco, undated

From the collection of the Lynchburg Museum System

Until the mid-1800s, one of the most common ways of shipping and buying tobacco was in twists—made by twisting and rolling leaves into a braided rope. Colonial Virginians preferred to smoke tobacco in pipes. During the 1800s, smokeless uses—either chewing or inhaling ground leaves (snuff)—grew in popularity.

Brass weight, 1773

From the collection of the Fredericksburg Area Museum

This weight marked "Falmouth Warehouses" was likely used to measure tobacco and other crops at merchant warehouses in Falmouth, located across the Rappahannock River from Fredericksburg. It is among the earliest known artifacts associated with the tobacco trade from that area.

***Slave Auction, Virginia,* 1860–1**

Lefevre Cranstone (artist)

VMHC Collection

A domestic slave trade flourished when the international slave trade ended in the United States (1808). Richmond became the largest slave-trading center in the Upper South, and the slave trade was Virginia's largest industry—surpassing the production of tobacco. Dehumanizing auctions like the one depicted by Cranstone accounted for the sale—and resulting destruction of families and social networks—of as many as one million Black people from Richmond to the Deep South, where the cotton industry provided a market for enslaved labor.

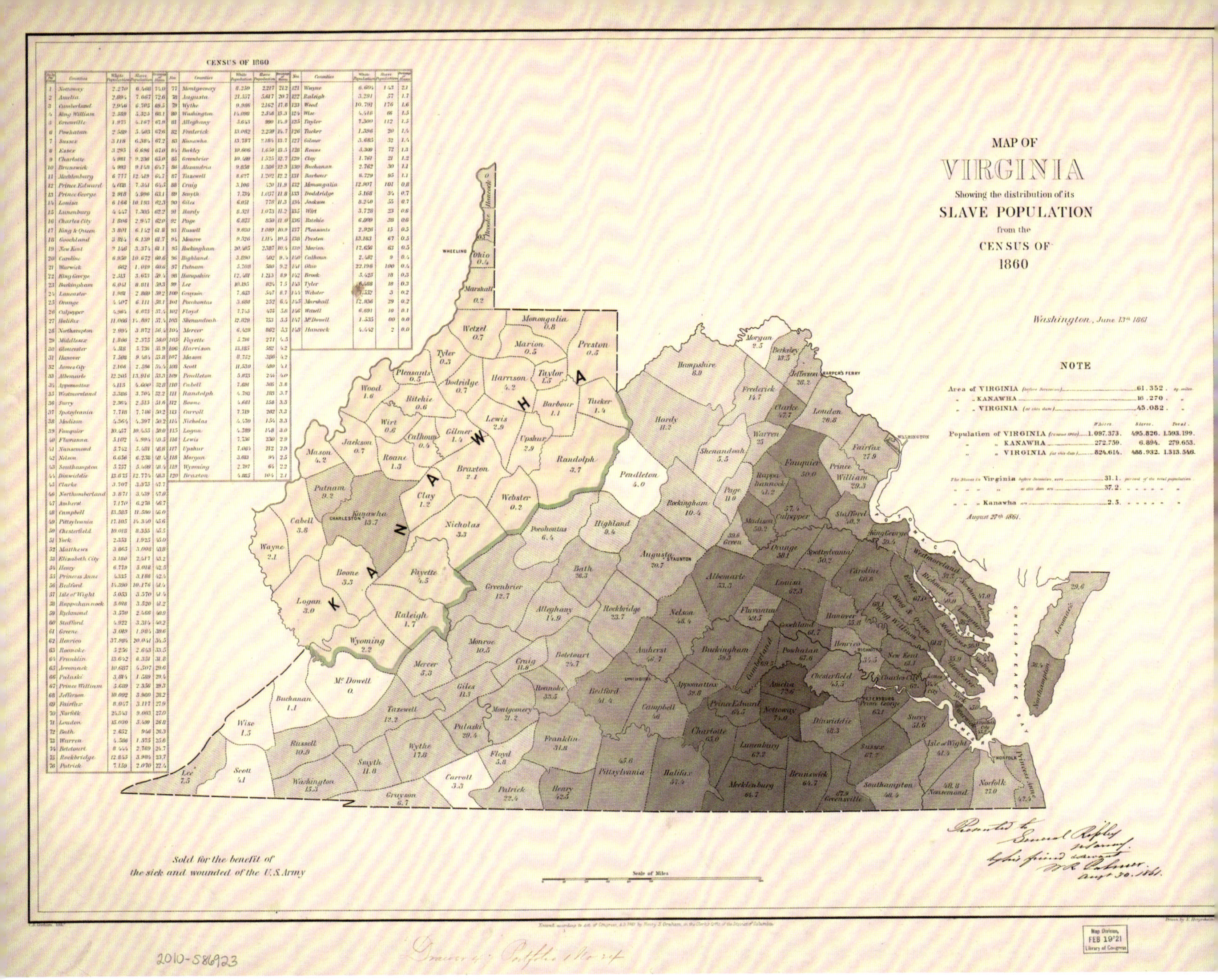

Map of Virginia: Showing the Distribution of its Slave Population from the Census of 1860 (detail), 1861

Henry S. Graham (publisher)

Library of Congress, Geography and Map Division

As tobacco cultivation expanded in colonial Virginia, planters increasingly used enslaved Black people for this work—linking Virginians to the transatlantic slave trade. Published the year the American Civil War began, this map shows the percentage of the enslaved population in each Virginia county. It also illustrates that the mountainous counties of western Virginia (now West Virginia) relied less on enslaved labor—one reason many in that region chose not to support the Confederacy and ultimately formed the new state of West Virginia.

The high quality of Virginia tobacco led colonial merchants to promote it by wrapping it with branded paper. By the late 1800s, manufacturers promoted their brands by attaching small metal tags to their tobacco bricks and twists.

Tobacco label (R. Mascall's Best Virginia), late 1600s or early 1700s
VMHC Collection

Colonial tobacco labels frequently depicted Black men, women, and children in the process of growing, harvesting, packing, and smoking tobacco. The figures tend to be a hybridized caricature of Africans depicted in Indigenous dress—symbolizing the enslaved people who grew the tobacco and the American origin of the plant. These stereotypes would be used to market tobacco well into the 1900s.

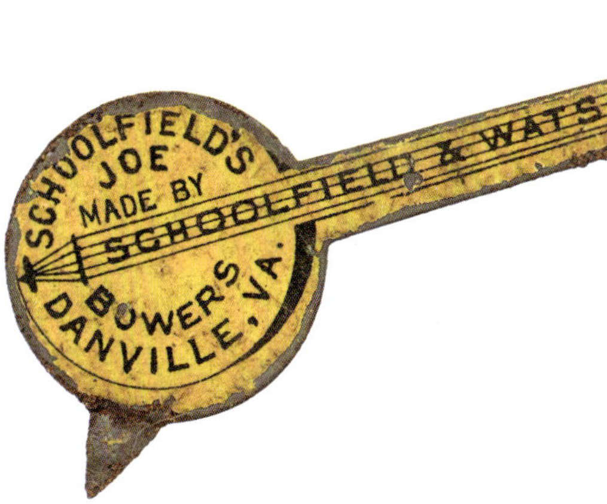

Schoolfield's "Joe Bowers" tobacco tag, late 1800s to early 1900s
Schoolfield & Watson
VMHC Collection

John H. Schoolfield (1838–1920) founded Danville's Schoolfield & Watson Tobacco Factory in 1870. This tobacco tag's brand name and banjo shape likely refer to "Joe Bowers," a popular folk song about a man who travels to California during the Gold Rush to finance a home for his fiancée, only to learn that in his absence she married another man.

Lucky Strike tobacco tag, late 1800s to early 1900s
R.A. Patterson Tobacco Company
VMHC Collection

Founded by Richard A. Patterson (1826–1912) in 1856 and based in Richmond, the R.A. Patterson Company is most famous for introducing the Lucky Strike brand of plug tobacco and cigarettes. "Lucky Strike" may refer to miners fortunate enough to strike gold during the California Gold Rush. North Carolina-based American Tobacco purchased the Patterson company in 1905.

Richmond Gem cigarette tin, about 1900
The American Tobacco Company
VMHC Collection, Gift of Mr. and Mrs. J. Madison Macon IV

After the Civil War, Richmond entrepreneur Lewis Ginter (1824–1897) helped to revolutionize the cigarette industry. Using less expensive local, rather than imported, tobacco, Allen & Ginter released Richmond Gem, one of the first mass-produced cigarette brands. In 1875, Ginter offered a prize to whoever could invent an automated cigarette-rolling machine. Fellow Virginian James Bonsack succeeded in 1881, but Ginter rejected it. Instead, James Duke of Durham, North Carolina, bought the machine, acquired many of his competitors (including Allen & Ginter), and formed the American Tobacco Company in 1890.

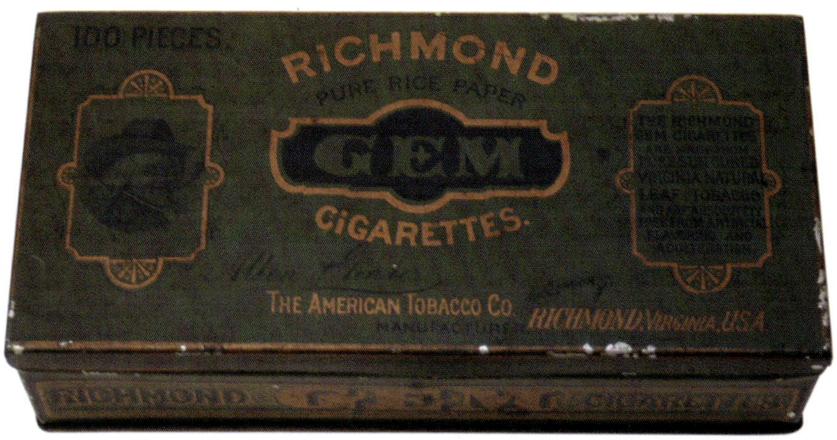

Migrant worker topping tobacco plants on a Virginia farm, 2018

rkadams / Stockimo / Alamy Stock Photo

Tobacco plants concentrate much of their energy into producing flowers containing seeds necessary for reproduction. For centuries, Virginia's tobacco farmers have removed the flowers by hand—a process known as topping—to redirect the plant's energy into its valuable leaves.

Bernie Dollarhite hanging tobacco in a curing barn, 1978

Library of Congress, Blue Ridge Parkway Folklife Project Collection, American Folklife Center

Tobacco needs to be cured (dried) to remove moisture from the leaves after harvesting. Beginning in the 1600s, Virginia tobacco was primarily dried using small fires built inside tall log barns. During the late 1800s, many farmers switched to "flue-cured" tobacco by using heat carried into the barn through pipes. The resulting tobacco is sweeter without a smokey flavor. To obtain a more earthy flavor, some tobacco is cured by air instead of heat.

Workers—likely at Philip Morris—processing cigarettes, 1968

Dennis Brack (photographer)

Courtesy of Dennis Brack

Tobacco farming in Virginia has been shrinking since the 1970s. When the U.S. government ended the Depression-era policy of regulating tobacco prices, small farmers increasingly sold their land to larger companies. From 2002 to 2022, annual tobacco production in Virginia declined from 63 million pounds to 30. Central Virginia continues to be a major producer of tobacco products. Philip Morris USA, a subsidiary of Altria, produces almost half of all the cigarettes sold in the United States, and its Richmond plant is one of the largest in the world.

Tobacco auctioneer Bob Cage (center, with hand over mouth), 1969

A. Bruce Dodson / Danville Historical Society

The end of government regulations on inspection warehouses after the Civil War allowed individual farmers to directly sell their crops—including by auction. Auction callers, like Bob Cage (1929–2020), and their distinctive chants became part of the folk traditions in the south-central region of Virginia.

"172 Hey seventy two, what'll I do, seventy two, three, four, five, seventy five, seventy eight, seventy eight dollar, Ginger!
162 Hey sixty two, toodee doodly doo-doo-doo, sickity three, sicky five, L and M.
185 Eighty five dollars, eighty five, eighty five, eighty seven, eighty seven, eighty, ninety dollars, send it to the Queen!"

A portion of a chant recorded by Bob Cage, 2007

Workers sorting and stemming tobacco at T.C. Williams & Company in Richmond, about 1899

Library of Congress, Prints and Photographs Division

Richmond native Thomas C. Williams (1831–1889) entered the tobacco business in the 1850s. By 1889, his company had two factory buildings in Richmond and employed 700 people who produced as much as 4 million pounds of plug and twist tobacco each year. By 1903, T.C. Williams Company was one of the United States's largest tobacco exporters.

"Preachers don't know nothing about hell; they ain't worked in no tobacco factory."

Louise Harris, Richmond tobacco stemmer and tobacco workers' rights activist, 1940

Horn, about 1850

From the collection of the Lynchburg Museum System

Horns like this one were blown to announce and open daily tobacco sales at warehouses. This one was used at Friend's Warehouse in Lynchburg.

BUILDING INDUSTRIES

Central Virginia has been a prime location for agriculture and manufacturing. The region's fertile soil allowed for the cultivation of tobacco, wheat, and other crops. Its waterways, roads, and later railroads brought goods from across Virginia to the world beyond. As Virginia transitioned from an agricultural economy to an industrial one in the late 1800s, the region became a manufacturing hub. Factories around Fredericksburg and Richmond created new products like synthetics and aluminum. Martinsville and Danville led the South in textile manufacturing. The region remains a critical center for industry, including steel production, chemical engineering, and biotechnology.

***View from Gambles Hill, Richmond, Va.*, 1857**
Edward Beyer (artist)
VMHC Collection, Gift of David Tennant Bryan

The James River powered some of Virginia's largest flour mills, iron works, and foundries. By 1860, Richmond was the most industrialized city in the South. Tredegar Iron Works (far left), the largest of its kind in the South, used free and enslaved labor to produce railroad track, locomotives, steam engines, and weapons for the U.S. government. Tredegar was also the largest manufacturer of artillery in the Confederacy during the Civil War. The iron works continued to do business until 1957.

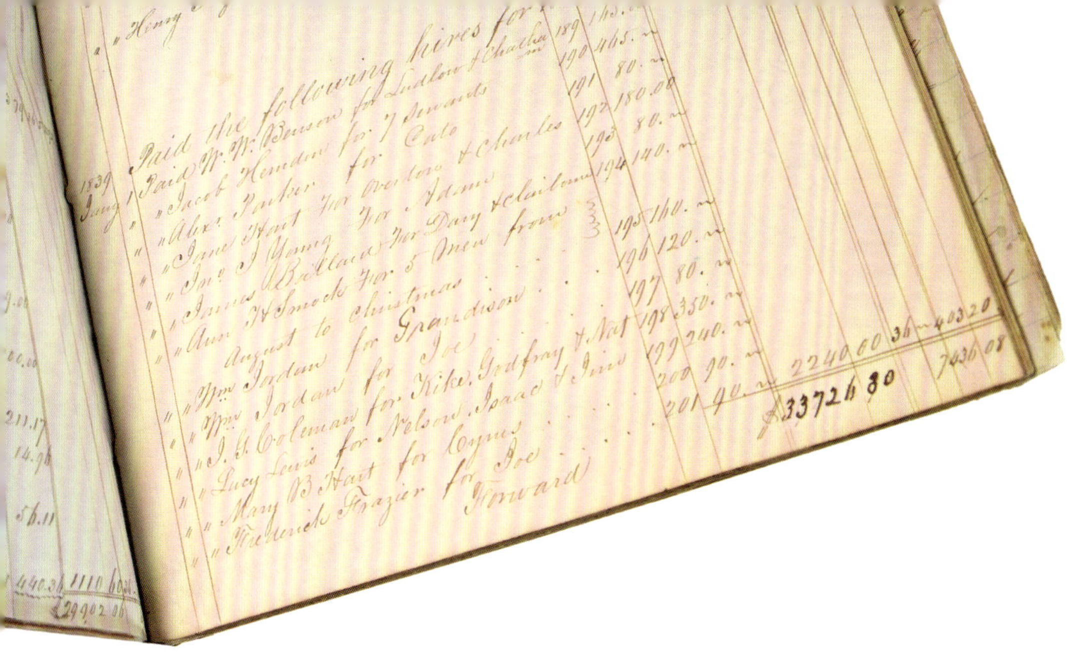

Account book for Catharine Furnace, 1837–47

From the collection of the Fredericksburg Area Museum

In 1836, John S. Wellford (1783–1846) named his new blast iron furnace in Spotsylvania County after his mother. Catharine Furnace produced crude "pig" iron to sell to the growing U.S. military and iron works as far away as Boston. Wellford beat his competitors' pricing by capitalizing on Central Virginia's abundance of enslaved laborers. As shown here, all payments for the work accomplished by Adam, Grandison, Joe, Nat, Cato, and many others, were made to their enslavers.

Jim Brown cutting steel for One World Trade Center, 2013

© Banker Steel Company, 2019

"I am a part of that building. . . . We had to put it back. We couldn't have left it, just like it was, at ground level; we had to put something back. And that reinforces the grain of the American people."

Jim Brown, Banker Steel employee, Lynchburg, 2013

Section of steel beam manufactured for the Freedom Tower in New York City, 2006

Banker Steel

VMHC Collection, Gift of Lieutenant Governor Bill Bolling

Based in Lynchburg, Banker Steel produced nearly one-tenth of the total steel (3,300 tons) used in the foundation of One World Trade Center, also known as the Freedom Tower. Completed in 2013, the skyscraper now stands on the site of the September 11, 2001, terrorist attacks in New York City, which destroyed the World Trade Center and other buildings.

Kline Kar, Seven Passenger Touring Car, Series 6-38, 1918
Kline Motor Car Company
VMHC Collection, Partial gift of Debbie and Tim Crowder, purchased through the Paul Mellon Acquisitions Fund, Restoration supported by Mr. & Mrs. Gerald F. Smith, Jr.

This is one of two surviving automobiles made by the Kline Motor Car Company. Founded in 1909 in York, Pennsylvania, the company moved to Richmond in 1911 and produced about 6,000 cars before closing in 1924. Renowned for its outstanding performance and workmanship, the Kline Kar could not compete with the less expensive Model-T Ford. This car was owned by A.D. (Alfred Douglas) Price (1860–1921), a Black businessman, philanthropist, and civic leader in Richmond.

Man's boot (above) and woman's lace-up boot, late 1800s to early 1900s
Craddock-Terry Shoe Company
From the collection of the Lynchburg Museum System

John W. Craddock (1857–1941) of Halifax County came to Lynchburg in the 1880s. He, his brother, and Thaddeus McGhee Terry founded the Craddock-Terry Shoe Company in 1888. The company grew into the fifth-largest shoe company in the world. Built along the James River, its factory became the backbone of Lynchburg's economy. At its peak, the company produced over 100,000 pairs of shoes a day.

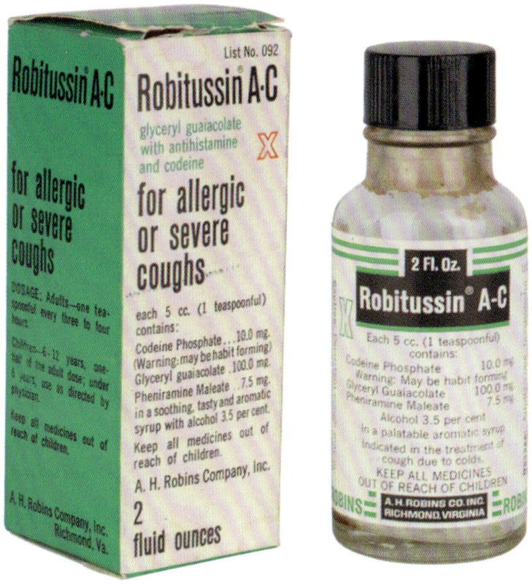

ChapStick Medicated Dry Skin Balm, about 1963

Morton Manufacturing Company

VMHC Collection, Gift of Helen B. Reveley

Lynchburg pharmacist Dr. Charles Browne Fleet (1843–1916) created a balm for chapped lips in the 1890s. It didn't sell well. He sold the formula to his friend John Morton, whose wife developed the pocketable, tube-shaped ChapStick we know today. The Morton Manufacturing Company operated in Lynchburg until 1963, when it was sold to A.H. Robins Company.

Robitussin A-C medicine box and bottle, 1950s–70s

A.H. Robins Company

VMHC Collection, Gift of E. Claiborne Robins, Jr.

In 1936, shortly after E. Claiborne Robins, Sr. (1910–1995) graduated from pharmacy school, he took over the Richmond business begun by his father in 1906 and turned it into a pharmaceutical empire. In 1949, A.H. Robins Company introduced the cough-suppressant Robitussin. The company continued under family control until 1989, when it was sold to American Home Products.

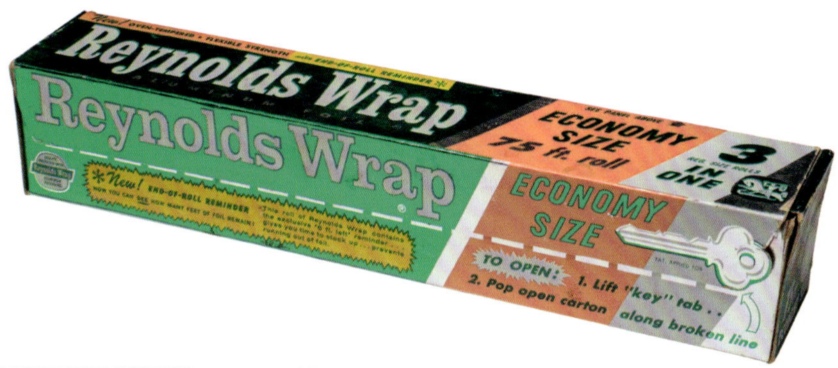

Reynolds Wrap, 1960s

Reynolds Metals Company

VMHC Collection

In 1919, Richard S. Reynolds (1881–1955)—nephew of tobacco magnate R.J. Reynolds—founded what would become Reynolds Metals Company to manufacture tin foil for cigarette packaging. It became an innovator in uses for aluminum—from house siding to yarn for clothing. The company moved its headquarters to the Richmond area in 1938, and its best-known product, Reynolds Wrap, hit stores in 1947. Before being purchased by Pittsburgh-based Alcoa in 2000, Reynolds was the second-largest aluminum company in the United States and the third largest in the world.

Geraldine Cox tests aluminum cans at Reynolds Metals Company, 1962

© *Richmond Times-Dispatch*

An expert in bacteriology, Geraldine Cox (1921–2016) helped set up the test kitchen in the Reynolds Metals Research and Packaging division, where she was involved in the development of oven bags and other household products.

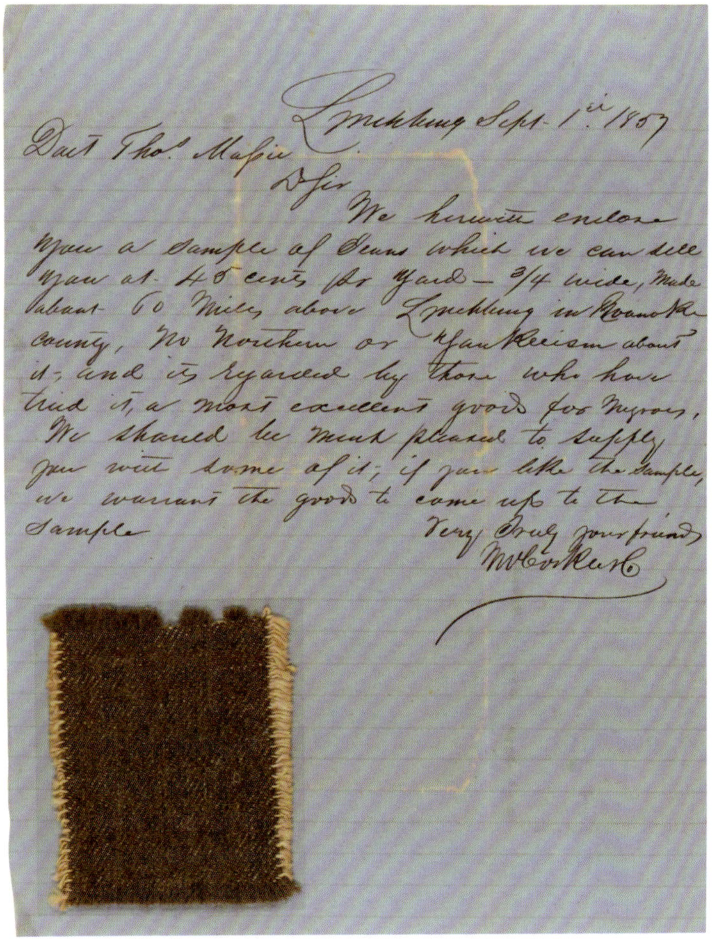

Lynchburg Sept 1st 1857
Capt Thos. Massie
D Sir
We herewith enclose you a sample of Jeans which we can sell you at 40 cents per yard — 3/4 wide, Made about 60 Miles above Lynchburg in Roanoke county, No Northern or Yankeeism about it; and is regarded by those who have tried it, a most excellent goods for Negroes, We should be much pleased to supply you with some of it; if you like the sample, we warrant the goods to come up to the sample
Very Truly your friends
McCorkle & Co

Letter to Thomas Massie from McCorkle & Co. of Lynchburg, with fabric sample, 1857

VMHC Collection, Gift of David T. Massie

In the 1800s, some textile mills specialized in producing "slave cloth," usually coarse, inexpensive textiles that were marketed to enslavers to use as clothing fabric and to be issued as garments to enslaved people.

"Dan Flair Preset Dan Press" fabric sample, mid-1900s

Dan River Mills, Inc.

Possibly designed by Victor Lobl

VMHC Collection, Gift of the American Textile History Museum, courtesy of Victor Lobl

Victor Lobl (1902–1990) immigrated to the United States from Austria in 1939. At the Dan River Mills in Danville, he managed multiple divisions and served as a lead designer, supervising the textile production on over 4,000 looms.

"I graduated [in Austria] in 1926 . . . in Textile Manufacturing and Designing. . . . In 1942 I received an invitation for employment with Dan River. . . . At my suggestion we replaced inefficient machinery with more up to date units and revitalized the procedures. I started to teach evening classes for training supervisors before I could express myself properly [in] English."

Victor Lobl, recalling his work at the Dan River Mills after retiring in 1967

***New Riverside Cotton Mill, Danville, VA*, 1923**

Parker's Bookstore (publisher); Liberty Flyers (photographer)

VMHC Collection

Riverside Cotton Mills opened in 1882 and grew into the Dan River Mills, which, by the 1950s, was the world's largest textile mill. During World War II, the company attracted Jewish textile workers from Eastern and Central Europe. The mill closed in 2006.

Woman packing spools of Kevlar yarn at DuPont Kevlar plant, 1998

Rob Crandall / Alamy Stock Photo

Built in 1929 to produce the new synthetic material of Rayon®, the DuPont Spruance factory in Chesterfield County is now the largest DuPont manufacturing facility in the world. Today, the Spruance factory produces more than 80 percent of the world's Kevlar fibers, which are used in body armor, cut-resistant materials, and sporting goods.

***UVA Rotunda Sunrise*, 2019**
Joshua Crane (photographer)
Courtesy of Joshua Crane (Hoowithaview)

Thomas Jefferson's (1743–1826) desire to reform public education in Virginia was partly realized with the establishment of the University of Virginia (Charlottesville) in 1819. As architect, Jefferson sought to promote discussion and collaboration. The library—housed in the Rotunda—stood at the head of a revolutionary U-shaped "Academical Village" where faculty and students lived around a shared lawn. Still a public university, UVA's continued success is based, in part, on Jefferson's founding ideals.

FOUNDING OUR RIGHTS

Central Virginia has been the birthplace of America's founding documents, and a battleground for testing American ideals. Thomas Jefferson took inspiration from George Mason's Virginia Declaration of Rights when he declared American independence from British rule. James Madison's Bill of Rights, which codified the principles of liberty, equality, and individual freedoms, forms the core of the U.S. Constitution.

Many Virginians have also fought to expand these rights to all Americans. Sophie Meredith was arrested to secure voting rights for women, Mildred and Richard Loving paved a way for people to be able to marry who they want, and lawyer Oliver W. Hill, Sr., led key court cases that helped dismantle racial segregation.

Today, Americans continue to debate the core rights expressed at our founding. As the capital region, Central Virginia bears witness to many of Virginia's hotly debated issues.

***Patrick Henry Arguing the Parson's Cause at the Hanover County Courthouse*, about 1831**
George Cooke (artist)
VMHC Collection

Patrick Henry (1736–1799) earned acclaim as a skilled orator and staunch defender of colonists' rights as a young lawyer. In the Parson's Cause case of 1763, he challenged Britain's authority to veto laws passed by Virginia's legislature. His arguments spurred colonial resistance. As revolutionary tensions grew, Henry became a leading voice for American independence—most famously in his "give me liberty or give me death!" speech delivered in Richmond at St. John's Church in 1775. Like many of America's Founding Fathers, Henry embodied the contradictory ideas about liberty. He championed individual freedoms yet enslaved Black people.

Eyeglasses owned by Patrick Henry, about 1760–99
VMHC Collection, Gift of John A. Lancaster

After interviewing contemporaries who had heard Patrick Henry speak and had watched him entrance his audiences, one historian noted that, "If his remarks were to be brief, his spectacles remained on his nose. But if he ever was seen to give his spectacles a cant to the top of his wig, it was a declaration of war, and his adversaries must stand clear." These spectacles played a role in Henry's oratorical theatrics.

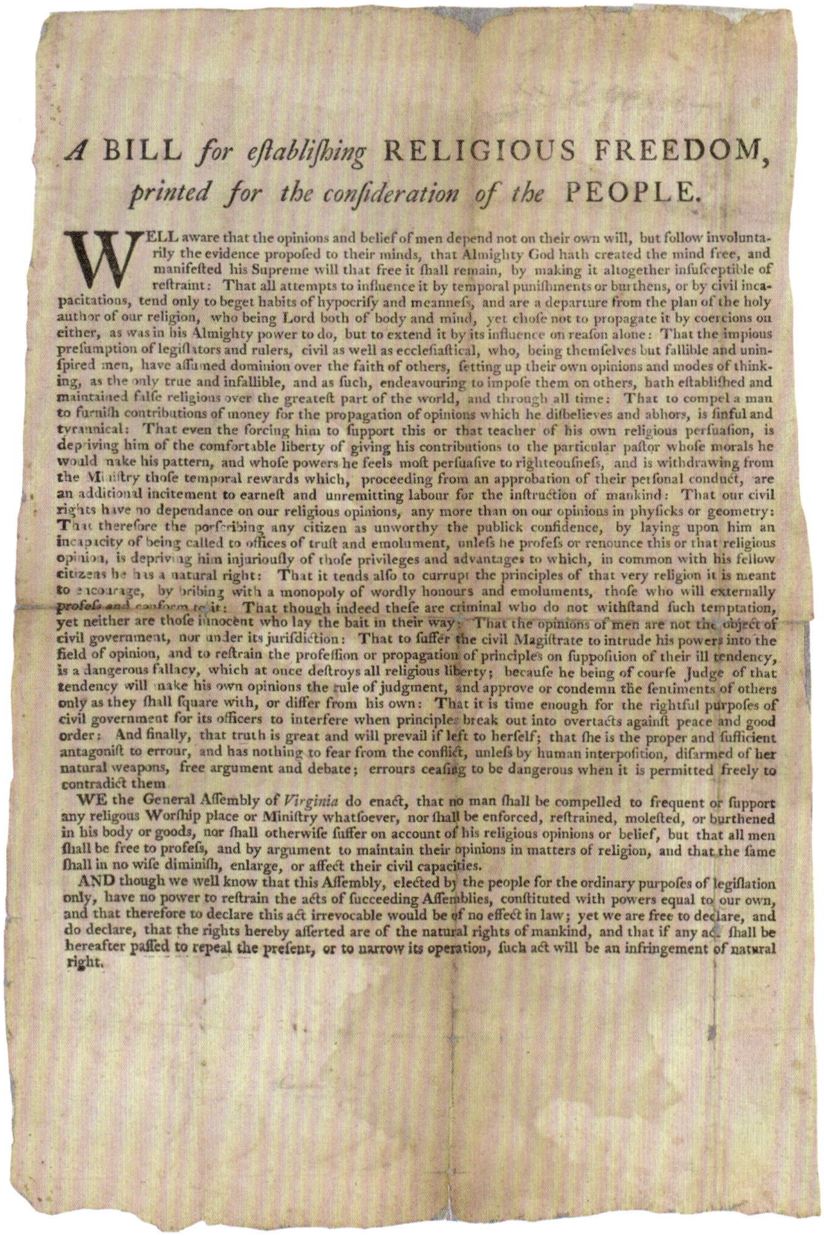

A BILL *for eſtabliſhing* RELIGIOUS FREEDOM, *printed for the conſideration of the* PEOPLE.

WELL aware that the opinions and belief of men depend not on their own will, but follow involuntarily the evidence propoſed to their minds, that Almighty God hath created the mind free, and manifeſted his Supreme will that free it ſhall remain, by making it altogether inſuſceptible of reſtraint: That all attempts to influence it by temporal puniſhments or burthens, or by civil incapacitations, tend only to beget habits of hypocriſy and meanneſs, and are a departure from the plan of the holy author of our religion, who being Lord both of body and mind, yet choſe not to propagate it by coercions on either, as was in his Almighty power to do, but to extend it by its influence on reaſon alone: That the impious preſumption of legiſlators and rulers, civil as well as eccleſiaſtical, who, being themſelves but fallible and uninſpired men, have aſſumed dominion over the faith of others, ſetting up their own opinions and modes of thinking, as the only true and infallible, and as ſuch, endeavouring to impoſe them on others, hath eſtabliſhed and maintained falſe religions over the greateſt part of the world, and through all time: That to compel a man to furniſh contributions of money for the propagation of opinions which he diſbelieves and abhors, is ſinful and tyrannical: That even the forcing him to ſupport this or that teacher of his own religious perſuaſion, is depriving him of the comfortable liberty of giving his contributions to the particular paſtor whoſe morals he would make his pattern, and whoſe powers he feels moſt perſuaſive to righteouſneſs, and is withdrawing from the Miniſtry thoſe temporal rewards which, proceeding from an approbation of their perſonal conduct, are an additional incitement to earneſt and unremitting labour for the inſtruction of mankind: That our civil rights have no dependance on our religious opinions, any more than on our opinions in phyſicks or geometry: That therefore the porſcribing any citizen as unworthy the publick confidence, by laying upon him an incapacity of being called to offices of truſt and emolument, unleſs he profeſs or renounce this or that religious opinion, is depriving him injuriouſly of thoſe privileges and advantages to which, in common with his fellow citizens he has a natural right: That it tends alſo to currupt the principles of that very religion it is meant to encourage, by bribing with a monopoly of wordly honours and emoluments, thoſe who will externally profeſs and conform to it: That though indeed theſe are criminal who do not withſtand ſuch temptation, yet neither are thoſe innocent who lay the bait in their way: That the opinions of men are not the object of civil government, nor under its juriſdiction: That to ſuffer the civil Magiſtrate to intrude his powers into the field of opinion, and to reſtrain the profeſſion or propagation of principles on ſuppoſition of their ill tendency, is a dangerous fallacy, which at once deſtroys all religious liberty; becauſe he being of courſe Judge of that tendency will make his own opinions the rule of judgment, and approve or condemn the ſentiments of others only as they ſhall ſquare with, or differ from his own: That it is time enough for the rightful purpoſes of civil government for its officers to interfere when principles break out into overtacts againſt peace and good order: And finally, that truth is great and will prevail if left to herſelf; that ſhe is the proper and ſufficient antagoniſt to errour, and has nothing to fear from the conflict, unleſs by human interpoſition, diſarmed of her natural weapons, free argument and debate; errours ceaſing to be dangerous when it is permitted freely to contradict them

WE the General Aſſembly of *Virginia* do enact, that no man ſhall be compelled to frequent or ſupport any religous Worſhip place or Miniſtry whatſoever, nor ſhall be enforced, reſtrained, moleſted, or burthened in his body or goods, nor ſhall otherwiſe ſuffer on account of his religious opinions or belief, but that all men ſhall be free to profeſs, and by argument to maintain their opinions in matters of religion, and that the ſame ſhall in no wiſe diminiſh, enlarge, or affect their civil capacities.

AND though we well know that this Aſſembly, elected by the people for the ordinary purpoſes of legiſlation only, have no power to reſtrain the acts of ſucceeding Aſſemblies, conſtituted with powers equal to our own, and that therefore to declare this act irrevocable would be of no effect in law; yet we are free to declare, and do declare, that the rights hereby aſſerted are of the natural rights of mankind, and that if any act ſhall be hereafter paſſed to repeal the preſent, or to narrow its operation, ſuch act will be an infringement of natural right.

***Thomas Jefferson*, about 1786–1820**

Attributed to John Trumbull

VMHC Collection, Gift of Dr. Frederick D. Gillespie

This portrait of Jefferson is related to Trumbull's famous painting of the presentation to Congress of the Declaration of Independence—of which Jefferson was the principal author. Although the principles he eloquently expressed in that document would remain a challenge across time, they have had a profound influence around the world.

***A Bill for Establishing Religious Freedom, printed for the Consideration of the People*, 1779**

Thomas Jefferson (author)

Trustees of the Boston Public Library

Before the American Revolution, the Church of England was the established church in Virginia. Colonists were required to attend services and pay taxes to support it. Growing dissent—particularly from Presbyterians and Baptists—stirred Thomas Jefferson (1743–1826) to propose a bill advocating religious freedom in 1777, which was adopted in 1786. Jefferson's concept of religious liberty and the separation of church and state influenced the U.S. Constitution and the U.S. Supreme Court's understanding of religious freedom.

"[O]ur civil rights have no dependance on our religious opinions . . . the proscribing any citizen as unworthy the public confidence . . . unless he profess or renounce this or that religious opinion, is depriving him injuriously of those privileges and advantages to which, in common with his fellow citizens, he has a natural right."

Excerpt from *A Bill for Establishing Religious Freedom*, 1779

John Marshall, 1832
James Reid Lambdin (artist)
VMHC Collection, Purchased with funds provided by Hunton & Williams in honor of Justice Lewis F. Powell, Jr.

John Marshall (1755–1835) fought in the American Revolution, established a law practice in Richmond, and served in all three branches of the federal government before becoming the fourth Chief Justice of the U.S. Supreme Court (1801). When he wrote "a law repugnant to the Constitution is void," in *Marbury* v. *Madison* (1803), it was the first time the court declared a law unconstitutional. During his 34-year tenure as chief justice he developed the court into what it is today—a co-equal branch of the federal government.

> *WHEREAS George the third, king of* Great Britain and Ireland, *and elector of* Hanover, *heretofore intrusted with the exercise of the kingly office in this government, hath endeavoured to pervert the same into a detestable and insupportable tyranny . . . the government of this country, as formerly exercised under the crown of* Great Britain, *is TOTALLY DISSOLVED.*

Virginia Constitution, 1776

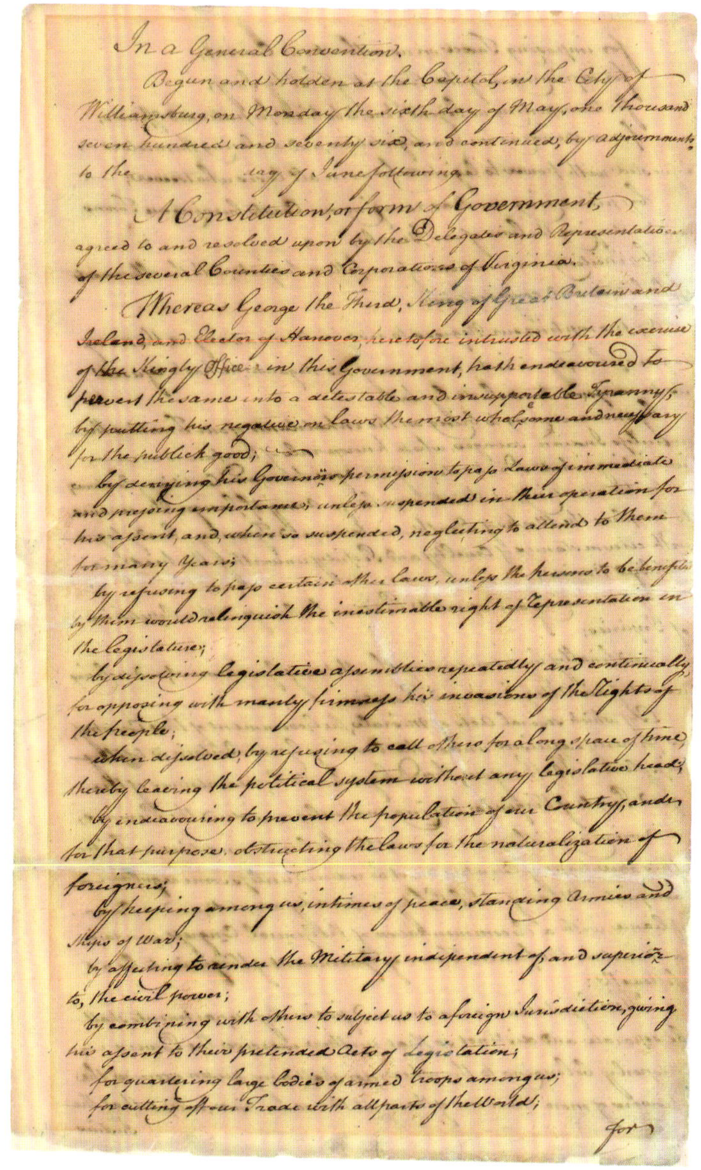

In a General Convention,
Begun and holden at the Capitol, in the City of Williamsburg, on Monday the sixth day of May, one thousand seven hundred and seventy six, and continued, by adjournments, to the day of June following.

A Constitution, or form of Government, agreed to and resolved upon by the Delegates and Representatives of the several Counties and Corporations of Virginia.

Whereas George the Third, King of Great Britain and Ireland, and Elector of Hanover, heretofore intrusted with the exercise of the Kingly Office in this Government, hath endeavoured to pervert the same into a detestable and insupportable Tyranny; by putting his negative on laws the most wholesome and necessary for the publick good;
by denying his Governors permission to pass Laws of immediate and pressing importance, unless suspended in their operation for his assent, and, when so suspended, neglecting to attend to them for many years;
by refusing to pass certain other laws, unless the persons to be benefited by them would relinquish the inestimable right of representation in the Legislature;
by dissolving legislative assemblies repeatedly and continually, for opposing with manly firmness his invasions of the rights of the people;
when dissolved, by refusing to call others for a long space of time, thereby leaving the political system without any legislative head;
by endeavouring to prevent the population of our Country, and, for that purpose, obstructing the laws for the naturalization of foreigners;
by keeping among us, in times of peace, standing Armies and Ships of War;
by affecting to render the Military independent of, and superior to, the civil power;
by combining with others to subject us to a foreign Jurisdiction, giving his assent to their pretended acts of Legislation;
for quartering large bodies of armed troops among us;
for cutting off our Trade with all parts of the World;
for

Constitution of the State of Virginia, 1776
Fifth Virginia Convention (May 6 – July 5, 1776)
Courtesy of the Library of Virginia

On June 29, 1776, five days before the Continental Congress approved the Declaration of Independence, Virginia adopted its first "Constitution or Form of Government." It established the separation of governmental powers and was the first state constitution to include a declaration of rights. Virginia's Constitution served as a model for other states and the U.S. Constitution.

Congressional Union of Virginia banner, about 1916

From the collection of Sophie Meredith Sides Cowan

This banner belonged to Richmond suffragist Sophie H. Meredith (1851 – 1928), who helped establish the Equal Suffrage League of Virginia in 1909. Realizing that the Virginia legislature would not give women the right to vote, she directed her efforts toward the ratification of a constitutional amendment and in 1915 organized the Virginia branch of the Congressional Union for Woman Suffrage. In 1920, the United States ratified the Nineteenth Amendment guaranteeing women the right to vote and ushered in a new age of women's civic activism.

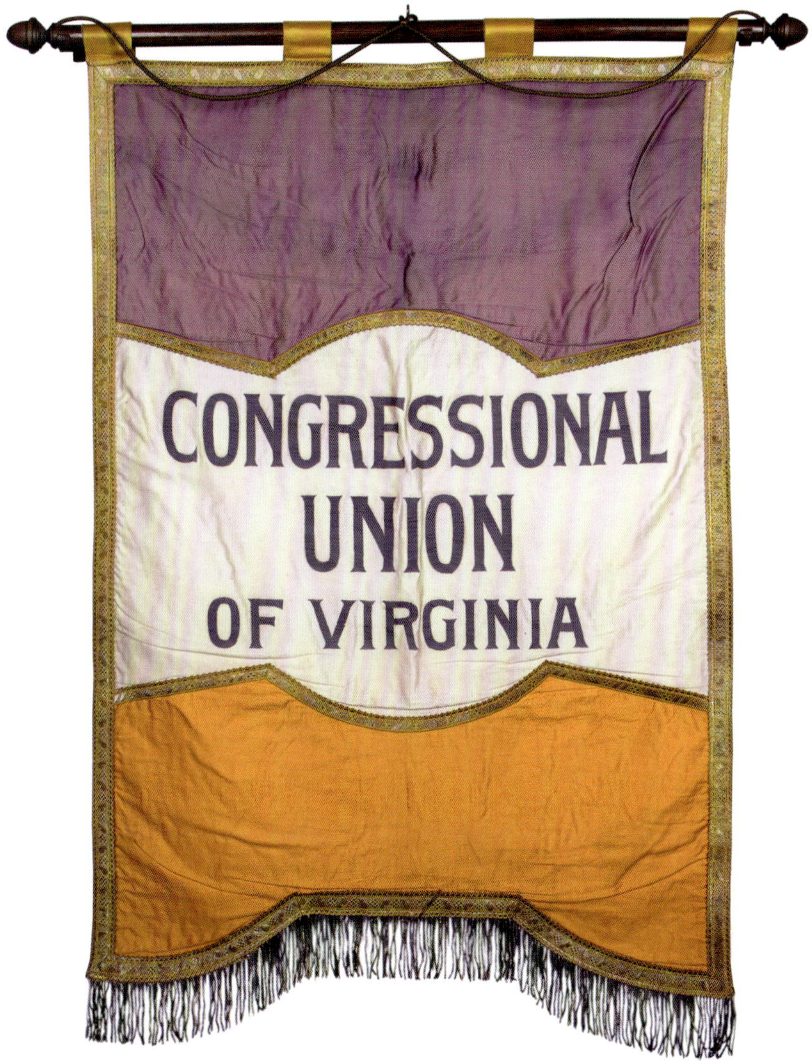

Members of the Congressional Union for Woman Suffrage at the steps of the Virginia Capitol in Richmond, about 1915

William Washington Foster (photographer)

VMHC Collection

"Votes for Women" pin, about 1910

VMHC Collection

By giving speeches, wielding campaign signs, and wearing pins like this one, suffrage activists challenged traditional conceptions of white southern femininity as genteel, demure, and confined to the domestic sphere.

Mildred and Richard Loving after the Supreme Court decision, 1967

Bettmann / Getty Images

In the 1960s, Richard (1933–1975) and Mildred (1939–2008) Loving of Caroline County fought Virginia's laws prohibiting interracial marriage. The U.S. Supreme Court declared such laws unconstitutional in *Loving* v. *Virginia* (1967). This landmark civil rights case ended centuries of restrictions on interracial unions and also paved the way for same-sex marriage equality.

> *"I think that marrying who you want to is a right that no man should have anything to do with. It's a god-given right."*
>
> Mildred Loving, 1967

Carol Schall (center), Mary Townley (right), and their daughter Emily Schall-Townley, 2014

Steve Helber / AP / Shutterstock

Chesterfield County couple, Carol Schall and Mary Townley, had been together for decades and had a daughter, Emily. Although married in California, Virginia did not recognize their union or Carol as Emily's legal guardian. In 2014, they helped overturn Virginia's ban on same-sex marriage as plaintiffs in *Bostic* v. *Shaefer*, and the following year, the U.S. Supreme Court legalized same-sex marriage nationwide.

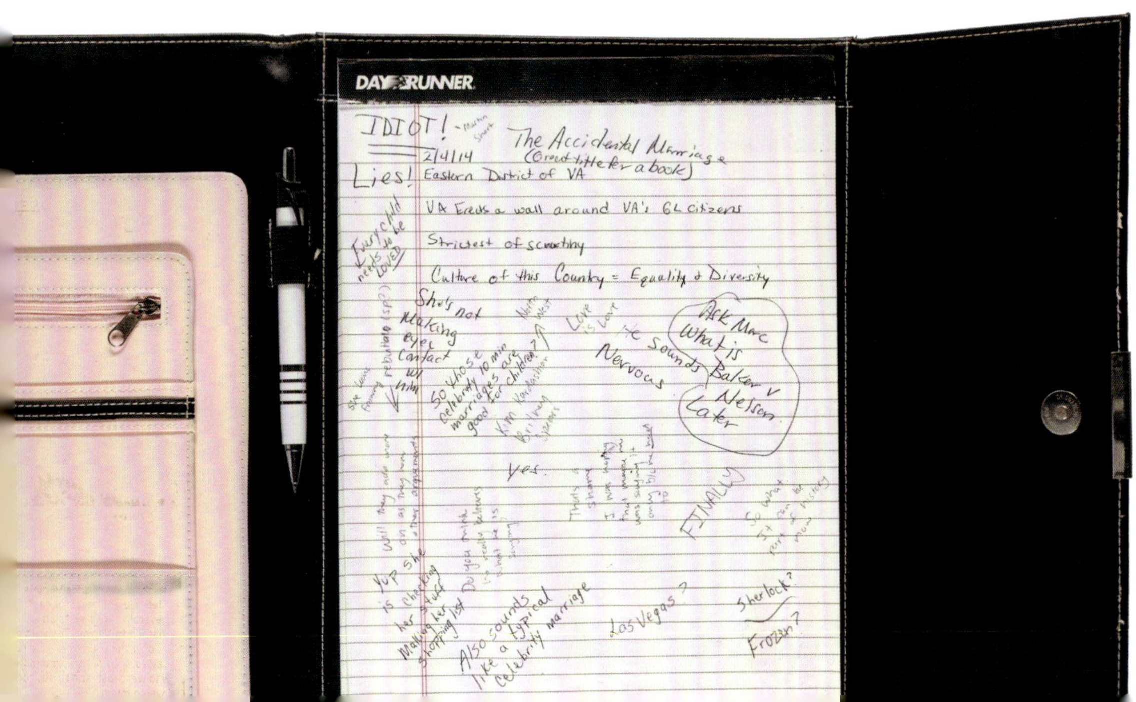

DayRunner notebook used during the 2014 hearing on Virginia's same-sex marriage ban, 2014

VMHC Collection, Gift of Carol Schall, Mary Townley, and Emily Schall-Townley

In the courtroom, Schall, Townley, and their daughter Emily, wrote, "Culture of this Country = Equality & Diversity," "VA Erects a wall around VA's GL [gay and lesbian] citizens," and other notes to one another using this notebook.

Some of the more than 100 students named in *Davis* v. *Prince Edward County*, 1953

Hank Walker / Time & Life Pictures / Getty Images

In 1951, sixteen-year-old Barbara Johns (1935–1991) led a student protest against the poor conditions, lack of supplies, and overcrowding in her segregated Farmville (Prince Edward County) high school. Their actions drew the attention of the NAACP, which took the case to the U.S. Supreme Court. The landmark *Brown* v. *Board of Education* decision (1954) ruled that school segregation was unconstitutional and undermined the "separate but equal" doctrine that had legalized racial segregation in Jim Crow America. Virginia officials responded by instituting a series of systematic methods to resist integration—referred to as Massive Resistance.

Attorneys Oliver W. Hill, Sr. (right) and Spottswood Robinson III (left) representing students from West Point, Virginia, 1953

Scott L. Henderson (photographer)

Library of Congress, Prints and Photographs Division

Richmond lawyers Oliver W. Hill, Sr. (1907–2007) and Spottswood Robinson III (1916–1998) represented the Farmville students and played vital roles in *Brown* v. *Board of Education*, among other key legal cases. During their careers, they became two of America's most celebrated civil rights attorneys. Oliver Hill received the Presidential Medal of Freedom in 1999.

Lunch counter and stools from Richmond's F.W. Woolworth Store, about 1950

From the collection of the Black History Museum and Cultural Center of Virginia

Sit-ins, marches, and other non-violent protests were a key part of the civil rights movement. On February 20, 1960, Black students from Virginia Union University led protests at Richmond stores, including Woolworth's. When they occupied "whites-only" dining areas, they were denied service and verbally abused. By 1964, when the U.S. Congress passed the Civil Rights Act banning racial discrimination, more than one quarter of Richmond's restaurants had integrated.

Leroy Bray, Jr., being arrested during the Thalhimers department store sit-in, 1960

Cook Collection, The Valentine

Leroy M. Bray, Jr., was the first of thirty-four Virginia Union University students to be arrested for attempting to integrate the dining facilities at Richmond's Thalhimers department store. The arrests sparked the Campaign for Human Dignity, which organized boycotts and picketed Richmond businesses.

Black Lives Matter protesters, 2020

Crixell Matthews (photographer)

VPM News

Following the murder by police of George Floyd in May 2020, members of Richmond's Black community and their supporters took to the streets to protest police violence and systemic racism. During the following month, demonstrators clashed with police. Since that summer, individuals, community groups, and city government in the former capital of the Confederacy have worked to reconcile with the city's troubled history.

Chiefs Gerald A. Stewart (Chickahominy Tribe Eastern Division); Lee Lockamy (Nansemond Indian Nation); Anne Richardson (Rappahannock Tribe); then-Secretary of the Interior Ryan Zinke; W. Frank Adams (Upper Mattaponi Tribe); Stephen R. Adkins (Chickahominy Indian Tribe); Dean Branham (Monacan Indian Nation); and Robert Gray (Pamunkey Indian Tribe) at a ceremony commemorating federal recognition, 2018

Department of the Interior

Virginia's Indigenous communities have consistently struggled to have their tribal sovereignty recognized by the Commonwealth. This was made more difficult when Virginia passed the Racial Integrity Act (1924) and effectively erased Virginia Indian identity from official records. Since the act's repeal in the 1960s, tribes have advocated for recognition by the state and federal government. By 2018, seven tribes had received federal recognition and four tribes—the Mattaponi, Patawomeck Indian Tribe of Virginia, Nottoway Tribe of Virginia, and Cheroenhaka (Nottoway) Indian Tribe—had been recognized by the Commonwealth.

"Save Rassawek" shirt, 2021

VMHC Collection

Located where the James and Rivanna rivers meet, Rassawek was the historic capital of the Monacan Indian Nation. In 2017, the James River Water Authority announced plans to place a water intake and pump station at that location. The tribe spent years advocating for the preservation of the sacred site—which included the sale of these "Save Rassawek" shirts. Their efforts, and those of their supporters, successfully pressured the JRWA to select an alternative site in 2022.

"This fight has been long and hard, but we are filled with joy to see Rassawek preserved, and our ancestors respected. We have always said, if we can't save Rassawek, there's nowhere in Virginia that's safe. And indeed, this is a victory not just for the Monacans, but for all Virginians."

Tribal Chief Kenneth Branham, Monacan Indian Nation, 2022

EXPRESSING YOURSELF

Across the centuries, Central Virginians have embraced the power of craft, words, dance, music, performance, and art to bridge gaps, express new ideas, and find common ground. This region, as the seat of state government and because of its diversity, has inspired people to speak their minds and share their perspectives in the hope of influencing others.

Hundreds of years ago, finding common ground meant sharing traditions for survival and for marking important occasions. On the eve of the American Revolution, outspoken Virginians articulated a vision of liberty and fundamental human rights. More recently, Central Virginia has brought like-minded people together through letter-writing campaigns, street art, and annual gatherings.

Sappony quilting bee, 2019
Mrs. Carrie Martin (maker of original 1970s quilt top)
Courtesy of Kara Stewart

Quilting has a long history among the Sappony—whose homelands span the North Carolina and Virginia border. Historically, women individually sewed pieces of their quilt in preparation for quilting bees held in fall or winter. Moving house-to-house, quilters shared work, food, and company as they completed each family's quilts. Contemporary quilting bees continue that tradition. With participation from both women and men, they strengthen community relationships and pass on learning to new generations.

"[T]he women make a great many patchwork quilts for use at home. These quilts are quite artistic, sometimes having original patterns and sometimes in such standard patterns as the Log Cabin and Sunburst designs. The quilts show a feeling for originality in color and design. . ."

Louise Nunn in *A Comparison of the Social Situation of Two Isolated Indian Groups in Northern North Carolina*, 1937

Artist Hamilton Glass (foreground) paints the "In Conversation" mural at 4 West Broad Street, Richmond, with Matt Lively, 2020

Katrina Hecksher-Jones (photographer)

Courtesy of Taekia and Hamilton Glass

A visible sign of social justice protests in May 2020 was graffiti on Richmond's monuments, plywood-covered windows, and other public and private property. In response, mural artist Hamilton Glass launched the Mending Walls project. By 2023, artists from different cultures and backgrounds collaboratively painted twenty-six murals around the city to inspire conversations about race and racism.

"We Need to Talk . . ." stencil, 2020

Noah Scalin (artist)

VMHC Collection, Gift of Hamilton Glass

Working with local business owners, artists participating in the Mending Walls project painted this stencil designed by Noah Scalin on plywood-covered windows throughout downtown Richmond to commemorate Juneteenth.

"As an artist, I needed to create to process all of the emotions that have been heightened with the pandemic and the social unrest. I knew that if I was feeling that way, my fellow creatives were feeling that way, and the community as well."

Mural artist Hamilton Glass about starting the Mending Walls project, 2020

Jeans worn by Hamilton Glass during the Mending Walls project, 2020

Courtesy of Taekia and Hamilton Glass

Solange Oliver in front of Meadowbrook High School, 2018
Scott Elmquist (photographer)
Courtesy of Scott Elmquist

In 2018, 15-year-old Solange Oliver founded the "Girls Code" club at Meadowbrook High School (Chesterfield County) to encourage girls to learn about different cultures and to advocate for a more culturally sensitive dress code.

"[S]ome days I don't have my hair figured out and I just want to throw on a turban. All hairstyles are not accessible to me, so I do what I can. We're taught from a Eurocentric perspective so when they have rules and guidelines they don't have to integrate you embracing your culture. I motivate girls to wear headscarves when they can if they want to. You'll get stopped and sent to [in-school detention], but I motivate more students to advocate for themselves."
Solange Oliver, Girls for a Change member, 2018

Limited-edition women's sneaker designed by Girls for a Change, 2022
Girls for a Change and COMUNITYmade (manufacturer)
VMHC Collection

Founded in 2000, the Richmond-based Girls for a Change (GFAC) organization aims to empower Black girls in Central Virginia to envision bright futures for themselves through discovery, development, innovation, and social change in their communities. GFAC members of Richmond's Thomas Jefferson High School designed these shoes and partnered with a company that produces locally made shoes to benefit community groups.

***Virginia Pride #1*, about 2018**
Ben Workman (Jumper Maybach) (artist)
VHMC Collection, Gift of Virginia Pride

Workman was commissioned to create this painting featuring the Virginia State Capitol for the organization Virginia Pride, which plans Virginia PrideFest. The first "Richmond Lesbian and Gay Pride Day" event was held at the city's Byrd Park on June 23, 1979—the tenth anniversary of the Stonewall Riots in New York City. Pride events became an annual event in the city in 1986. Today, Virginia Pride's PrideFest is one of the state's largest LGBTQ+ festivals, attracting more than 30,000 people.

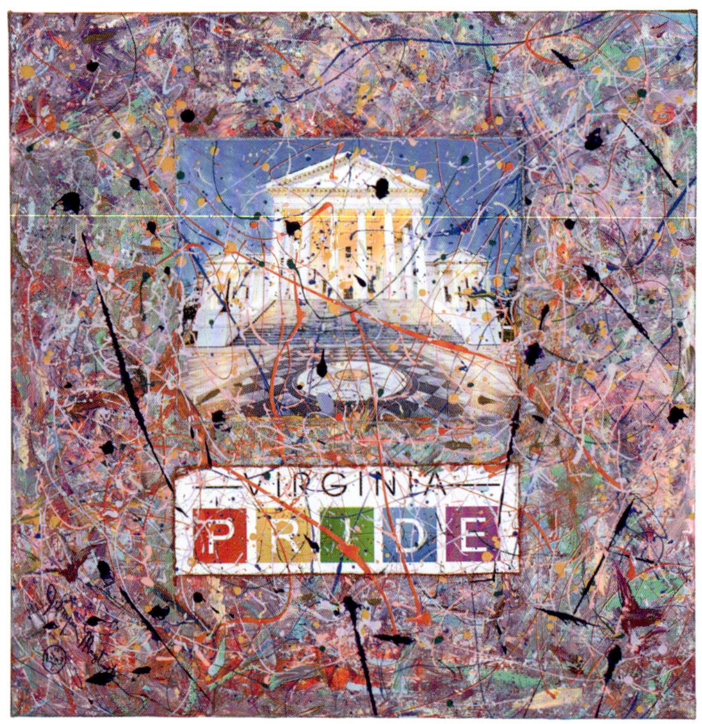

Adèle Clark (bottom center), Nora Houston (left), Mae Schaill, and Mary Eugenia Benson Jobson, 1915

Foster Studios (photographer)

Special Collections and Archives, James Branch Cabell Library, VCU Libraries

"[A]rt is a language and expresses a person's philosophy."

Nora Houston, 1940

Richmond Art Club exhibition catalog, 1898

VMHC Collection

Established in 1895, by attorney and industrialist James H. Dooley (1841 – 1922), the Art Club of Richmond offered opportunities for local artists to teach and practice art. Adèle Clark and Nora Houston met at the Art Club and began a relationship that lasted for forty years. In 1917, they left the Club to start their own art school, the Atelier of the Virginia League of Fine Arts and Handicrafts.

***The Children's Amendment*, about 1920**

Eleanora "Nora" Houston (artist)

Courtesy of Richmond Conservation Studio & The Nora Houston Foundation, Inc.

Eleanora "Nora" Houston (1883 – 1942) and Adèle Clark (1882 – 1983) were companions in life, art, and activism. Through art they sought to improve conditions for women, Black people, and children. *The Children's Amendment* reflects Houston's efforts to improve child labor laws and healthcare access.

Fence and playground in Jackson Ward, 2019

Lanai Benn (photographer)

From the collection of the Black History Museum and Cultural Center of Virginia

Oakwood Arts helps art students learn how self-expression can transition into creative careers, opening professional opportunities to previously marginalized communities. This photograph was taken as part of a photography course in which students explored the history of Jackson Ward, a historic Richmond neighborhood that was a center of Black enterprise, culture, and civic activism during the Jim Crow era.

Mask designed by Helen McGehee Umaña, about 1967

VMHC Collection, Gift of Helen McGehee Umaña

Umaña designed this mask for the character of Cuchulain in *The Only Jealousy of Emer*, a work that she choreographed in the 1960s.

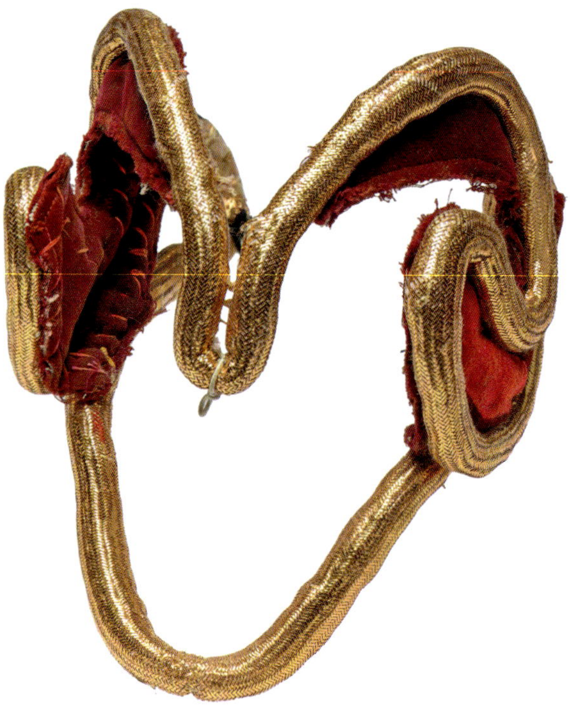

Helen McGehee Umaña, 1940s–50s

VMHC Collection, Gift of Helen McGehee Umaña

Born in Lynchburg, Helen McGehee Umaña (1920–2021) was a gifted dancer, choreographer, costume designer, and member of the renowned Martha Graham Dance Company. She began her career in modern dance at Randolph-Macon Woman's College (now Randolph College) and later taught dancers at Juilliard and her alma mater, encouraging them to express themselves in new ways to forward the art form.

"Helen was in possession of this remarkable vibrancy and creativity, and she was until the end of her life."

Pam Risenhoover, professor of dance at Randolph College and former student of Helen McGehee Umaña, 2021

Lynchburg's Academy of Music program for *The Beauty Shop*, 1926

From the collection of the Lynchburg Museum System

Lynchburg's Academy Center of the Arts, 2019

Camden Littleton (photographer)

Camden Littleton Photography

During World War II, the Academy of Music became a venue for movies. By the 1950s, television and suburbanization led people to find entertainment elsewhere. The Academy of Arts closed its doors in 1958. After being added to the National Register of Historic Places, it was refurbished and reinvigorated as the Academy Center of the Arts in 2018.

Ava Holloway (right) and Kennedy George pose at Richmond's Robert E. Lee monument, 2020

Julia Rendleman / Reuters

Graceful and defiant, 14-year-old ballerinas Ava Holloway and Kennedy George raise their clenched fists in support of the Black Lives Matter movement at the graffiti-covered Robert E. Lee monument. Their image went viral on social media. Using their sudden fame, they founded Brown Ballerinas for Change to promote social justice and increase opportunities for underrepresented communities in ballet.

"I never really expected for our photo to be as viral as it was. But I've learned that you can advocate in your own way. You can speak up using the gifts that you're given. . . . We're promoting social justice. We're able to advocate in a different way using an art form."

Ava Holloway, ballerina, activist, and author, 2020

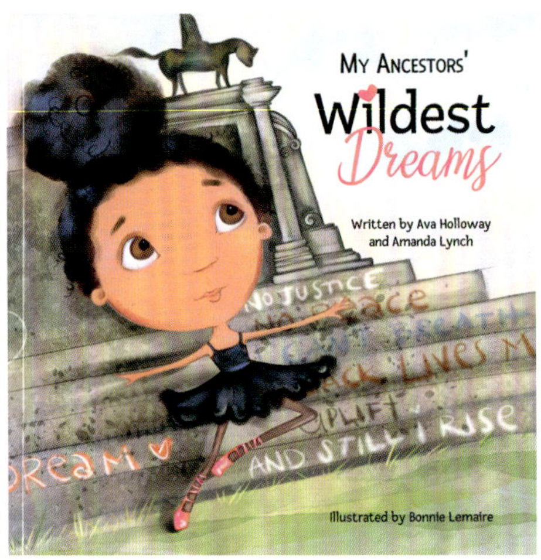

***My Ancestors' Wildest Dreams*, 2020**

Ava Holloway and Amanda Lynch (authors); Bonnie Lemaire (illustrator)

VMHC Education Collection

Holloway and her mother Amanda Lynch published a children's book about their experience to inspire future ballerinas of color.

Bio Ritmo performs at Friday Cheers, Richmond, 2015

David Parrish Photography

Formed in 1991, Bio Ritmo is an ensemble band based in Richmond and known for its unique approach to Latin music.

"La banda nació de esta próspera comunidad cruda, artística que sigue caracterizando a Richmond hoy. . . . Pero todos compartimos la pasión por la 'salsa', una música que abarca tantos estilos e influencias diferentes."

"The band was born out of this thriving, raw, artistic community that continues to characterize Richmond today. . . . But we all share a passion for 'salsa,' a music that encompasses so many different styles and influences."

Marlysse Simmons, Bio Ritmo pianist, composer, and producer, 2014

Members of GWAR, 2010

Rebecca and Dave Kendry (photographers)

Pit Records, Inc.

GWAR was formed in 1984 from a Richmond artist collective known as the "Slave Pit." Claiming to be a group of intergalactic "chaos warriors," the heavy metal rock band mixes satire and political commentary with grotesque costumes, simulated onstage violence, and elaborate props and sets. With a rotating line-up of performers, the band has built an international fanbase and opened a GWARbar in Richmond in 2014.

***Autumn on the Vine* (Afton Mountain Vineyard), 2016**
Deb Snelson (photographer)
Courtesy of Scenic Virginia

Virginia's oppressive humidity and destructive pests doomed efforts by Thomas Jefferson (1743–1826) and other early vintners to cultivate popular European grapes. With the introduction of new varieties and improved growing techniques, growers are overcoming those obstacles. Central Virginia is now home to more than one-third of the Commonwealth's 300 wineries and is the state's largest winemaking region.

COMING TO THE TABLE

Food is not only about survival; it is also a primary way we connect with our culture, our families, and our communities. Some of the most iconic Southern foods—cornbread, collard greens, and smoked meats—are the result of the cultural collision between American Indians, enslaved Africans, and European colonists. New food traditions have been introduced by successive waves of immigrants from Eastern Europe, South America, and Asia. Professional and home chefs alike are sharing traditional foods and creating new ones that nourish both body and spirit.

Whether breaking bread over a home-cooked meal, joining friends at a local restaurant or tasting room, or attending one of the many cultural food festivals, Central Virginians cherish gathering around food and drink.

"I have kept thinking about the people that I grew up with and about our way of life. Whenever I go back to visit my sisters and brothers, we relive old times . . . we share again in gathering wild strawberries, canning, rendering lard, finding walnuts, picking persimmons, making fruitcake. I realize how much the bond that held us had to do with food."

Edna Lewis, *The Taste of Country Cooking*, 1976

Edna Lewis (right) arranging dinner for the annual reunion of former Freetown residents at the Bethel Baptist Church in Unionville, 1977

Photograph by John T. Hill

Acclaimed chef, teacher, and cookbook author Edna Lewis (1916–2006) grew up in Freetown, an Orange County community founded by Black Virginians who seized freedom after the Civil War. Lewis's book, *The Taste of Country Cooking*, was one of the first written by a Black woman to reach a national audience. The book rekindled interest in Southern cooking and shared recipes and her childhood memories about how the community's seasonal, farm-to-table cooking traditions were intertwined with family meals, holidays, and communal events.

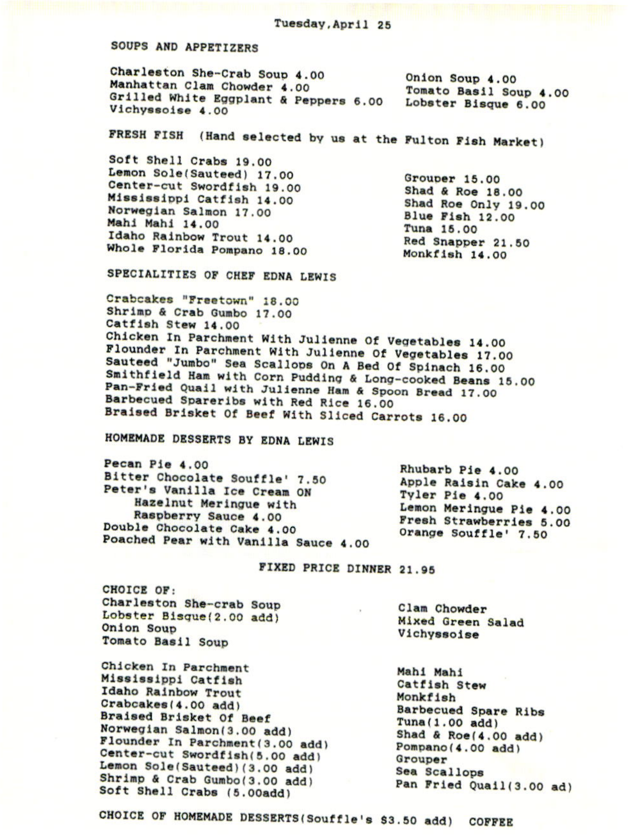

Tuesday,April 25

SOUPS AND APPETIZERS

Charleston She-Crab Soup 4.00
Manhattan Clam Chowder 4.00
Grilled White Eggplant & Peppers 6.00
Vichyssoise 4.00
Onion Soup 4.00
Tomato Basil Soup 4.00
Lobster Bisque 6.00

FRESH FISH (Hand selected by us at the Fulton Fish Market)

Soft Shell Crabs 19.00
Lemon Sole(Sauteed) 17.00
Center-cut Swordfish 19.00
Mississippi Catfish 14.00
Norwegian Salmon 17.00
Mahi Mahi 14.00
Idaho Rainbow Trout 14.00
Whole Florida Pompano 18.00
Grouper 15.00
Shad & Roe 18.00
Shad Roe Only 19.00
Blue Fish 12.00
Tuna 15.00
Red Snapper 21.50
Monkfish 14.00

SPECIALITIES OF CHEF EDNA LEWIS

Crabcakes "Freetown" 18.00
Shrimp & Crab Gumbo 17.00
Catfish Stew 14.00
Chicken In Parchment With Julienne Of Vegetables 14.00
Flounder In Parchment With Julienne Of Vegetables 17.00
Sauteed "Jumbo" Sea Scallops On A Bed Of Spinach 16.00
Smithfield Ham with Corn Pudding & Long-cooked Beans 15.00
Pan-Fried Quail with Julienne Ham & Spoon Bread 17.00
Barbecued Spareribs with Red Rice 16.00
Braised Brisket Of Beef With Sliced Carrots 16.00

HOMEMADE DESSERTS BY EDNA LEWIS

Pecan Pie 4.00
Bitter Chocolate Souffle' 7.50
Peter's Vanilla Ice Cream ON Hazelnut Meringue with Raspberry Sauce 4.00
Double Chocolate Cake 4.00
Poached Pear with Vanilla Sauce 4.00
Rhubarb Pie 4.00
Apple Raisin Cake 4.00
Tyler Pie 4.00
Lemon Meringue Pie 4.00
Fresh Strawberries 5.00
Orange Souffle' 7.50

FIXED PRICE DINNER 21.95

CHOICE OF:
Charleston She-crab Soup
Lobster Bisque(2.00 add)
Onion Soup
Tomato Basil Soup
Clam Chowder
Mixed Green Salad
Vichyssoise

Chicken In Parchment
Mississippi Catfish
Idaho Rainbow Trout
Crabcakes(4.00 add)
Braised Brisket Of Beef
Norwegian Salmon(3.00 add)
Flounder In Parchment(3.00 add)
Center-cut Swordfish(5.00 add)
Lemon Sole(Sauteed)(3.00 add)
Shrimp & Crab Gumbo(3.00 add)
Soft Shell Crabs (5.00add)
Mahi Mahi
Catfish Stew
Monkfish
Barbecued Spare Ribs
Tuna(1.00 add)
Shad & Roe(4.00 add)
Pompano(4.00 add)
Grouper
Sea Scallops
Pan Fried Quail(3.00 ad)

CHOICE OF HOMEMADE DESSERTS(Souffle's $3.50 add) COFFEE

Gage & Tollner menu featuring dishes prepared by Chef Edna Lewis, about 1990

Gage & Tollner (printer)

From the collection of the Brooklyn Public Library, Center for Brooklyn History

Gage & Tollner became renowned for authentic Southern food when Edna Lewis became the New York restaurant's head chef at the age of 72. During her three-year tenure, her menus were typewritten, dated, and reflected her use of seasonal ingredients available at the city's markets.

A pot of Brunswick Stew being made at the Brunswick Stew Festival, 2019

TVNewsBadge (licensed under CC 2.0)

Made from readily available meats and vegetables, Brunswick Stew was a traditional food for European settlers in this region. The tradition continues at stew competitions and community fundraisers, where it is made in a large caldron, with a "stewmaster" overseeing the stirring team. When the stew is thick enough to allow the paddle to stand upright, it is ready! Although many places—including Brunswick, Georgia—claim the stew's origins, in 1988 the Virginia General Assembly officially proclaimed Brunswick County as its birthplace.

Mrs. Fearnow's Delicious Brunswick Stew can label, late 1900s

VMHC Collection

Lillie Pearl Hovermale Fearnow (1881 – 1970) turned her home recipe for Brunswick Stew into a thriving business in Hanover County. Her sons established the Fearnow Brothers Cannery in Mechanicsville to expand the enterprise during the 1940s. In the following decades, her canned stew became a customer favorite in regional stores.

Luz Maria López (left) and Princey Reyes, 2019

Courtesy of Luz López

López grew up in Quintana Roo on Mexico's Yucatan Peninsula and learned to cook traditional dishes of the region—cochinita piblil, tamales de hoja de planto, and panchuros—from her mother. After moving to Charlottesville in 2002, López became an active member of the city's Mexican community and continues the tradition of passing along traditional Yucatecan-style recipes to family and friends.

"Since I can remember, I was in the kitchen helping my mom cook . . . [learning] how to make a perfect handmade tortilla . . . the exact time to flip it and not be afraid of the hot comal [griddle]. I'm trying to teach [my two daughters] everything I know about our traditions."

Luz Maria López, teaching her daughter Princey Reyes how to make traditional Yucatecan-style dishes, 2019

Legend Brewing Company growler, 2021

Breweries across Virginia have become community-gathering spaces. Tom Martin opened Richmond's Legend Brewing Company in 1994. It is the oldest operating craft brewery in Virginia.

James River Distillery's Commonwealth Gin bottle, 2015

VMHC Collection, Gift of Jamison Davis

Although Southwest Virginia is well-known for its moonshining history, Central Virginia boasts many modern distilleries such as James River Distillery, which was founded in 2013 in Richmond.

Barboursville Vineyards wine bottle, 2021

VMHC Education Collection

Considered as a possible revenue-generating industry, wine production was attempted by the Jamestown colonists, but the European grapes failed to grow in Virginia's soil. A disease-resistant hybrid grape developed in the 1830s resurrected Virginia's wine industry until Prohibition in 1920. Founded in 1976, Barboursville Vineyards is the first in the modern era of Virginia winemaking to successfully plant *Vitis vinifera* (a type of grape). The vineyard sits on the former estate of Virginia's 18th governor, James Barbour, in Orange County.

Chef Patrick O'Connell (center) in the kitchen of the Inn at Little Washington, 2015

Scott Suchman (photographer)

Scott Suchman Photography

The small town of Washington (Rappahannock County) is the humble home to one of the world's best restaurants. A self-taught chef, Patrick O'Connell (b. 1945) opened the Inn at Little Washington in an abandoned garage in 1978. An early adopter of using farm-to-table ingredients, O'Connell masterfully blends French-style cooking with regional American cuisine. He earned the James Beard Lifetime Achievement Award in 2019 and, as of 2023, the Inn is one of only thirteen restaurants in the U.S. to receive three Michelin Stars.

CHEERING ON THE TEAM

Although Virginia is the most populous state without a major sports franchise, Central Virginia is home to many teams and with deeply loyal fans. Charlottesville hosts University of Virginia alumni as they rally around their college football and basketball teams. Danville and Richmond celebrate "America's pastime" at their minor league stadiums and welcome racing fans to their tracks. Fredericksburg and Lynchburg show off their corporate and military pride along the routes of their annual road races. Lacrosse fans across the region root for players as they continue an ancient Virginia Indigenous game into the 21st century.

Cheering alongside one another brings people from Central Virginia's diverse communities together.

Richmond-Korean Youth Soccer Goal Shooting Contest trophy, 2005
VMHC Collection

Coaches for the Richmond-Korean Youth Soccer League signed the soccer ball on this trophy for a goal shooting contest.

Bloomers used by Josephine V. Weyand while playing basketball at the Richmond YWCA, 1920s
VMHC Collection, Gift of Barbara L. McRae

Richmond YWCA basketball team, 1920s
VMHC Collection, Gift of Barbara L. McRae

Josephine V. Weyand (1902–1988) was among the many women who enjoyed the programs, including basketball, offered by the Richmond Young Women's Christian Association (YWCA). Founded in 1887, the Richmond YWCA sought to empower women, but membership and services were restricted to white women. In 1911, the Phyllis Wheatley Branch opened in the city, one of the first YWCAs to serve Black women in the country.

Richmond Virginians player at Parker Field, Richmond, early 1960s
Adolph B. Rice Studio (photographer)
Courtesy of the Library of Virginia

Richmond has long supported minor league baseball. Area baseball fans enjoyed watching the Richmond Virginians—a minor league team affiliated with the New York Yankees—in the 1950s and 1960s. After the team moved to Ohio in 1964, the Richmond Braves thrilled fans until 2008. The following year, the Richmond Flying Squirrels landed in Richmond.

One-half of a silk boating scarf, 1888
VMHC Collection, Gift of D. Tennant Bryan

Although it has faded over time, this scarf inspired the University of Virginia's (UVA) school colors of orange and blue. In the fall of 1888, UVA star athlete Allen Potts (1867–1930) wore it to a rally about changing the school's colors of red and gray. A fellow student reportedly grabbed the scarf and yelled, "How will these colors do?" and the crowd roared its approval. Generations of UVA fans have worn orange and blue ever since.

TM

Richmond Flying Squirrels team logo, 2009
Brandiose (designer)
Richmond Flying Squirrels

Following the departure of the Richmond Braves, Richmond's new minor league baseball team flew into town in 2009. To engage the community, the team—formerly the Connecticut Defenders—held a contest in which the public could propose suggestions for a new name. Brad Mead of Prince George County submitted the winning entry. With their mascot "Nutzy," the Flying Squirrels have built a loyal following.

Arthur Ashe at the U.S. National Championship in Forest Hills, Queens, New York, 1965
Bob Gomel (photographer)
LIFE Images Collection / Getty Images

Arthur Ashe's (1943–1993) remarkable career began on Richmond's segregated tennis courts and reached the world's top arenas. He was the first Black male tennis player to win the singles title at Wimbledon (1975), the U.S. Open (1968), and the Australian Open (1970). Off the court, Ashe championed a range of humanitarian causes, including fighting apartheid in South Africa and supporting AIDS advocacy.

"Winning a place on our national team [marked] my ultimate triumph over those people who had opposed my career . . . in the name of segregation."
Arthur Ashe, tennis champion and humanitarian, 1993

Davis Cup championship ring awarded to Arthur Ashe, 1970
VMHC Collection

In 1963, Ashe became the first Black player to represent the United States at the Davis Cup. As a member of the 1970 championship team, he received this ring.

Players gather for the Labor Day challenge at Dr. Robert Johnson's court in Lynchburg, 1950s
Courtesy of the Whirlwind Johnson Foundation

Dr. Robert Walter "Whirlwind" Johnson (1899–1971) set up a tennis boot camp for Black athletes at his home in Lynchburg in the 1940s. He helped launch the careers of tennis greats Althea Gibson (1927–2003) and Richmond-native Arthur Ashe. This image shows Johnson—8th from the right—with a gathering of players on his court.

Emily Bower at Special Olympics Virginia, 2018
Courtesy of the Bower Family

Emily Bower's gold medal in javelin from the Summer Games, Special Olympics Virginia, 2022
From the collection of Emily Bower

Emily Bower (b. 1986) of Richmond did not imagine herself as an athlete until she joined the Global Messenger program of Special Olympics Virginia. While developing leadership and public speaking skills, she also met athletes with disabilities who inspired her to compete. She won two gold medals and one silver in swimming at her first Special Olympics in 2018, and has continued her success at subsequent games.

Virginia Union University megaphone, late 1930s
VMHC Collection, Gift of Dr. Francis M. Foster, Sr.

Clemenceau Givings (1919–1944) used this megaphone to cheer on the teams at Virginia Union University, a historically Black college in Richmond, where he played tennis and was secretary of the Varsity Club. Givings served as a Tuskegee Airman during World War II and was killed in action in Italy in 1944.

Clemenceau Givings, 1943
VMHC Collection, Gift of Dr. Francis M. Foster, Sr.

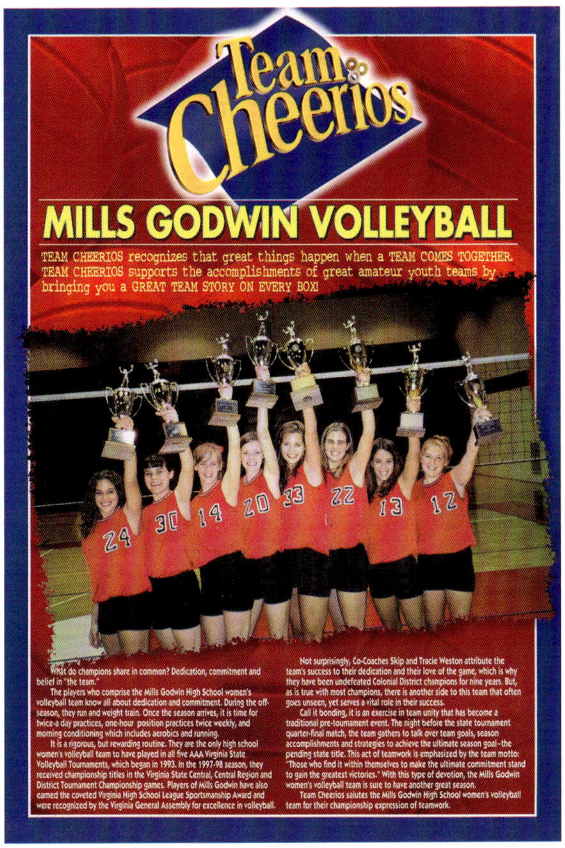

Team Cheerios cereal box, 1998

VMHC Collection

Only a decade after its creation, the Women's Volleyball team of Mills Godwin High School earned two state championships and a feature on a Cheerios cereal box. The team also earned the Virginia High School League Sportsmanship Award and a commendation from Virginia's General Assembly.

Tip-off between the Richmond Spiders and VCU Rams during a women's basketball game, 2017

University of Richmond Athletics

Virginia Commonwealth University (VCU) students, alumni, and fans rally around their basketball team. With campuses separated by only six miles, when the University of Richmond and VCU play one another, it can excite the area.

Shenandoah VALLEY

The Shenandoah Valley provides a natural passageway through the Blue Ridge and Allegheny mountains, and the region offers a rich history and breathtaking vistas. In the period before the arrival of Europeans, the Iroquois, Shawnee, Catawba, Cherokee, Delaware, and Susquehannock competed for control of the Valley and passed frequently through it for trade and war. European settlers later traveled the same routes as they moved from Pennsylvania into Virginia and points south. The fertile soil and lush landscape nurtured hunting, fishing, farming, recreation, and industry. Here, cultures have clashed and combined to create local crafts and a distinctive way of life.

Many stories exist about the origin of the word "Shenandoah." The name, as we know it, has its roots in words of Indigenous people for both a type of place and a person. Some believe it may be derived from Schin-han-dowi, the "River Through the Spruces"; On-an-da-goa, the "River of High Mountains" or "Silver Water"; or an Iroquois word for "Big Meadow." Another legend suggests that it is derived from the name of an Iroquoian chief, Sherando. Perhaps the most popular, romanticized belief is that the name comes from an expression for "Beautiful Daughter of the Stars."

Sunlight streaming through clouds over the Shenandoah Valley, 2013
Nick Roush / Cavan Images

Apple orchard in Stephens City (Frederick County), 2011
Pat & Chuck Blackley / Alamy Stock Photo

Shenandoah Valley Independent Cities

1. Buena Vista
2. Covington
3. Harrisonburg
4. Lexington
5. Staunton
6. Waynesboro
7. Winchester

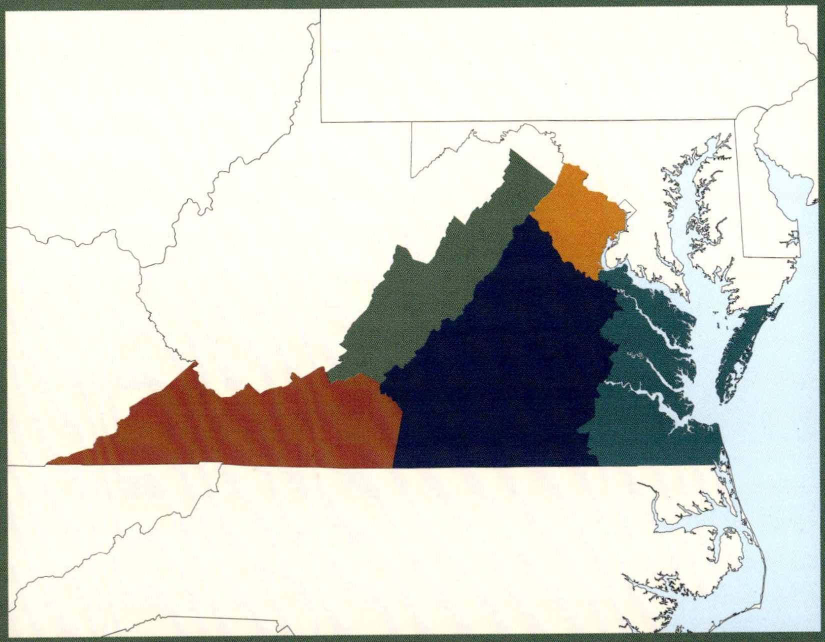

PERFECTING A CRAFT

Each cultural group that made the Valley home brought with them essential survival skills. Each had a way to make pottery or baskets to hold food. Each had ways of felling trees and making tools. Each had ways to hunt and trap. Through generations, these skills were shaped by natural resources, time-honored familial traditions, and interactions between craftspeople from diverse cultural, ethnic, and religious groups. Crafts that once were born out of necessity—quilting, glass blowing, furniture making, blacksmithing—are now sought out for their artistry and cherished as heirlooms. Small-town shops and regional festivals offer glimpses into past ways of life and help artisans express their cultural and Valley origins.

Woodcrafting

Server safe, 1875
William F. Petefish (maker)
From the collection of the Museum of the Shenandoah Valley

Food safes—cabinets with doors featuring punched-tin panels—kept food safe from pests and could often be found in kitchens or cellars. By the mid-1800s, Valley families used decorative server safes in dining rooms or parlors for displaying and serving food. Featuring floral tin panel designs, this safe is distinctive for bearing the signature of the cabinetmaker William F. Petefish (1846–about 1920), who owned a shop in Honeyville (Page County).

Punched-tin safe panel featuring George Washington, about 1830

From the collection of the Museum of the Shenandoah Valley, photo by William H. McGuffin, courtesy of Jeffrey S. Evans & Associates

A group of safes attributed to the Lexington shop of Matthew S. Kahle (cabinetmaker) and John Henson (tinsmith) feature panels with political motifs.

Safe panel, mid-1800s

Attributed to the Alexander family

Photo by William H. McGuffin, courtesy of Jeffrey S. Evans & Associates

Augusta County tinsmiths often created panels with elaborate floral or geometric patterns, like this one on a mid-1800s safe attributed to the Alexander family's shop in Waynesboro.

Carousel horse, 1875–85

Attributed to James William Sheetz

From the collection of the Museum of the Shenandoah Valley

Descended from some of the earliest German settlers in Shenandoah County, James Sheetz (1851–1923) carved an entire carousel that traveled to Confederate veteran reunions and festivals throughout the region. The Sheetz family still boasts woodworkers in their lineage today.

Robert Cross with Castle sculpture, 1960s

Courtesy of Cross Family / Museum of the Shenandoah Valley

Folk artist Robert Cross (b. 1926) grew up in Webbtown (Clarke County), a community founded by formerly enslaved people after the Civil War. He later lived and worked in Winchester. The hallmark of his craft is his use of found items, scrap parts, and recycled materials.

***Tree House*, 1960–74**

Robert Cross (artist)

From the collection of the Museum of the Shenandoah Valley

Cross sculpted this miniature tree house from a stump of locust wood that he found on his family's farm in Webbtown. Locust wood is difficult to carve, so Cross sought out pieces hollowed out by insects. He transformed natural gaps in the wood into working windows and doors.

"We all worked together. [The termites] helped me on the inside and I did my work on the outside."

Robert Cross, sculptor, 2019

Basket Making

White oak basket with handle, about 1887–1936
Attributed to Thomas Jackson "Happy Jack" Nicholson
From the collection of the Museum of the Shenandoah Valley

The Nicholsons of Page and Shenandoah counties established themselves as skilled, prolific basketmakers. Thomas Jackson "Happy Jack" Nicholson (1867–1936) supported his family with the craft and passed the skill along to his children.

Coiled rye grass basket with oak handle, late 1800s to early 1900s
Unknown maker
From the collection of the Museum of the Shenandoah Valley

This type of basket was made by gathering grasses, tree needles, and straw into bundles that were then coiled into the desired shape. Although designs and materials may have differed, the Indigenous, European, and African people who came to live and work in the Valley all brought this technique with them. Basketmaking remained a common part of rural life until the mid-1900s.

Clyde Jenkins splits white oak for basketmaking, 2005
Morgan Miller / Virginia Humanities

"I saw my father and my grandfather work wood as a child, and I wanted to learn how to do it, too. Learning how to do things using these old methods, well it's really served me my whole life. The way my family lives our life, to be honest, is really not all that different from how my grandfather and his grandfather lived. And it's important for me to pass these traditions along because if I don't do it, who will?"
Clyde Jenkins, basketmaker from Page County, 2005

Ceramics

Potters at the S. Bell pottery in Strasburg, about 1885
John A Kubil / Allentown Photographic Studio (photographer)
Courtesy of Crocker Farm Auction

In the 1800s, stoneware and earthenware production became a thriving industry in the region after numerous potters of European descent established shops there. The Bell family ran successful potteries in Winchester and Strasburg, employing other Valley potters to meet the demand.

Three-gallon stoneware jar, 1840s
Solomon Bell (maker)
VMHC Collection, Gift of J.F. Wine, M.D.

Solomon Bell (1817–1882) learned the pottery trade from his father Peter (1775–1847), who moved the family from Maryland to Winchester in 1824. Solomon made this cobalt-decorated stoneware jar early in his career, either in Winchester or in Strasburg, where he worked with his brother Samuel.

Crock, 1860–73
Attributed to Abraham Spencer
From the collection of the Museum of the Shenandoah Valley

The large inverted "A" inscribed on this crock indicates it as the work of free Black potter Abraham Spencer (1806–1873). Spencer likely learned the trade in New Market (Shenandoah County) and worked for multiple Valley potters, including Samuel Bell of Strasburg.

Detail of inverted "A" on crock attributed to Abraham Spencer, 1860–73
From the collection of the Museum of the Shenandoah Valley

Wall pocket, late 1870s to 1880s
Anthony Bacher (maker)
VMHC Collection, Gift of J.F. Wine, M.D.

Anthony Bacher (1824–1889) immigrated from Germany and set up a pottery in Frederick County. This cornucopia-shaped wall pocket or vase shows his skilled use of applied floral decoration and striking glaze treatments.

Vase, 1930–3
Round Hill Pottery (maker)
VMHC Collection, Gift of J.F. Wine, M.D.

This vase was created at the Round Hill Pottery (active 1927–33), a short-lived shop in Winchester that carried on regional pottery traditions in an age of mechanized mass production of ceramic wares. The dissolution of Round Hill—likely forced to close as a result of the Great Depression—ended over a century of commercial pottery production in the Valley.

Kassy Newman at her potter's wheel, 2018
Courtesy of Buddy Harlow

"I have been inspired by the colors in nature, the landscapes, and the friendly community of people that live here. . . . As I share my passion for ceramics, I hope to inspire others and share the therapeutic benefits of turning a chunk of clay into a finished piece of art."

Kassy Newman, ceramic artist and Harrisonburg resident, 2018

Quilting

Sharon Tindall (left) teaching the details of quilting to Nancy Chilton, 2014
Pat Jarrett / Virginia Humanities

Sharon Tindall works on the centerpiece of a quilt, 2014
Pat Jarrett / Virginia Humanities

Practiced for thousands of years, quilting often includes intricate patterns that hold quilt layers together and express the creativity and skills of the maker or makers. The craft continues to thrive and remains an important part of creating and maintaining social networks and community. Sharon Tindall has been making quilts for nearly 30 years.

Connie Broy stands in front of her quilt titled *A Dazzle of Zebras*, 2023

Rich Cooley / *The Daily News-Record*

Connie Broy (b. 1940) of Toms Brook (Shenandoah County) began her sewing career as a seamstress. Her original designs represent the freedom enjoyed by modern quilters who abandon traditional patterns to make their own designs.

"The creative quilter stands for nothing short of perfection. Her points are perfectly matched and her stitching is precise. But the talent that sets her aside is the way she looks at pieces of fabric and swirls the ideas that perk her imaginative mind."

Virginia Quilt Museum description of Connie Broy, 2023

Log cabin quilt, late 1800s to early 1900s

Cora Snapp Blackburn (maker)

VMHC Collection, Gift of Mrs. Marjorie Simmons Crump, granddaughter of Cora Snapp Blackburn

Staunton resident Cora Snapp Blackburn (1868–1926) created this intricately patterned quilt with small rectangular strips of silk and other fabrics. By the second half of the 1800s, the log cabin was a symbol of individual prosperity and conquering the frontier. In this popular design, the diamond shape represents the hearth and the surrounding strips the walls of the cabin.

Four "T" quilt, about 1890–1900
Rena Effinger Coyner Koiner (maker)
VMHC Collection, Gift of Dennis and Kay Stockdale

Augusta county native, Rena Koiner (1869–1949), carefully sewed 1,776 pieces of fabric together by hand to create the decorative panel of this quilt. The pattern features four capital letter "T"s that may symbolize "temperance" or "teetotaler." With calls for the prohibition of alcohol growing stronger in the early 1900s, quilt designs emerged with names like Double T, Capital T, Imperial T, and Kansas T. These quilts were sometimes used to show support for the temperance movement which was driven largely by women.

Quilt block strip and pieces, late 1800s
Attributed to Nannie Edwards Finley White
VMHC Collection, Gift of Eleanor Bear Wallace in memory of Nannie Edwards Finley White

The unfinished strip of hexagonal star-patterned blocks has been attributed to Nannie Edwards Finley White (1861–1900) of Bath County. Using the process of English piece work, she wrapped and stitched fabric around diamond-shaped bits of paper—once letters from family and friends—and then sewed the pieces together to form the block. The recycled letters served as shape templates and added support as she meticulously joined the pieces and then the blocks together.

MIGRATING TO A NEW LAND

Archaeologists report that 10,000 years ago Indigenous people migrated through the Valley along a system of footpaths. More than 1,000 years ago, Siouan-speaking people followed the Mishimayagat ("Great Warrior Trail") and set up agricultural villages along its route. White European settlers to this region—including English, German, and Scots-Irish immigrants—followed this trail. They established towns—often bringing enslaved people with them—along what they called the "Great Wagon Trail," which is today's Route 11. Migration into the Valley continues today by people drawn by the many universities, seasonal agricultural jobs, and other opportunities. Immigrants from Central and South America, in particular, have established robust new communities in the Valley.

***A Mapp of Virginia Discouered to Ye Hills . . .*, 1651**
Virginia Farrer (cartographer), after a map by John Farrer
VMHC Collection, Gift of Henry C. Taylor

In the mid-1600s "Virginia"—labeled "Ould Virginia" to differentiate it from Maryland and "Noua Francia"—still encompassed nearly the entire continent of North America. Throughout the century, the extent of the continent remained unknown to explorers. Here (at the top), the Pacific Ocean appears just beyond the Appalachian Mountains, and a Northwest Passage (the waterway at the right) connects to "The Sea of China and the Indies."

Map showing route of the Great Wagon Road

Initially a trail used by Indigenous people for hunting, trade, and war, the "Great Wagon Road" became the most important frontier road in the 1700s. Many European immigrants who disembarked in Philadelphia and then headed west used the road to travel into the southern "backcountry" in search of land. The road continued along the Shenandoah Valley, through the Carolinas, and into Georgia.

Conestoga wagon, about 1830
John B. Kiger, Sperryville, Virginia (maker)
VMHC Collection

Beginning in the mid 1700s, many migrants traveling on the "Great Wagon Road" used Conestoga wagons like the one shown here. This sturdy vehicle was developed near Conestoga, Pennsylvania, and is thought to have been introduced by German settlers. The curved floor prevented contents from tipping and shifting as it traveled over rough roads. By the 1850s, railroads began to supplement Conestoga wagons.

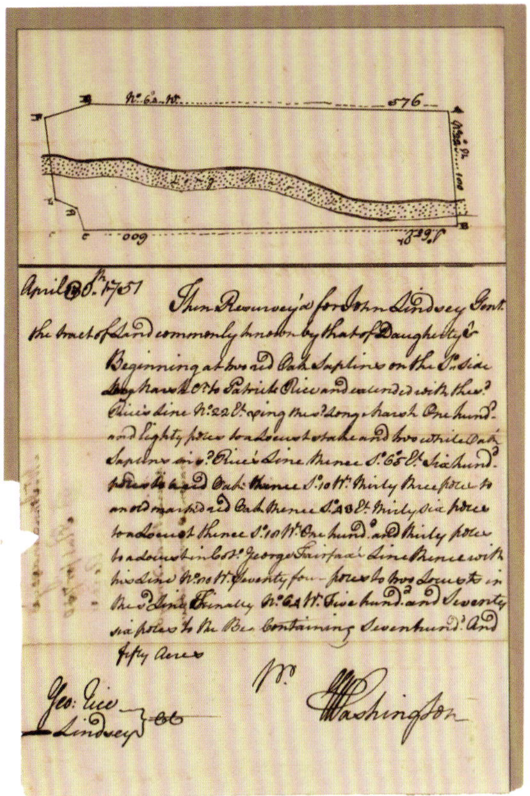

Survey of 750 acres in Frederick County owned by John Lindsey, 1751

George Washington (draftsman)

VMHC Collection, Gift of Alice Hanauer Strauss in memory of Admiral Lewis Lichtenstein Strauss

Before George Washington (1732–1799) served as a soldier or president, he was a land surveyor. Starting when he was seventeen years old, he conducted much of his work in the Valley. Former German and Scots-Irish servants from Pennsylvania and wealthy planters from eastern Virginia were encouraged to migrate to the Valley to secure the colony from Indian attacks and incursions by the French. Washington eventually owned land in the Valley and drew upon his understanding of maps to inform military strategy.

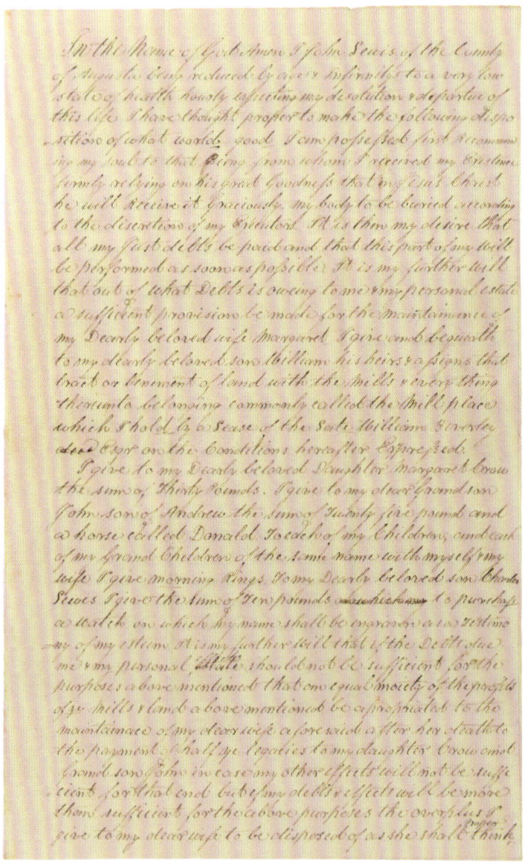

Inventory of the estate of Thomas Lewis (1718–1790), about 1790

VMHC Collection

The earliest waves of Scots-Irish settlers arrived in the Valley during the 1730s. Among these Presbyterians of Scottish descent from Northern Ireland were members of the Lewis family who helped found Augusta and Rockingham counties. Enslaved African Americans mentioned in this document were forced to work their extensive land holdings.

Taufschein (baptismal certificate) fraktur, 1814

Attributed to Henry Heltzel

VMHC Collection

German-speaking communities throughout the Valley created fraktur, a form of illuminated drawing with decorative calligraphy derived from German script. These documents commemorated births, baptisms, marriages, and deaths. This fraktur was created for the baptism of Jacob Lantz (1814–?) of Shenandoah County.

William F. Rupp, 1860

VMHC Collection

Artist William F. Rupp (1834–1908) immigrated to New Market, Virginia, from Germany in 1854. He completed frescoes and other decorative painting projects in private and public buildings throughout the Valley. His business letterhead noted how his skills included "frescoing, sign, and all kinds of plain and ornamental painting."

Paint brush and box of brushes used by William F. Rupp, late 1800s to early 1900s

Unknown manufacturers

VMHC Collection

Stencil created and used by William F. Rupp, late 1800s to early 1900s

VMHC Collection

Interpretation headset used by the Harrisonburg City Public Schools system, 2021

Courtesy of the Harrisonburg City Public Schools

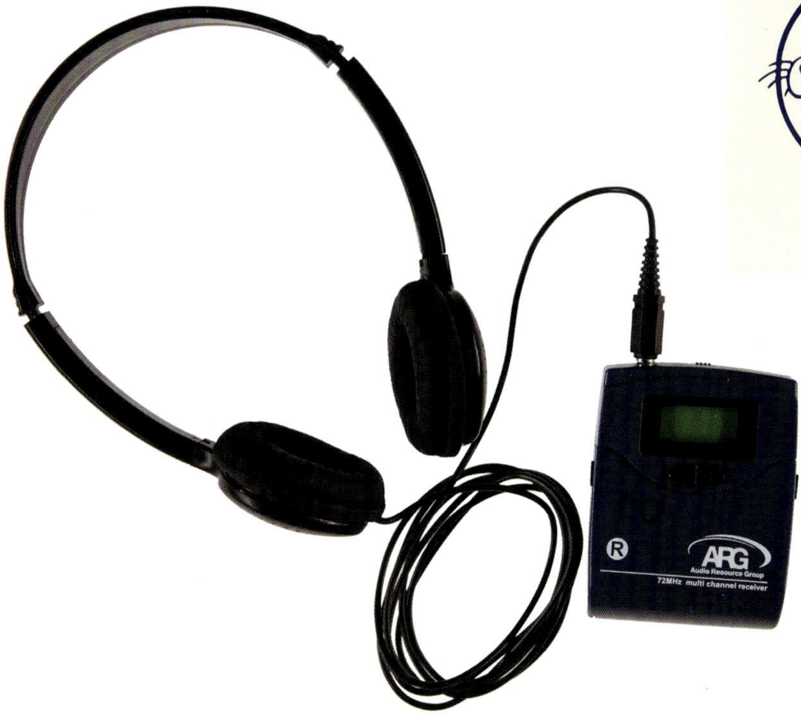

Keister Elementary School sign, about 2021

Courtesy of the Harrisonburg City Public Schools

Harrisonburg City Public Schools has one of the most diverse student bodies in the state. Students speak more than seventy languages, with Spanish being the most spoken, followed by English, Tigrinya, Kurdish, and Russian. Multilingual signs and translation equipment, like the ones shown here, assist the district's students.

Karina Kline-Gabel, 2018

Courtesy of The Breeze, James Madison University

In 2021, people of Hispanic or Latino heritage represented more than half of the 1 million residents of the Shenandoah Valley. Karina Kline-Gabel (center) grew up in a bicultural and bilingual Harrisonburg home with Colombian heritage. A faculty member at James Madison University, she has created several community programs benefiting the Valley's Latino population, including leadership programs, lecture series, and film festivals.

"I knew that we were starting to get a major population shift and I wanted to be here to support my community through it. . . . I try to really focus on how important it is to realize that there's a huge significance in having a Latino population, and we need to make sure we are supporting and educating one another."

Karina Kline-Gabel, educator, 2018

Shenandoah Autumn (Andy Guest State Park, Warren County), 2014
Chester Lewandowski (photographer)
Courtesy of Scenic Virginia

ALLURING NATURE

The Shenandoah Valley's natural beauty and bounty have enticed visitors and settlers for generations. Spectacular views have long captivated travelers, whether crossing on horseback hundreds of years ago, or perching atop Skyline Drive in an RV today. The 1800s witnessed the growth of hotels and resorts to support a burgeoning tourism industry. Rolling fog over the Valley and a spectacle of colors on tree-lined mountainsides inspire artists to capture the splendid views. Streams filled with fish and pick-your-own orchards also draw tourists for rejuvenating getaways.

Shenandoah National Park

Tourists visiting cottages at the Black Rock Springs Hotel, about 1900
National Park Service

For centuries, people have been drawn to the waters of the Valley's mineral springs. Augusta County's Black Rock Springs Hotel, built in 1885, offered access to the spring's "healing" waters and other pastimes to those seeking a weekend retreat. The resort's buildings no longer stand, and the land was incorporated into Shenandoah National Park in 1936.

"The time was spent in all kinds of amusements and at noon a delightful lunch was enjoyed by all on the ground in the shade of the trees. Afternoon and evening was spent in sight seeing, rolling ten pins, photo striking, and many other amusements. At 4:30 o'clock the gay crowd left for home after enjoyed a delightful day."
Staunton Daily Leader, 1908

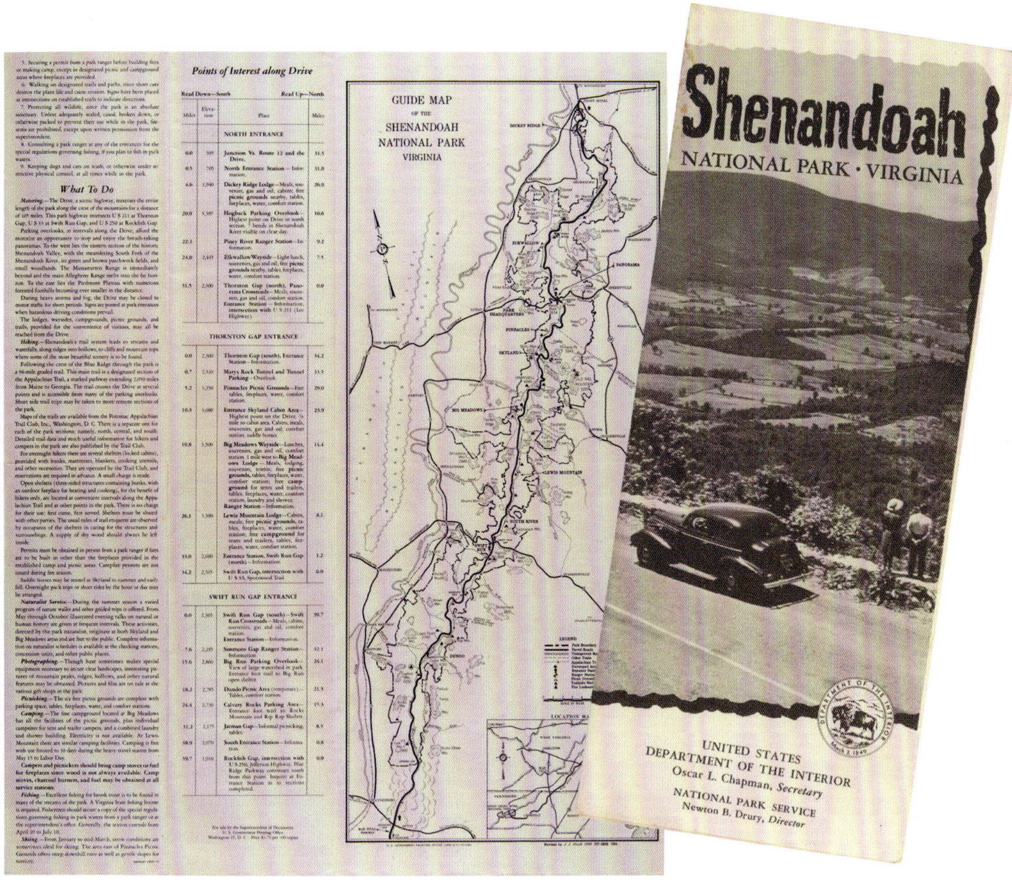

Shenandoah National Park brochure, 1949–53
National Park Service
VMHC Collection

Shenandoah National Park was created in 1926 to preserve an area of natural beauty and provide recreational opportunities for the people in the surrounding region. Virginia purchased 3,000 tracts of land to donate to the federal government. Despite their appeals, at least 500 families living there were displaced from their homes. The 160,000-acre park (now 200,000 acres) was dedicated in 1936. Today, Shenandoah National Park is one of the most popular parks in the country.

Civilian Conservation Corps workers in the soon-to-be-dedicated Shenandoah National Park, 1934
VMHC Collection, Gift of Linden Hughes

During the Great Depression, the Civilian Conservation Corps (CCC) established six camps in Shenandoah National Park. The CCC workers conducted surveys, constructed roads, and improved forest landscaping and wildlife conditions.

Natural Bridge

***Breath of the Ancestors,* 2019**
Victoria Ferguson (photographer)
Courtesy of Victoria Ferguson

Long before the arrival of Europeans, Natural Bridge was a sacred site to the Indigenous people of the region—particularly the Siouan-speaking Monacan Nation. Seeing the ethereal light through the mist, Victoria Ferguson, a member of the Monacan Nation, took this photograph and wondered "if the breath of those ancestors buried and disturbed above the Bridge was among the breath Mother Nature was showing me that day."

***Natural Bridge,* 1882**
Flavius Fisher (artist)
VMHC Collection, Purchased with funds provided by Lora M. Robins

The 215-foot-tall Natural Bridge is a limestone gorge carved out by Cedar Creek. It was made famous by Thomas Jefferson, who once owned it and described it as "the most sublime of Nature's works." Following the Civil War, new railroads made it accessible to tourists.

Natural Bridge pennant, second half 1900s
Unknown manufacturer
VMHC Collection, Gift of William Z. Schenck

Luray Caverns

***Virginia.—The Grandest of American Caverns—Scene in the ballroom in the newly-discovered cave at Luray, Page County,* 1878**
***Frank Leslie's Illustrated Newspaper* (publisher)**
Library of Congress, Prints and Photographs Division

Luray Caverns, a 64-acre underground cave system in Page County, has been a popular tourist attraction since the 1870s. The awe-inspiring stalactite formations in the "ballroom" also include the Great Stalacpipe Organ. Installed in 1954, an organ-like console controls the tapping of stalactites of varying sizes with rubber mallets to produce musical tones.

Cave formations at Luray Caverns, 2014
Jan Gorzynik / Alamy Stock Photo

One of the best-known features of Luray Caverns is a drapery called "Saracen's Tent" (center). These formations are created when water flows down overhanging portions of a cave wall. This is considered one of the best examples of this natural phenomenon in the world.

Driving through the Valley

Skyline Drive near the Shenandoah Valley Overlook, 2009

H. Mark Weidman Photography / Alamy Stock Photo

When the National Park Service expressed interest in a park in the Appalachian Mountains, a group of Virginia businessmen championed a "skyline" drive. The 105-mile road runs along the entire length of Shenandoah National Park, from Front Royal to Rockfish Gap. Completed in 1939, it provides spectacular views of the Shenandoah Valley to the west and the Piedmont to the east.

***Cocktail Hour, Star Gables Motor Court*, 2016–17**

Barry Vance (artist)

From the collection of the Museum of the Shenandoah Valley

Even today, travelers driving along Route 11 encounter some of the many "motor courts" that became popular after the automobile era began. Vance, whose ancestors settled in the region in the 1700s, has been composing paintings of idyllic Shenandoah Valley scenes since 1971. This motor court, once located north of Harrisonburg, no longer stands.

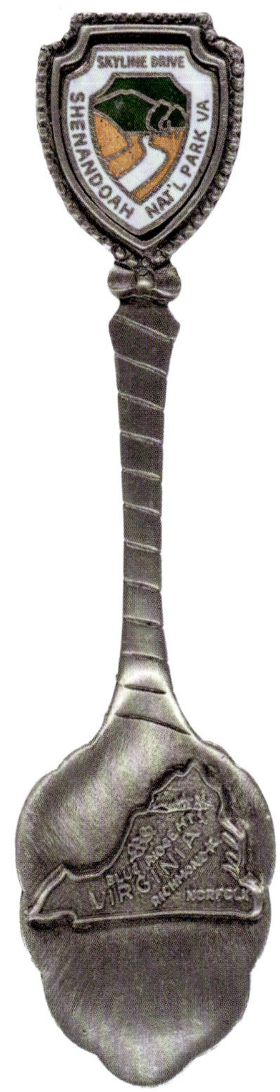

Skyline Drive souvenir spoon, second half 1900s

Unknown manufacturer

VMHC Collection, Gift of Raymond Schreiner

Fly Fishing

Harry Murray shows off a smallmouth bass caught on the South Fork of the Shenandoah River, 2019

Photo courtesy of Harry Murray

The Valley's rivers and streams offer many opportunities for anglers to catch trout and bass. Harry Murray (b. 1939) started fly fishing when he was ten years old and has designed over thirty types of flies, the lures for fly-fishing. As a master fishing guide, fly tyer, and author, he has passed on his knowledge about fishing in the region through numerous books, workshops, and guided trips organized by his shop in Edinburg (Shenandoah County).

Murray's Mr. Rapidan Streamer fly, 2021

Harry W. Murray (maker)

VMHC Collection, Gift of Harry W. Murray, Murray's Fly Shop (murraysflyshop.com)

Murray developed the Mr. Rapidan fly family in the early 1970s. Made from moose and calf hair, it floats, can easily be seen on the water's surface, and simulates the shape and color of the mayflies that hatch early in the season.

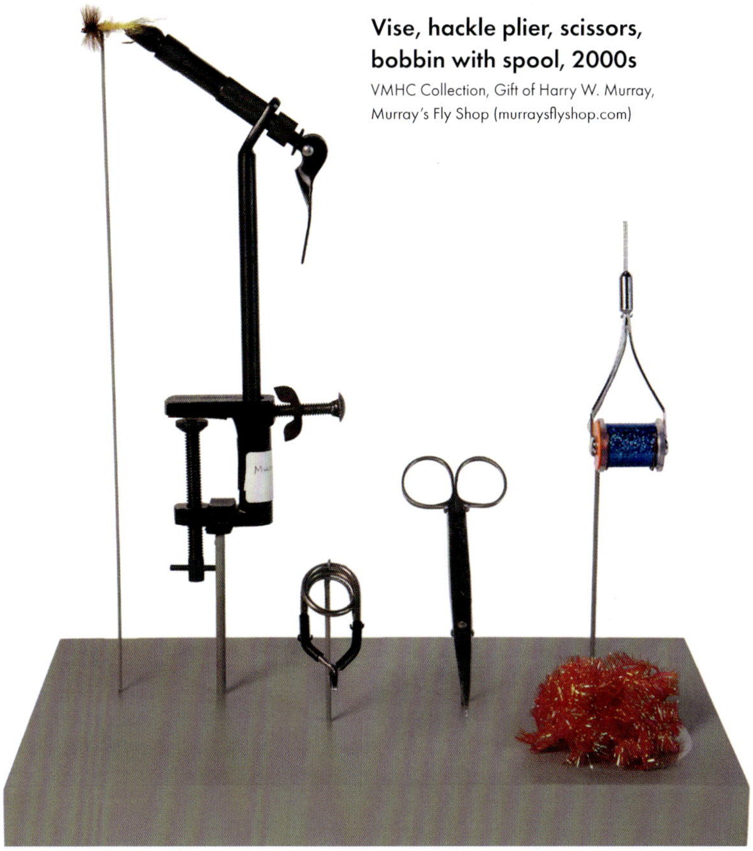

Vise, hackle plier, scissors, bobbin with spool, 2000s

VMHC Collection, Gift of Harry W. Murray, Murray's Fly Shop (murraysflyshop.com)

JOURNEYING THROUGH THE VALLEY

For over 10,000 years, people have traveled up and down the Valley by foot, horse, train, and car. For some, the region served as a pathway to new opportunities in Virginia and points further west. Many have come here seeking a respite in the natural beauty of the Shenandoah. Today, the region's mountain peaks and lowland valleys remain rich with opportunities for rejuvenation and personal growth.

"I gained a profound respect for the wilderness and nature. . . . I understand now, in a way I never did before, the colossal scale of the world. I found patience and fortitude that I didn't know I had."

Bill Bryson, *A Walk in the Woods*, 1998

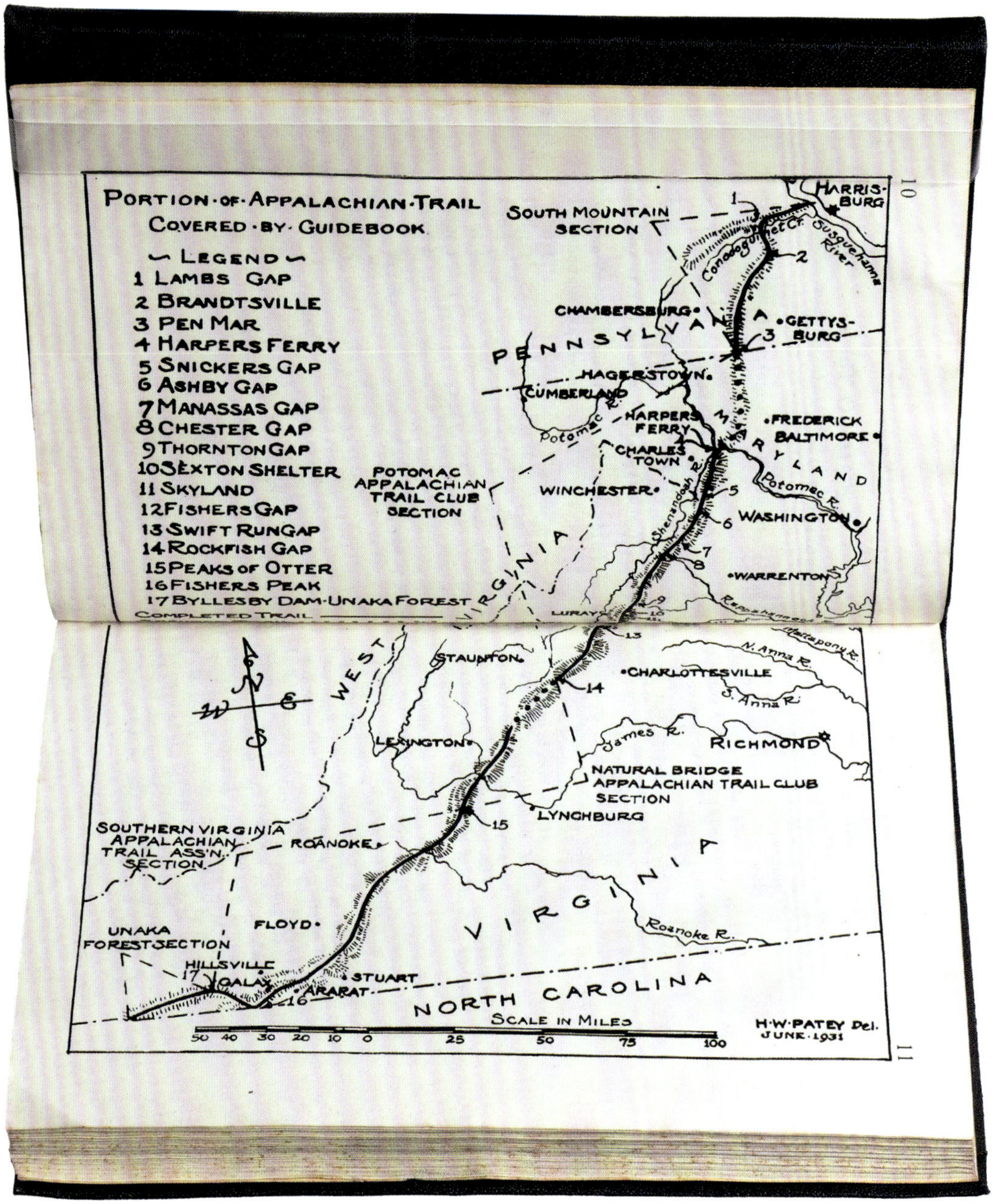

***Guide to Paths in the Blue Ridge*, 1931**

Potomac Appalachian Trail Club

VMHC Collection

Completed in 1939, the Appalachian Trail passes through Virginia and thirteen states from Georgia to Maine. Today's hikers enjoy the benefits of satellite mapping and clearly blazed trails, but early travelers relied on the hand-drawn maps and detailed written instructions outlined in guidebooks like this one.

"Turn left opposite entrance to cabin and pass through alder-grown section where brook overflows the Trail, then pass through gate. Road climbs hill, passing the Frank Weakley place on left at 16.02 m., and goes through gate at top of hill at 16.22 m."

From *Guide to Paths in the Blue Ridge*, 1931

Sean Gobin, 2015
Dan Addison (photographer)
University of Virginia Communications

"I got back from Afghanistan in 2012 and decided to hike the Appalachian Trail. It was a really therapeutic experience. About two-thirds of the way through, I had an epiphany and realized a hiking program could be designed as therapy for returning veterans. I started Warrior Expeditions in 2013 to offer long-distance outdoor expeditions and help other warriors walk off the war like I did."

Sean Gobin, Warrior Expeditions founder and U.S. Marine Corps veteran, 2022

Backpack, boots, and trekking poles used by Sean Gobin during his 2,181-mile through-hike of the Appalachian Trail, 2012
VMHC Collection, Gift of Sean Gobin

The Virginia Military Institute Color Guard leads the Corps of Cadets in the New Market Day parade, 2019

Virginia Military Institute Archives

Founded in 1839, the Virginia Military Institute (VMI) in Lexington was the nation's first state military college. In 1864, the 257 members of the Cadet Corps marched 84 miles along the Valley Turnpike (Route 11) to join Confederate forces at the Civil War Battle of New Market. Ten cadets were killed or mortally wounded—including Cadet Jaqueline Beverly Stanard (1845–1864).

"[W]e fixed up and left on Wednesday Morning at half past 8, marched 18 miles by half past 2, when we camped. The roads were very good but were quite dusty and it was very warm. This morning we left camp under quite different circumstances, it having rained during the night and has continued to do so all day. The roads were awful perfect loblolly [swamp] all the way and we had to wade through like hogs."

VMI Cadet Jaqueline B. Stanard, May 12, 1864

Virginia Military Institute cartridge box, 1861–5

VMHC Collection, Maryland Steuart Collection, Gift of Richard D. Steuart

Cartridge boxes like this one would have held thirty rounds of ammunition and been worn on a sling by VMI cadets while on parade and during their engagement at the Battle of New Market.

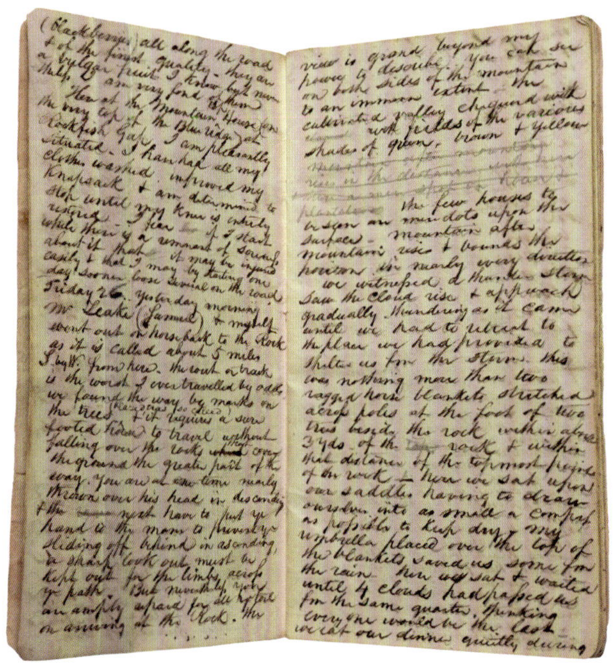

Pocket diary of Isaac Gorham Peck, 1833

VMHC Collection, Gift of Lemuel Houston

"Yesterday morning [I] went out on horseback to the Rock, as it is called. . . . The view is grand beyond my power to describe. You can see on both sides of the mountain to an immense extent the cultivated valley chequered with fields of the various shades of green, brown and yellow. The few houses to be seen are mere dots upon the surface. Mountain after mountain rises and bounds the horizon in nearly every direction."

Isaac Gorham Peck, describing a vista near Waynesboro on his journey from Fredericksburg through the Shenandoah Valley, 1833

Chesapeake & Ohio Railway publicity photograph for *The Chessie* passenger train, 1948

From the collection of the C&O Historical Society, cohs.org

Chesapeake & Ohio Railway passenger schedule, 1955

VMHC Collection, Gift of the Heirs of A.C. Gordon

The history of the Chesapeake & Ohio Railway can be traced in part to a Louisa County railroad built in the 1830s. Renamed Virginia Central, it expanded both east and west in the 1850s, connecting Richmond to the Shenandoah Valley counties of Augusta, Bath, and Alleghany. Once it reached the Ohio River, it became known as the Chesapeake & Ohio Railway. It continued to grow before merging with other lines to form the CSX Corporation in 1980.

Norvel Lee (center) preparing to receive the Olympic gold medal in light-heavyweight boxing, 1952

The Sports Museum of Finland

A Botetourt County native, Lee (1924–1992) served with the Tuskegee Airmen during World War II. After the war he attended Howard University and became a championship boxer, winning a gold medal and the Val Barker Trophy at the 1952 Olympic Games. In 1948, Lee refused to leave the whites-only section of a train car and was arrested in Covington. His sentence was overturned by the Virginia Supreme Court of Appeals the following year. Lee dedicated the rest of his life to serving as an educator in Maryland and Washington, D.C.

Service plate from *The George Washington* passenger train dinner service, 1932
Syracuse China (manufacturer)
From the collection of the C&O Historical Society, cohs.org

C&O's premier passenger train *The George Washington* went into service in 1932, the bicentennial of Washington's birth. Its dining cars used a custom dinner service designed with Washington's image.

Chessie System sign, 1970s
VMHC Collection, Gift of Joseph Robertson

After the Chesapeake & Ohio Railroad merged with two other mid-Atlantic railways in the early 1970s, the combined companies took on the name "Chessie System" and included a silhouette of the iconic kitten in the "C."

Chesapeake & Ohio Lines "Sleep like a Kitten" advertisement, about 1933
From the collection of the C&O Historical Society, cohs.org

Chessie the kitten is one of the most enduring company symbols in the United States. Chessie's first "Sleep like a Kitten" ad appeared in the September 1933 issue of *Fortune* magazine to promote Chesapeake & Ohio's new air-conditioned sleeper coaches. Chessie's family grew over time to include her mate Peake and kittens Nip and Tuck.

"A year ago we found you, a lonely little kitten looking for a home. You found one, and we found a friend. When we published your picture, a lot of folks said: 'Who ever heard of using a gol darned cat to advertise a railroad!' . . . Overnight, you became The Kitten of the Hour."

Acknowledgments to Chessie the sleeping kitten by the Chesapeake & Ohio Lines Company, about 1935

ENJOYING FESTIVALS

People throughout the Valley take time each year to celebrate the things that make their communities unique. Annual festivals—some of which date back to the 1800s—pay tribute to the key agricultural products, the beauty of the landscape, local folklore, and the changing of the seasons.

Queen City Mischief and Magic Festival, 2020

Kate Simon / Lifestyle Photography

The 19th-century architecture of downtown Staunton reminded local coffee shop owner Sarah Lynch of the fictional town of Hogsmeade described in J.K. Rowling's Harry Potter series. Since 2016, the Queen City Mischief and Magic Festival that Lynch founded transforms downtown Staunton into an enchanted village in celebration of everything Potter.

Matthew Henerson performing in *Hamlet* at the Blackfriars Playhouse, 2023

October Grace Media (photographer)

American Shakespeare Center in Staunton, Virginia

The world's first modern re-creation of William Shakespeare's indoor London theater can be found in Staunton. Built in 2001, it is home to the American Shakespeare Center and in addition to an annual conference, they offer weekly performances of Shakespeare's works, those of his contemporaries, and creative modern interpretations.

Houston Kibler, of Edinburg, shows his steer at the Shenandoah County Fair, 2019

Rich Cooley / *The Northern Virginia Daily*

Shenandoah County Agricultural Society fair pass, 1887

From the collection of the Shenandoah County Library – Truban Archive

Organized in 1886, the Shenandoah County Agricultural Society sponsored a local fair until they disbanded in 1915. The following year, a group of 338 investors organized the Shenandoah County Fair Association. Since 1917, they have held fairs nearly every year—except during World War II—to highlight the region's agricultural products, local businesses, and crafts.

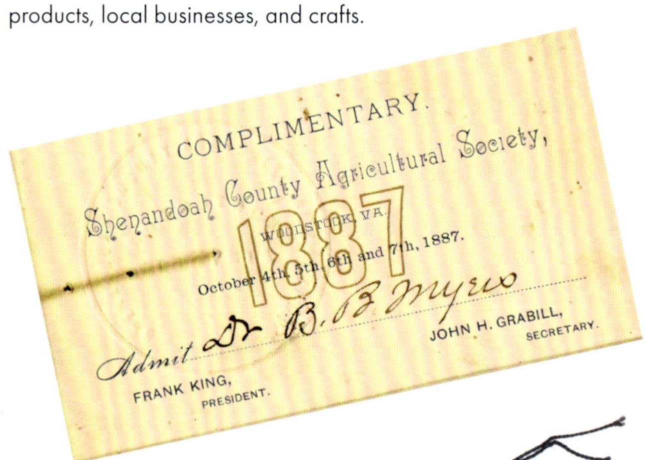

Rockingham County Fair poster, 2003

From the collection of Rocktown History | HRHS

Established as an annual event in 1949, the Rockingham County Fair is considered one of the world's leading agricultural fairs. Today, the fairgrounds include exhibit halls, barns, a farm museum, and buildings for horticulture, crop, and flower displays.

Rockingham County Fair ribbon, 1923

VMHC Collection

Although the annual Rockingham County Fair was established in the 1940s, smaller fairs have been held periodically in the county as far back as 1891.

Highland County Fair poster, 2021

VMHC Collection, Gift of Highland County Chamber of Commerce

Rockingham Turkey Festival ribbon, 1939

From the Collection of Rocktown History | HRHS

The inaugural Rockingham Turkey Festival was intended to promote the county's multi-million-dollar poultry industry. Events included a turkey exhibit hall, turkey stunts, a turkey throw, a turkey race, and many opportunities to eat turkey. In 2017, Rockingham's 112 farms made it the Commonwealth's largest producer of turkeys.

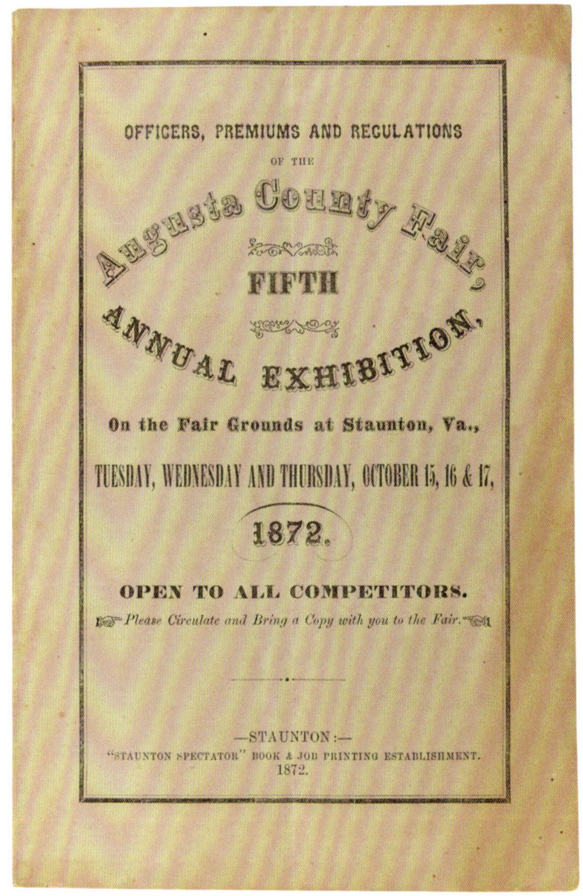

OFFICERS, PREMIUMS AND REGULATIONS

OF THE

Augusta County Fair,

FIFTH

ANNUAL EXHIBITION,

On the Fair Grounds at Staunton, Va.,

TUESDAY, WEDNESDAY AND THURSDAY, OCTOBER 15, 16 & 17,

1872.

OPEN TO ALL COMPETITORS.

Please Circulate and Bring a Copy with you to the Fair.

—STAUNTON:—

"STAUNTON SPECTATOR" BOOK & JOB PRINTING ESTABLISHMENT.

1872.

Augusta County Fair premium list, 1872

VMHC Collection, Gift/purchase of Dr. Thornton Tayloe Perry and Eleanor C. Read

"The [Augusta County Fair's] first exhibition was, in every respect, a most triumphant success . . . the most entertaining Fair which has ever been held in this State. . . . [T]he thousands assembled . . . gratified their curiosity in examining the horses, cattle, sheep, swine, poultry, farming Implements, Agricultural machinery, House-hold Implements, Domestic manufactures, Fruits and fruit trees, Flowers, Vegetables, Wines, Liquors, Butter, Grain, Waddell's patent Churn, Cave specimens, Minerals, Embroidery, Oil Paintings, and the thousand and one specimens of Art and Nature on exhibition."

Staunton Spectator, 1868

Shenandoah Apple Blossom Festival pin, after 1927

VMHC Collection, Gift of Mrs. Joseph P. Crenshaw

Highland County Maple Festival button, 1983

VMHC Collection, Gift of Highland County Chamber of Commerce

GROWING CROPS

The unique geography of the Shenandoah Valley has created soil that is particularly fertile for agriculture. Crops thrive in this bountiful land. Over a thousand years ago, Siouan-speaking people grew the "Three Sisters"—corn, beans, and squash. In the mid-1700s, European settlers pushed into "the frontier" and set up farmsteads and orchards. They built mills to process grains and raised livestock. The Civil War devastated the most productive wheat-growing region in the South, but it recovered after the war. Across the Valley today, farmers focus on grain, apples, and raising livestock and poultry.

Union troops burning out the Shenandoah Valley, 1864
Theodore R. Davis (artist)
VMHC Collection, Gift of Robert M. Hicklin, Jr., Inc.

Known as the "breadbasket of the Confederacy," the Shenandoah Valley became a prime target for the U.S. Army in 1864. In what became known as "The Burning," soldiers targeted and destroyed supplies that could support the Confederate armies in an attempt to weaken the will of Southern people and hasten the end to the war.

"[T]he whole country from the Blue Ridge to the North Mountain has been made untenable for a rebel army. I have destroyed over two thousand barns filled with wheat, hay, and farming implements, and over seventy mills filled with flour and wheat, have driven in front of this army over four thousand head of stock, and have killed and issued to the troops over three thousand sheep. . . . When this is completed the valley, from Winchester up to Staunton, 92 miles, will have but little in it for man or beast."
United States general Philip H. Sheridan, October 1864

The restored Burwell-Morgan Mill, 2019

Carol M. Highsmith (photographer)

Library of Congress, Prints and Photographs Division

Among the largest in the region, the Burwell-Morgan Mill in Clarke County operated—all day every day—from 1785 to 1943. At its peak, mill workers processed more than 60,000 bushels of wheat per year. Today, the grist mill is operational again and open to the public as a historic site run by the Clarke County Historical Association.

Winchester Milling Corporation "Crystal" Enriched Self-Rising Flour bag, 1900s

VMHC Collection

Burwell-Morgan Mill grain bag, early 2000s

VMHC Collection

Hernesto Sanchez, a migrant worker, harvests apples for Fruit Hill Orchard, Winchester, 2020

Jeff Taylor / *The Winchester Star*

The apple orchards around Winchester are harvested by domestic as well as Latino and Jamaican migrant workers. From September through October, the Frederick County Fruit Growers Association operates a camp to house these workers and transports them to orchards in the area.

Sky Line Drive Apple Juice can, mid-1900s

VMHC Collection

The buildings of Sperryville's (Rappahannock County) River District were once part of a fruit-growers cooperative. The juicing plant, where Sky Line Drive Apple Juice was produced, is now home to a distillery.

Newtown Pippin (*Malus domestica*), 1910

Ellen Isham Schutt (artist)

U.S. Department of Agriculture Pomological Watercolor Collection. Rare and Special Collections, National Agricultural Library

The Albemarle or Newtown Pippin was one of Thomas Jefferson's two favorite dessert apples. In 1838, Sallie Coles Stevenson (1789–1848), wife of the American minister to the Court of St. James in England, received a shipment of Albemarle Pippin apples from her family farm in Virginia. The apples kept well on long voyages, had a distinctive flavor, and were a treasured "American" dessert. Easier-to-grow varieties replaced this apple and today it is difficult to find.

Julian W. Glass apple crate stencil, 1880–1930

From the collection of the Museum of the Shenandoah Valley

"[N]ever did a barrel of apples obtain so much reputation for the fruits of our country. They were eaten & praised by Royal lips, and swallowed by many aristocratic throats. Mr. Stevenson proposed sending two dozen to the Queen, accordingly they were put into a beautiful basket. . . . Lord Durham . . . told me my apples had created a great sensation at the Palace."

Sallie Coles Stevenson, in a letter to her family, 1838

Judith McCann-Slaughter feeding some of the cattle on her 150-acre farm, 2017
Scott Mason / *The Winchester Star*

McCann-Slaughter is the fifth generation of her family to farm the land in Stephenson (Frederick County) that has been in her family since the late 1800s.

"Honestly, I think that having grown up on a farm, I have such an appreciation of how hard my ancestors worked. And you are out in nature every day. I've really felt blessed to be able to walk in the same steps and do the same things that my ancestors have done."
Judith McCann-Slaughter, 2017

Tim Rothwell of Mountain Haven Farm, Fulks Run (Rockingham County), 2017
Katie Schmid (photographer)
Courtesy of Farmer Focus

Tim and Sasha Rothwell, from Fulks Run, partner with other like-minded family-owned farms across the region. Together they focus on sustainable, organic, humanely raised poultry.

Southwest VIRGINIA

Framed by the Blue Ridge Mountains to the east and the Appalachian Plateau to the west, the isolated nature of this mountainous region challenges the independent and resourceful people who settle here.

The region was a crossroads of Indigenous cultures. Mississippian people moved into and through the area along the Tennessee River, Ohio Valley groups by the New River, and Piedmont cultures up the Roanoke River. Although Europeans began settling along the eastern seaboard in the early 1600s, white settlers did not reach Southwest Virginia until the 1740s. Some of the English, German, and Scots-Irish settlers continued southwest from the Shenandoah Valley and carved small farms out of the region's valleys. Others continued into Kentucky and Tennessee.

The arrival of railroads in the late 1800s transformed Southwest Virginia and connected its people and vast resources in coal and timber to the rest of the world. Miners and lumberjacks fueled the nation's growth for more than a century.

Today, the region attracts nature lovers with its spectacular scenery, and new industries based on rich natural resources, biological diversity, and the celebration of its people and places have grown to replace coal and timber.

***Dusk at Breaks Interstate Park*, 2020**
Don Sniegowski (photographer)
Courtesy of Don Sniegowski

The Roanoke Star, 2020
Aaron Spicer (photographer)
Aaron Spicer Photography

Perched atop Mill Mountain, the Roanoke Star is a Virginia icon. Originally constructed as a Christmas decoration, it is visible for 60 miles from the air and sits 1,045 feet above the city of Roanoke.

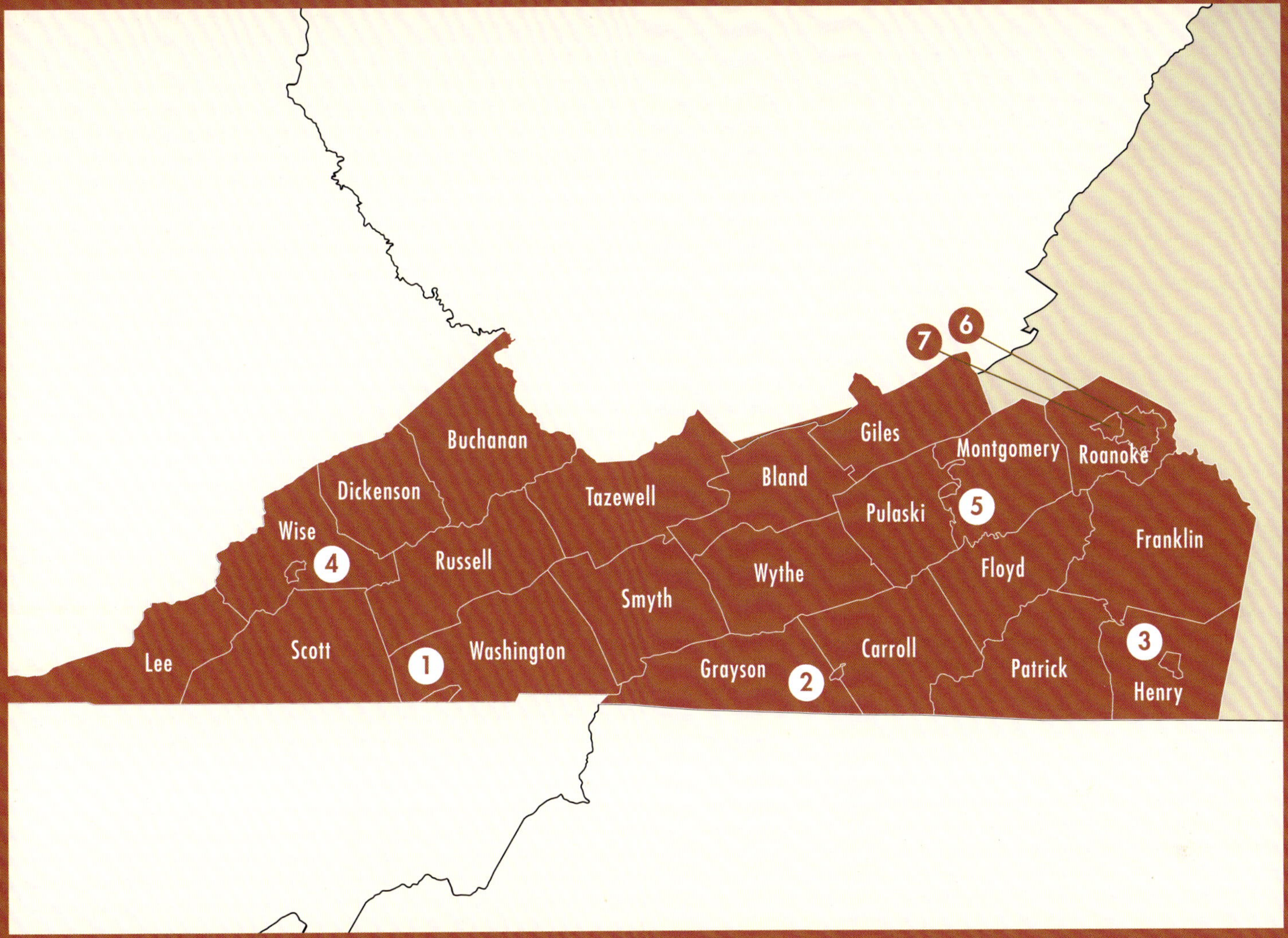

Southwest Virginia Independent Cities

1. Bristol
2. Galax
3. Martinsville
4. Norton
5. Radford
6. Roanoke
7. Salem

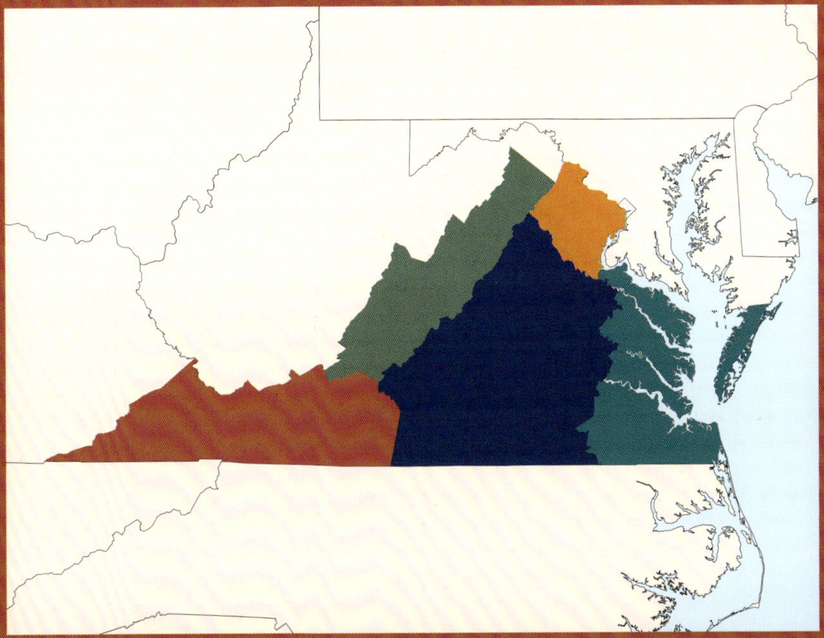

GATHERING TOGETHER

In small, isolated towns throughout Southwest Virginia, country stores, farmers' markets, dance halls, and makeshift stages provide lively venues for camaraderie and sharing folkways.

People are drawn from near and far by the folk melodies and dancing feet that vibrate throughout the region. Communities come together and show younger generations the ways of their Appalachian ancestors.

The Floyd Country Store "Friday Night Jamboree," 2010
Woody Crenshaw (photographer)
Courtesy Dylan Locke / The Floyd Country Store

In 1910, a farmers' supply store opened in Floyd (Floyd County). As it changed hands over time, this general store remained a place for locals to exchange stories and listen to music. Today, The Floyd Country Store is an internationally well-known venue for traditional folk musicians and dancers.

"Our Friday Night Jamboree is a celebration, our community's time to come together after a long week in communion. By dancing and playing music together, we are connecting in a deeper way to each other. Through these types of gatherings we are able to see our shared humanity and it is powerful and necessary medicine for this time in history."

Dylan Locke and Heather Krantz, owners of The Floyd Country Store, 2021

Pair of leather dancing shoes known as "taps," 1900s
From the collection of The Floyd Country Store

Clogging (from the Gaelic for "time") is a percussive folk dance born from interactions between people from the British Isles and Germany as they settled the Appalachians in the 1700s. Another popular dance style in the region is flatfooting. Although clogging is more rehearsed, flatfoot dance steps are specific to a family or community. Some dancers wear metal taps on the heels and toes of their shoes to create a signature jingling sound.

"I was born [during the Great Depression], and my family had just come up from Alabama into Virginia to work on the coal mines and railroad. . . . I learned to be much of who I am now by going to the [Baptist Church], which was on my street in Appalachia, Virginia. The church was at the end of the street and a row of homes for Black people was up the street from that. And I learned a lot about how to work with people and deal with people in that [church]. . . . How to get up in front of a group of people and speak and sing and work with children younger than I."

Jessie Reasor Zander, recalling her childhood in Appalachia, 2017

Mount Hermon Presbyterian Church, 1940s

Southwest Virginia Museum Historical State Park

Established in the late 1800s, Mount Hermon in Big Stone Gap (Wise County) and other historic Black churches became centers for spiritual and social gatherings. During Jim Crow segregation, they also served as schools for the Black community.

"Barter Theater," 2009

John Henley (photographer)

Courtesy of Barter Theatre

In 1933, Robert Porterfield (1905–1971) opened the Barter Theatre in Abingdon (Washington County). Throughout the Great Depression, theatergoers could pay for their tickets with produce from their farms and gardens—literally "trading Ham for Hamlet." Today, it is the State Theatre of Virginia and continues to host "Barter Days" when patrons can barter for tickets with canned goods for the local food bank.

MAKING MUSIC

People who worked side by side in Southwest Virginia's mines, forests, and factories often spoke different native tongues. Music broke language barriers. Traditional melodies, treasured homeland instruments, and folk-dance steps took on a new life in this remote region of Virginia. In small towns nestled between the mountains, diverse cultures harmonized to create a uniquely American musical style. They shared their folklore, faith, and the struggles of daily life to the sounds of fiddles, banjos, harmonicas, and dulcimers. Heard around the world, Appalachian music is among Southwest Virginia's most important exports.

Fiddlers from Hillsville playing at Jackson Ferry (Wythe County), undated

Bettman / Getty Images

Audrey Hash Ham (left), Albert Hash, and Emily Spencer, 1970s

Courtesy of Martha Spencer

Albert Hash (1917–1983), from Grayson County, was a renowned fiddle and dulcimer maker and player. He started the popular Whitetop Mountain Band to share his music with others. Hash also passed his passion and skills along to others, including his daughter Audrey Hash Ham (1949–2013) and sister-in-law Emily Spencer.

Fiddle, 1980

Audrey Hash Ham (maker)

From the collection of the Blue Ridge Institute & Museum

"I got the fiddle done, and I was so nervous when it was done. I knew it wouldn't play. I just knew it wouldn't. I handed it to Daddy, and it played. I gave the fiddle to Daddy for his birthday, and he said, 'I'd rather have that than a brand-new Cadillac.'"

Audrey Hash Ham, instrument maker, remembering the first fiddle she made after learning the craft from her father, 2013

The Carter Family: Maybelle Carter (left), Sara Carter, and A.P. Carter, about 1929

RCA Victor Records

Albert and Shirley Small Special Collections Library, University of Virginia

A.P. Carter (1891–1960), his wife Sara (1898–1979), and her cousin Maybelle Carter (1909–1978), from Maces Spring (Scott County), performed as the Carter Family. They started recording at the now-famous Bristol Sessions in 1927 and played together until 1943. The Carters were the first family of American folk music and the first country music stars. Consistently at the forefront of the American music industry during its first two decades, their music profoundly influenced bluegrass, country, Gospel, pop, and rock music.

"He's dressed in overalls and the women are country women from way back there. They looked like hillbillies. But as soon as I heard Sara's voice, that was it. I knew it was going to be wonderful."

Ralph Peer, recording engineer during the Bristol Sessions, on his first meeting with the Carter Family, 1959

Gibson L-5 guitar played by Maybelle Carter, 1928

Gibson (manufacturer)

From the collection of the Country Music Hall of Fame® and Museum

Carter used a humble Stella flat-top guitar during the legendary Bristol Sessions. When the Carter Family went to New Jersey to make new recordings in 1928, Maybelle and her husband Eck bought this guitar, the best they could find. She played it throughout the remainder of her career.

Kyle Creed, 1978
Terry Eiler (photographer)
Library of Congress, Prints and Photographs Division

Kyle Creed (1912–1982) crafted his first banjo when he was 16 years old. A skilled carpenter, he understood the qualities of wood and other materials that improved the sound of the old-time banjo. Famous for playing clawhammer style, he won multiple Old Fiddler's Convention banjo competitions in his hometown of Galax.

Earl White, 1970s
Jodi White (photographer)
Courtesy of Earl White

From instruments like the banjo to musical and vocal techniques, African and African American traditions are engrained in country music. Earl White (b. 1955) of Floyd County, shown here clogging in the 1970s, started the Green Grass Cloggers and the Earl White Stringband to carry on African Americans' contributions to traditional country music.

"[O]ld-time music is not a Black music, it's not a white music, it was always pretty much played together."
Earl White, fiddler and clogger, 2022

Banjo, 1974
Kyle Creed (maker)
From the collection of the Blue Ridge Institute & Museum

Mountain dulcimer from Patrick County, probably 1800s
VMHC Collection, Purchased through the Paul Mellon Acquisitions Fund

The origins of the mountain dulcimer can be found in the European lap instruments brought by German and Scandinavian immigrants to the region in the early 1800s. Virginia instrument makers typically designed a teardrop-shaped body with four or more strings—this example has five. Players created a sweet drone-like sound by moving a wooden dowel up and down the fretboard while strumming the strings with the right hand.

IMPACTING HISTORY

The people of Southwest Virginia have been at the nexus of our nation's history. Indigenous peoples trod the first Wilderness Road. European settlers followed to cross the Cumberland Gap and move into the American West. Local frontiersmen helped win the American Revolution. Pioneers farmed critical crops for the new country. Armies battled over vital regional saltworks during the Civil War. Appalachian musicians created legendary sounds. Coal miners helped fuel America's Industrial Revolution and led the fight for safer working conditions. These determined, motivated Southwest Virginians shifted the course of history and firmly placed their region at the heart of the nation's story.

***View of Christiansburg, Virginia,* 1855**

Edward Beyer (artist)

VMHC Collection, Gift of Lawrence Lewis, Jr.

In the mid-1850s, German artist Edward Beyer (1820–1865) traveled across Southwest Virginia. He found not only beautiful scenery to paint, but also growing market towns like Christiansburg that, with improved roads, served as centers of commerce, culture, and government. Many of the buildings featured in this painting are still part of the historic landscape.

Paint Lick Mountain pictograph, undated

Unknown Indigenous artist

Courtesy of the Library of Virginia and the Tazewell County Public Library and Historical Society

A group of twenty pictographs, including geometric shapes and figures suggesting humans and animals, can be found on a rock cliff in Tazewell County. Made using the soft mudstone in the area, the images may reflect spiritual or known aspects associated with the lives of the earliest people in Southwest Virginia.

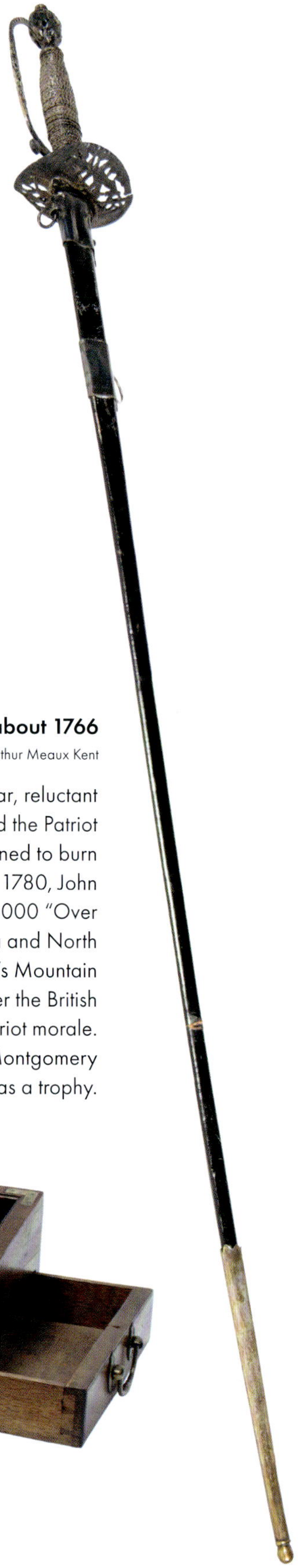

Scottish officer's small sword, about 1766

VMHC Collection, Gift of Arthur Meaux Kent

During the Revolutionary War, reluctant Southwest Virginians embraced the Patriot cause after the British threatened to burn their homes and communities. In 1780, John Kent (1761–about 1815) joined 1,000 "Over Mountain Men" from Virginia and North Carolina during the battle of King's Mountain (South Carolina). Their victory over the British provided a necessary boost to Patriot morale. Kent brought this sword home to Montgomery County as a trophy.

Field desk, about 1825

John Cording & Co. (manufacturer)

From the collection of the William King Museum of Art, Gift of Wallace and Liza Gusler

The Campbell family were among Southwest Virginia's earliest European settlers. John Campbell (about 1789–about 1866) grew up in Washington County and probably owned this field desk. He was the first U.S. treasurer to have been born a citizen of the United States, serving in the office from 1829 to 1839.

Ron and Jill Carson in the Appalachian African-American Cultural Center, 2019

Kevin Ridder / Appalachian Voices

In 1939, Rachel Scott of Pennington Gap sold 2.6 acres of land to Lee County to serve as the site of a primary school for Black children. It was the only school serving that community until 1965. Ron Carson—Scott's great-great-grandson—and his wife Jill restored the building to serve as the Appalachian African-American Cultural Center to collect and preserve the history of Black people in the region.

"Everything we do, we do [with the idea of documenting and preserving history] as a foundation. We started out with one specific goal, but it has branched out because we think it's important for everybody to know who they are and to have a strong foundation."

Jill Carson, 2019

***The Big Lick GayZette*, 1971**

Gay Alliance of the Roanoke Valley

Southwest Virginia LGBTQ+ History Project

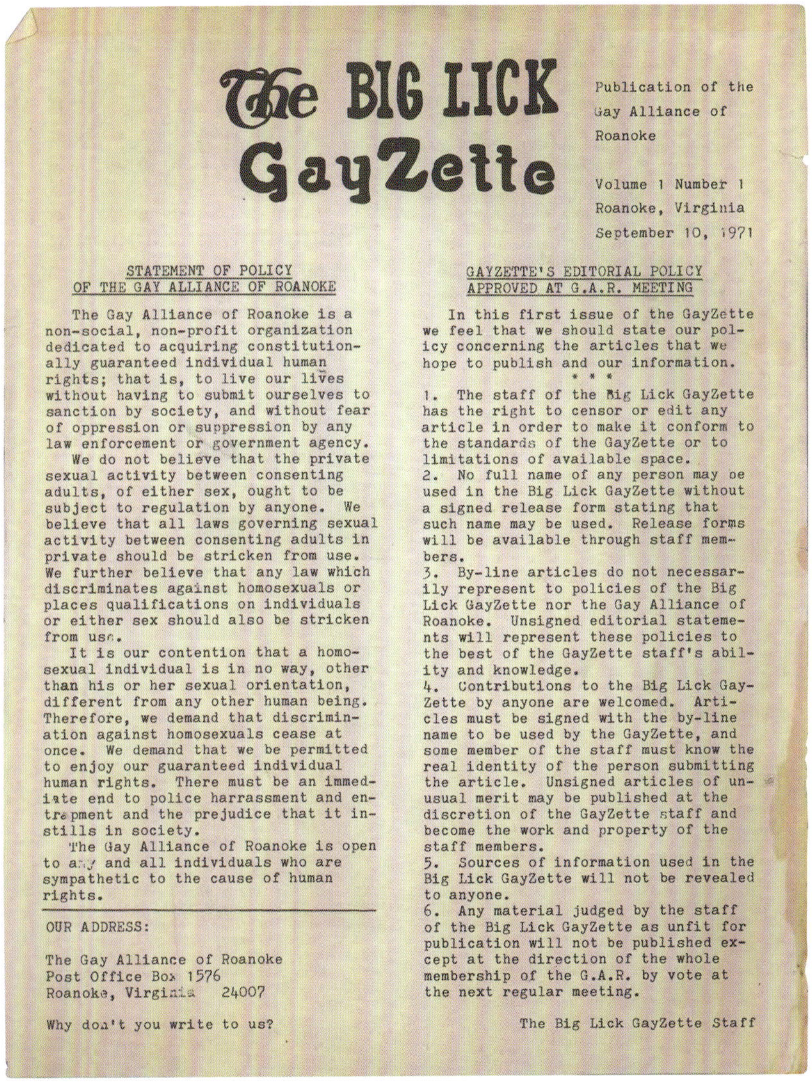

The BIG LICK GayZette

Publication of the Gay Alliance of Roanoke

Volume 1 Number 1
Roanoke, Virginia
September 10, 1971

STATEMENT OF POLICY
OF THE GAY ALLIANCE OF ROANOKE

The Gay Alliance of Roanoke is a non-social, non-profit organization dedicated to acquiring constitutionally guaranteed individual human rights; that is, to live our lives without having to submit ourselves to sanction by society, and without fear of oppression or suppression by any law enforcement or government agency.

We do not believe that the private sexual activity between consenting adults, of either sex, ought to be subject to regulation by anyone. We believe that all laws governing sexual activity between consenting adults in private should be stricken from use. We further believe that any law which discriminates against homosexuals or places qualifications on individuals or either sex should also be stricken from use.

It is our contention that a homosexual individual is in no way, other than his or her sexual orientation, different from any other human being. Therefore, we demand that discrimination against homosexuals cease at once. We demand that we be permitted to enjoy our guaranteed individual human rights. There must be an immediate end to police harrassment and entrapment and the prejudice that it instills in society.

The Gay Alliance of Roanoke is open to any and all individuals who are sympathetic to the cause of human rights.

OUR ADDRESS:

The Gay Alliance of Roanoke
Post Office Box 1576
Roanoke, Virginia 24007

Why don't you write to us?

GAYZETTE'S EDITORIAL POLICY
APPROVED AT G.A.R. MEETING

In this first issue of the GayZette we feel that we should state our policy concerning the articles that we hope to publish and our information.

* * *

1. The staff of the Big Lick GayZette has the right to censor or edit any article in order to make it conform to the standards of the GayZette or to limitations of available space.
2. No full name of any person may be used in the Big Lick GayZette without a signed release form stating that such name may be used. Release forms will be available through staff members.
3. By-line articles do not necessarily represent to policies of the Big Lick GayZette nor the Gay Alliance of Roanoke. Unsigned editorial statements will represent these policies to the best of the GayZette staff's ability and knowledge.
4. Contributions to the Big Lick GayZette by anyone are welcomed. Articles must be signed with the by-line name to be used by the GayZette, and some member of the staff must know the real identity of the person submitting the article. Unsigned articles of unusual merit may be published at the discretion of the GayZette staff and become the work and property of the staff members.
5. Sources of information used in the Big Lick GayZette will not be revealed to anyone.
6. Any material judged by the staff of the Big Lick GayZette as unfit for publication will not be published except at the direction of the whole membership of the G.A.R. by vote at the next regular meeting.

The Big Lick GayZette Staff

The Gay Alliance of the Roanoke Valley organized in Roanoke (formerly Big Lick) in the wake of New York City's 1969 Stonewall Riots. It was the region's first community-based gay liberation organization. Their publication, and others like it, provided news, organized protests, and shared opportunities in an era of rampant anti-gay discrimination. Today, the Southwest Virginia LGBTQ+ History Project, based at Roanoke College, is researching, collecting, and sharing stories from the region's LGBTQ+ community.

"I think the greatest success of the project is mobilizing queer people to be actors in their own history, to feel a sense of authorship over the story of our city, of our region, of our community."

Dr. G. Samantha Rosenthal (b. 1983), History Department at Roanoke College and a founder of the LGBTQ+ History Project, 2021

WORKING ON THE RAILROADS

In the mid-1800s, railroads began connecting towns and cities across the United States, but Southwest Virginia's rugged mountains and forests made the region inaccessible to the early lines. After a few failed attempts, trains finally reached Big Stone Gap in 1890. More dependable routes soon developed to keep up with the high demand for Southwest's coal and timber.

Building railroads in this mountainous region was difficult. Companies often exploited immigrants and other marginalized people, who performed this dangerous and arduous work for low wages. Many of these workers settled in the region. This influx of new people, as well as the freight and passenger trains coming through, forever changed many small towns.

In 2010, the Virginia General Assembly recognized Southwest's rich railroad story and established Virginia's Rail Heritage Region to preserve key sites.

Freight train at Elliston, Virginia, between Roanoke and Christiansburg, 1930s

Special Collections and University Archives, University Libraries, Virginia Polytechnic Institute and State University

"A faint whistle to the west was the first indication of its presence. . . . Sort of spooky sounding through the mountains. I took away the lasting impression of enormity: how the engine towered above its drivers, and how the boiler seemed to extend over the platform (and over my head)."

David Stephenson, train enthusiast recalling a freight train spotting near Elliston in 1957

Trainman cap belonging to Thomas Royal May, mid-1900s

VMHC Collection, Gift of the Family of Thomas Royal May

Thomas Royal May (1895–1970) worked as a "trainman" for the Norfolk and Western Railroad in Roanoke. On passenger trains he collected tickets, made announcements, and opened and closed car doors.

Crew Preparing to Move Old #7, Bluefield, West Virginia, 1955

O. Winston Link Museum and Winston Conway Link

Until the 1940s, work teams—primarily Black men—laid new rail, replaced rotten crossties, and repaired tracks for railroad companies. Known as "Gandy Dancers," they worked in unison wielding five-foot-long bars to inch the track back into line. One member of the gang synchronized the group's movements using song.

"There's a caller there . . . to synchronize the efforts. Cause if you don't . . . everybody is picking up at different times, no man can lift that rail. Now in lining track, you're not only moving the rail, you're moving the entire rail, ties, everything that's there. And that's why it called for tremendous coordination and strength. . . . It's the caller's task to motivate . . . to make certain calls . . . to call upon the strength that they didn't know they had."

Cornelius Wright, retired Gandy Dancer, 1994

NORFOLK AND WESTERN RY. CO.
Virginia Ticket Claim Coupon
V. P.-2
No 84617
To be Retained by Passenger
NOT GOOD FOR PASSAGE

Issued under an order of the Circuit Court of the United States for the Eastern District of Virginia in a suit in equity (No. 578) therein pending between Norfolk and Western Railway Company, Complainant, and Beverley T. Crump, et als., Defendants.

Norfolk and Western Railway Company has, on the date stamped hereon, received in connection with the sale of the ticket of corresponding form and number, the rate designated in the tariff of this Company in effect on date of sale, for travel between points designated hereon within the State of Virginia to which ticket this coupon is attached. This coupon is evidence only of a claim for the difference between the amount received and what would have been the amount if the distance covered by said ticket had been paid for at the rate fixed by the order of the Corporation Commission of Virginia of April 27, 1907, payable only on the order of said court, upon surrender of this coupon in such manner and upon such conditions, when, where and as the said court may by such order impose, provided it should be finally determined in said suit that the said claim is entitled to such payment.

In case the ticket with which this coupon corresponds is presented for redemption, it must be presented at the General Passenger Agent's office, accompanied by this coupon either for surrender or for appropriate notation.

W. B. Bevill
General Passenger Agent.

Norfolk and Western Railway Company ticket claim coupon, 1907

VMHC Collection, Gift of the heirs of A.C. Gordon

Norfolk and Western Railroad timetable pamphlet, 1892

VMHC Collection

NEW RIVER BRANCH.

STATIONS. — WESTBOUND.	No. 49. Daily.	No. 41. Daily.	No. 13. Daily.	No. 15. Daily.
Lv. EAST RADFORD			6.00 AM	11.30 AM
" RADFORD			6.04 "	11.34 "
" ‡New River			6.06 "	11.36 "
" Schooler			6.11 "	. . . "
" Belspring			6.20 "	11.50 "
" Dry Branch			6.30 "	. . . "
" Eggleston			6.41 "	12.11 PM
" Pembroke			6.51 "	12.21 "
" Ripplemead			6.58 "	12.28 "
" Curve			7.06 "	. . . "
" Pearisburg			7.15 "	12.45 "
" Shumate			7.19 "	. . . "
" Narrows			7.23 "	12.53 "
" Lurich			7.33 "	1.03 "
" Glen Lyn			7.38 "	1.08 "
" Wills			7.46 "	. . "
" Oakvale			8.01 "	1.30 "
" Ingleside			8.15 "	1.44 "
" Ada			8.30 "	2.00 "
Ar. BLUEFIELD			ǁ 8.40 "	2.10 "
Lv. BLUEFIELD	7.15 PM	4.20 PM	9.05 "	2.40 "
" Graham	7.22 "	4.27 "	9.12 "	2.47 "
" Falls Mills	7.33 "	4.38 "	9.19 "	2.57 "
" Abbs Valley	7.41 "	4.46 "	9.26 "	3.06 "
" Blue Stone Junc.	7.45 "	4.50 "	9.30 "	3.10 "
Ar. POCAHONTAS	7.50 PM	4.55 PM	9.35 AM	3.15 PM

NOTE. ‡ These trains stop only at West End Curve Bridge.

STATIONS. — EASTBOUND.	No. 14. Daily.	No. 16. Daily.	No. 36. Daily.
Lv. POCAHONTAS	6.50 AM	3.30 PM	1.25 PM
" Bluestone Junc.	6.55 "	3.35 "	1.30 "
" Abbs Valley	6.59 "	3.39 "	1.35 "
" Falls Mills	7.07 "	3.46 "	1.44 "
" Graham	7.18 "	3.58 "	1.53 "
Ar. BLUEFIELD	ǁ 7.25 "	4.05 "	2.00 PM
Lv. BLUEFIELD	7.50 "	4.20 "	
" Ada	8.00 "	4.30 "	
" Ingleside	8.15 "	4.46 "	
" Oakvale	8.30 "	5.01 "	
" Wills	8.41 "	5.12 "	
" Glen Lyn	8.47 "	5.18 "	
" Lurich	8.52 "	5.23 "	
" Narrows	9.02 "	5.33 "	
" Shumate	9.07 "	5.38 "	
" Pearisburg	9.12 "	5.43 "	
" Curve	9.21 "	5.52 "	
" Ripplemead	9.30 "	6.01 "	
" Pembroke	9.38 "	6.10 "	
" Eggleston	9.48 "	6.20 "	
" Dry Branch	10.00 "	6.32 "	
" Belspring	10.09 "	6.43 "	
" Schooler	10.20 "	6.55 "	
" ‡New River	10.24 "	7.00 "	
" RADFORD	10.26 "	7.01 "	
Ar. EAST RADFORD	10.30 AM	7.05 PM	

No. 48.—Daily.
Leave POCAHONTAS . 5.40 PM
Arrive Graham . . . . 6.10 "
Arrive BLUEFIELD . 6.17 "

SALTVILLE BRANCH.

STATIONS. — WESTBOUND.	MILES.	No. 41. Daily Ex. Sunday.	No. 43. Daily Ex. Sunday.
Lv. GLADE SPRING	0	7.30 AM	2.00 PM
Ar. SALTVILLE	8	8.00 "	2.30 "

STATIONS. — EASTBOUND.	MILES.	No. 42. Daily Ex. Sunday.	No. 44. Daily Ex. Sunday.
SALTVILLE	0	10.30 AM	4.00 PM
[illegible]	8	11.00 "	4.30 "

CITY POINT BRANC

Trains leave Petersburg for City Daily, except Sunday, at 8.45 A additional trains on Tuesday, 7 day and Saturday at 1.00 P. M on Tuesday and Friday at 6.00 connecting with Old Dominior Steamers for New York.

Trains leave City Point for burg on arrival of Steamers fror mond and Norfolk.

ON APPLICATION TO CONDUCTOR ONE STOP-OVER will be allowed on FIRST-CLASS THROUGH UNLIMITED TICKETS, stop-over at plea the passenger allowed to holders of SUMMER EXCURSION and WINTER TOURISTS' TICKETS, unless otherwise specified in contract of said .. Stop-over will also be allowed at LURAY, GROTTOES and NATURAL BRIDGE to holders of FIRST-CLASS THROUGH LIMITED TICKETS, and local excursion tickets (return trip), provided destination can be reached within the limit of tickets. No stop-over allowed on any other kind of ticket.

Botetourt Sprs.
Tinker
Mills Mt
Coyners
Bonsacks
PORTERS
Greens Knob
2563
2356
Round Hill
Lick Creek
Glade Creek
Stewarts Knob
2472
Howells Gap
Weaver Knob
Roanoke
Vinton
Wolf Creek
Horse Pen Mt
Ruddell Mt
Falling Creek
Stewartsville
1060
BELT LINE
940
ROANOKE RIVER
Blue Ridge Church
ROANOKE
Mill Mt
Garnard Br.
Mt Pleasant Church
Rorer Mines
Lester
BLACKWATER FORD
WEBBS FORD
HORN'S FORD
McVEIGH'S FORD
HARDYS FORD
Yellow Mt
2191
Windy Gap
Prater Creek
Tory Knob
Hardys Ford
Narrows Creek
Lynville Mountain
2286
Lynville Creek
Buck Mt
1892
Back Creek
2071
Crowell Gap
Little Lynville Creek
B

Restored Norfolk and Western No. 611 steam locomotive, 2019

Tyler Wenzel / Alamy Stock Photo

Norfolk and Western's Roanoke railway works built fourteen J Class steam locomotives between 1941 and 1950. Adorned with Tuscan red running boards and gold-leaf pinstriping, it is among the most powerful locomotives ever built and reached speeds of 110 miles per hour. Engine 611 (also known as the "Spirit of Roanoke") carried passengers from Norfolk, Virginia, to Cincinnati, Ohio, before being retired in 1959.

Topographical map of Roanoke, Virginia (detail), 1963

U.S. Geological Survey

Courtesy of the University of Texas Libraries, The University of Texas at Austin

Long before the railroads arrived, Big Lick was a series of salt marshes. Located along the "Great Wagon Road" used to travel from Philadelphia into the Deep South, a town began to take shape in the 1830s. In 1881, railroad executives chose Big Lick (now Roanoke) as the hub to connect the Shenandoah Valley Railroad and Norfolk and Western Railway. This momentous decision transformed the once small mountain town into an expansive city connecting raw materials, goods, and people from Ohio and Maryland to the port at Norfolk.

DRIVING HOT RODS

In 1916, Virginia banned the production and transportation of alcohol, followed by national Prohibition from 1920 to 1933. Many Southwest distillers risked losing their sole livelihood. They knew, however, that the mountainous terrain made it difficult for federal and state agents to enforce the Prohibition laws. "Moonshiners" hired skilled local drivers to outrun officers on the area's twisting roads in cars with engines modified—hot rodded—to increase speed. The popularity of the modern hot rod craft and the two NASCAR racetracks in Bristol and Martinsville grew out of these legendary mountain chases.

A 1960 Ford racing against a 1961 Chevy at the Roanoke Drag Strip, 1961

From the collection of the Blue Ridge Institute & Museum

SOUTHWEST VIRGINIA HOT ROD TERMS

Deuce: The slang for a 1932 Ford Coupe—a popular car for hot rodding—derived from the French word for "two."

Liquor Car/Hauler: A stock-looking car used to transport illegal whiskey.

Rake: An automobile with a front end lower than the back.

Rigger: A person who builds hot rods and street rods not used in racing.

Squirrel: A person who shows off an automobile at a stop light.

Three on Three: A three-speed transmission with the gear shift attached to the steering column.

Excerpts from *Full Throttle* courtesy of the Blue Ridge Institute & Museum

"[D]rivers would hot rod their cars. The drivers bragged about their racing and they raced each other. That was the beginning of racing as we know it today."

Scott Schumaker, distiller, Marion (Smyth County), 2019

Wendell Scott in his custom #34 car, mid-1960s

Bristol Motor Speedway Photo Archives

Danville native Wendell Scott (1921 – 1990) was an independent stock car racer during the Jim Crow era. He continued to race in the face of racism and threats of violence. Scott holds the distinction of being the first Black driver to win a NASCAR race.

"My brother, Frankie, a cousin and a couple friends came to Bristol with some uniforms we had made up. Our names were stenciled on the back along with Daddy's No. 34 car number. NASCAR officials came [and] . . . said that he couldn't race unless we all shaved our beards. Richard [Petty] just happened to walk by [and] said that all his crew members would grow beards the following week if they didn't let Daddy race. . . . NASCAR kept coming up with stuff like that against Daddy."

Wendell Scott, Jr., 2020, discussing his father's experience as a Black NASCAR driver in the 1960s

The 2019 STP 500 at Martinsville Speedway, 2019

Dough4872 / Wikimedia Commons

Built in 1947, Martinsville Speedway is actually in nearby Ridgeway, Virginia. It is the only racetrack that has been on the NASCAR circuit since its beginning. At a half-mile long, it is the shortest track on the NASCAR Cup Series tour. The track's popularity grew with that of the sport. About 6,000 people watched the first race held there. Today, the attendance is over 44,000.

John Rinehart, 2003

Morgan Miller / Virginia Humanities

John Rinehart (b. 1943) of Franklin County made his first run down the Roanoke Drag Strip in 1958—winning the regional Soap Box Derby. After building his first car in 1975, he became the first modern professional hot rod builder in the Roanoke Valley. Rinehart loves the innovation involved in the building process—making his own parts or hunting them down at junkyards. He built more than ten hot rods for friends and family.

Car quarter panel, 2021

Ford for Front Row Motorsports

VMHC Collection

With 115 laps to go, NASCAR driver Michael McDowell (b. 1984) was involved in a crash that included fifteen cars at Martinsville Speedway on April 11, 2021. Fortunately, none of the drivers was hurt, but this rear quarter panel shows some of the damage from that accident.

Bristol Virginia-Tennessee sign, 2022

Jon Bilious / Alamy Stock Photo

The state line that separates Virginia and Tennessee runs down the center of State Street in Bristol. Half of downtown is in Virginia and the other half is in Tennessee.

PRESERVING FOOD

Living among the rugged mountains of Southwest Virginia meant people had to be thrifty and industrious to have food supplies for the months when goods were not readily available. Taking skills learned from Indigenous people or passed down through their European ancestors, settlers in the area started a now time-honored tradition of preserving food to last throughout the year. Grains were fermented to make "moonshine." Garden fruits and vegetables were pickled. Forest trees were tapped for sweetening syrups, and hunted game and fish were preserved by drying and salting. Many of these foods are still found today at farmers' markets and farm-to-table restaurants.

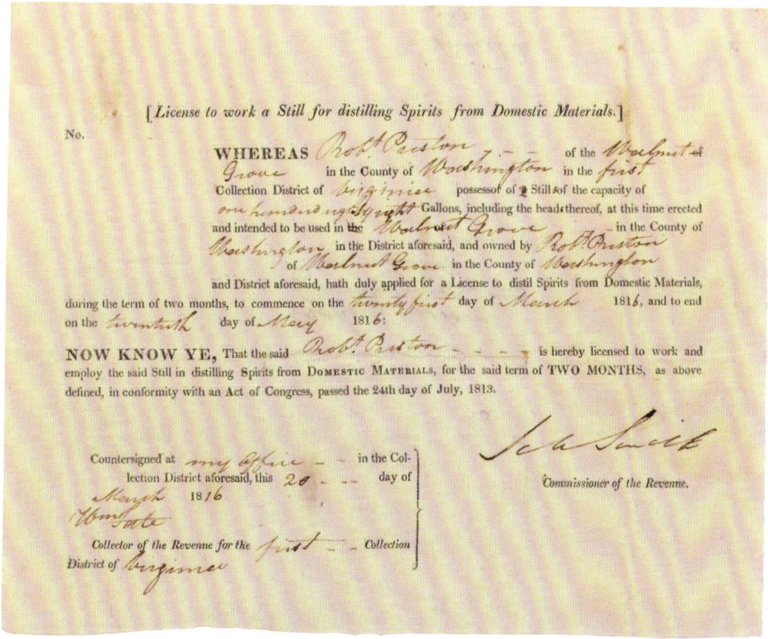

[*License to work a Still for distilling Spirits from Domestic Materials.*]

No.

WHEREAS Robt Preston of the Walnut Grove in the County of Washington in the first Collection District of Virginia possessor of 1 Still of the capacity of one hundred eighty Gallons, including the head thereof, at this time erected and intended to be used in the Walnut Grove in the County of Washington in the District aforesaid, and owned by Robt Preston of Walnut Grove in the County of Washington and District aforesaid, hath duly applied for a License to distil Spirits from Domestic Materials, during the term of two months, to commence on the twenty first day of March 1816, and to end on the twentieth day of May 1816:

NOW KNOW YE, That the said Robt Preston is hereby licensed to work and employ the said Still in distilling Spirits from DOMESTIC MATERIALS, for the said term of TWO MONTHS, as above defined, in conformity with an Act of Congress, passed the 24th day of July, 1813.

Countersigned at my office in the Collection District aforesaid, this 20 day of March 1816

Wm Tate

Collector of the Revenue for the first *Collection District of* Virginia

Commissioner of the Revenue.

Subject: **"PREPAREDNESS"**

The whole nation is talking "PREPAREDNESS," so why not the individual PREPARE? Prepare for the coming prohibition drouth that hits Virginia on November 1st, this year, 1916

On and after that date you will not have the privilege of fortifying your home with pure 100 proof Mountain Rose Corn Whiskey, made and sold strictly on its merits; nothing purer or better for medicinal purposes, regardless of the price you pay.

Good Whiskey will be Hard to Procure

at any price after our state goes dry, and if procured it will cost you three to five times the price I charge you. It will be no bad idea to lay away a ten years' supply of CORN WHISKEY strictly for medicinal purposes, and you will never regret it. Do not fail to include in your purchase ample supply for the coming Xmas holidays, as it is going to be hard on a supposed free people to conform abruptly to the fake prohibition measures. You had better

"Make Hay While the Sun Shines"

Now, in conclusion will say, get your orders in early and avoid the rush that will prevail during the last days of October. Remember that all orders to be delivered in Virginia will have to be placed in due time to be filled and delivered to you on or before October 31st.

Thanking my many friends and customers for their past patronage, and hoping to be of further service in the last days of my present business career, I remain,

Yours truly,

J. H. de-HART,

PROPRIETOR OF

THE MOUNTAIN ROSE DISTILLERY

PHILPOTT, VIRGINIA.

Distilling license issued to Robert Preston, 1816

Deposited by Robert Henley Lamb

In 1816, Robert Preston (1750–1833) obtained this license to distill liquor legally in Washington County. Three years earlier, Congress had imposed licensing taxes on distillers to raise funds for the War of 1812. Distillers who refused to pay the federal taxes could choose to secretly produce illegal spirits at night under the light of the moon—thus the term "moonshining."

"Preparedness" broadside, 1916

The Mountain Rose Distillery

From the collection of the Blue Ridge Institute & Museum

This Patrick County distiller warned locals to stock up on alcohol before new Prohibition laws went into effect in Virginia in 1916. National Prohibition was enacted in 1919 and repealed in 1933.

Copper still, about 1890

VMHC Collection, Purchased with Funds from the Betty Sams Christian Business History Fund

Moonshining is often a family operation, with skills and recipes passed from one generation to the next. This still belonged to the McConnell family of Washington County.

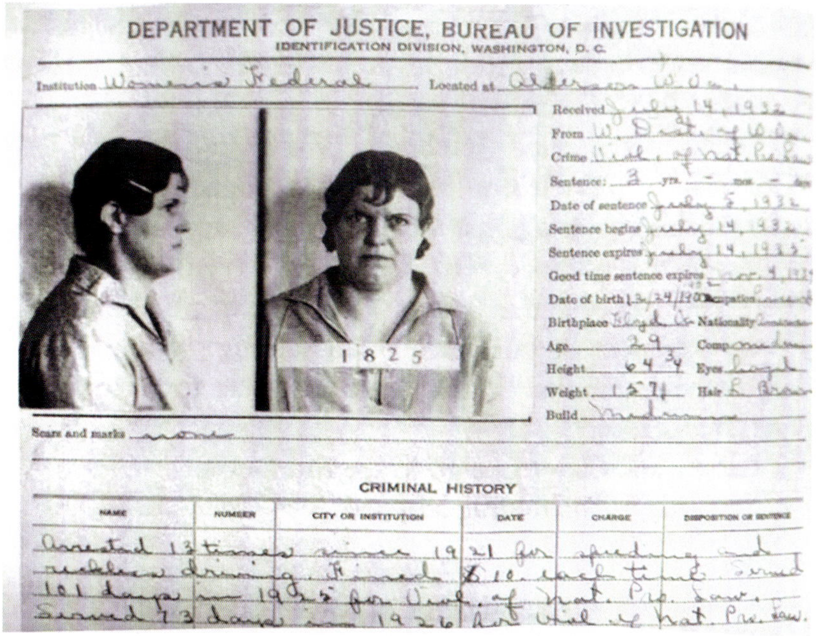
DEPARTMENT OF JUSTICE, BUREAU OF INVESTIGATION
IDENTIFICATION DIVISION, WASHINGTON, D. C.

Institution Women's Federal Located at Alderson W. Va.

Received July 14, 1932
From W. Dist. of W. Va.
Crime Viol. of Nat. Pro. Law
Sentence: 3 yrs. – mos. – days
Date of sentence July 5, 1932
Sentence begins July 14, 1932
Sentence expires July 14, 1935
Good time sentence expires
Date of birth
Birthplace Floyd Co.
Nationality
Age 29
Comp.
Height
Eyes
Weight
Hair
Build
Scars and marks none

1825

CRIMINAL HISTORY

NAME	NUMBER	CITY OR INSTITUTION	DATE	CHARGE	DISPOSITION OF SENTENCE

Arrested 13 times since 1921 for speeding and reckless driving. Fined $10. each time. Served 101 days in 1925 for Viol. of Nat. Pro. Law. Served 73 days in 1926 for Viol of Nat. Pro. Law.

Willie Carter Sharpe, 1932

Department of Justice, Bureau of Investigation

From *Moonshine: A Cultural History of America's Infamous Liquor*, by Jaime Joyce, 2014

Willie Carter Sharpe (1903–?), from Franklin County, was arrested in 1932. According to her criminal record, it was her fourteenth arrest. At her trial, prosecutors claimed that she distributed more than 220,000 gallons of illegal alcohol from 1926 to 1931. Unfortunately, Sharpe didn't smile to reveal a diamond-filled tooth in her mug-shot photograph.

"It was the excitement that got me, outwitting the feds. We were mostly kids who liked the excitement. Cars scattering, dashing along the streets."

Willie Carter Sharpe

Moonshine makers Chris Prillaman (right) and Tanner Talley, 2019

Pat Jarrett / Virginia Humanities

"Making liquor was a way of life around home. The equipment used at the production site is traditional to the mountains of the Blue Ridge. We do not use commercialized column stills. We build or use traditional-style pot stills true to the hills. We use fruit grown on a local lake here in our hometown."

Chris Prillaman, founder and head distiller at the Twin Creeks Distillery, 2020

1st Sugar Moonshine jar, 2020s

Twin Creeks Distillery

From the collection of the Blue Ridge Institute & Museum

When Twin Creeks Distillery began producing liquor in 2014, it became Franklin County's first legal distillery since the 1920s. Distiller Chris Prillaman's family has longtime ties to bootlegging. Some of his ancestors were among the eighty people indicted in "The Great Moonshine Conspiracy Trial" of 1935. The two-month trial exposed a system of bribery and extortion associated with illegal moonshining in Franklin County but did little to curtail it.

Alumni Mall

Torgersen Hall and Alumni Mall at Virginia Tech, 2013

Courtesy of Virginia Tech

In 1872, Addison Caldwell became the first of 132 students to enroll at the all-male Virginia Agricultural and Mechanical College in Blacksburg (Montgomery County). The school provided both classical education and military training. Today, with a diverse community of 37,000 students, the university (now Virginia Tech) is recognized for exceptional agriculture and engineering programs as well as its renowned football team, the Hokies.

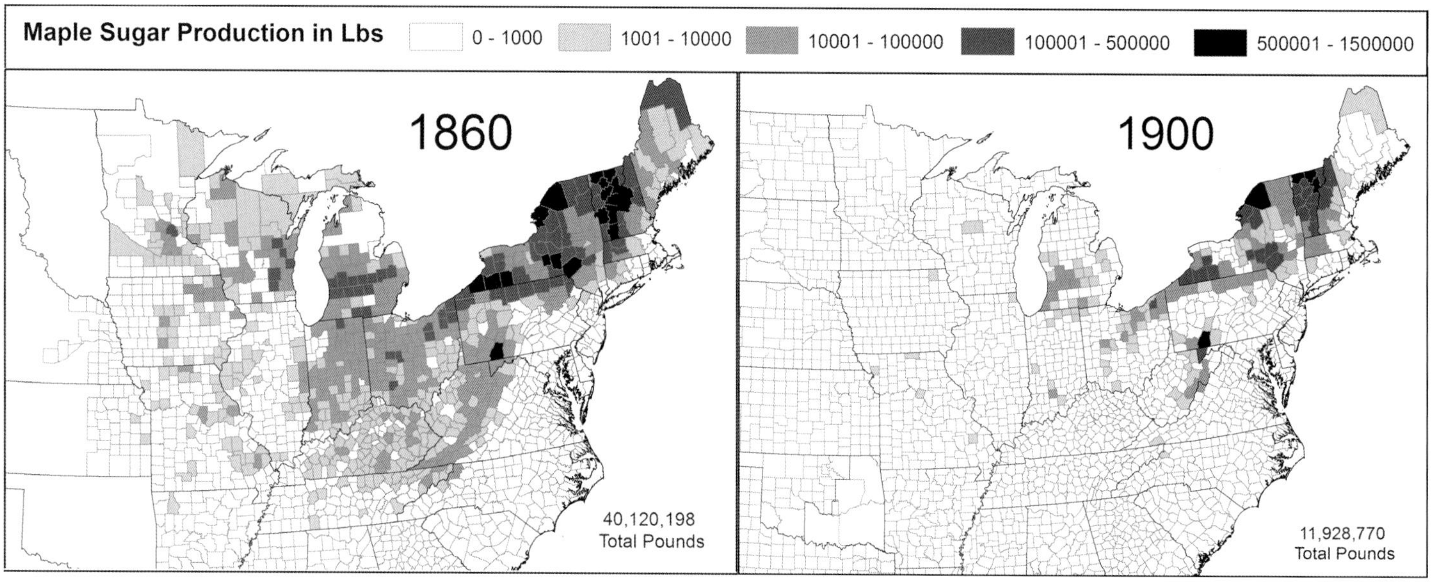

Maps comparing maple sugar production between 1860 and 1900, 2017

Luke Manget / The Southern Highlander

Indigenous people introduced European settlers in Virginia to the practice of tapping maple trees. For centuries, farmers gathered and processed maple sugar to supplement their income. Although many Americans associate Vermont with maple sugar, Southwest Virginia produced hundreds of thousands of pounds of sugar when the industry peaked around 1860. In the late 1800s, changing markets for sugar and the arrival of large-scale timber companies brought a decline in the maple sugar industry in Southwest Virginia.

***Interior View of the Salt-Works*, 1865**

David Hunter Strother (artist); *Harper's Weekly* (publisher)

VMHC Collection

Salt was an essential ingredient used to preserve foods before refrigeration. Since 1782, the residents of Saltville (Smyth and Washington counties) have turned the heavily salted water from underground deposits into usable forms. In the 1890s, the Mathieson Alkali Works began extracting deeper deposits. They produced chlorine, baking soda, and industrial chemicals before closing in 1972. Today, food-grade salt and chlorine for pools continue to be made in Saltville.

Food cellar of Fred and Martha June (Dutton) Hounshell, 1950

Special Collections and University Archives, University Libraries, Virginia Polytechnic Institute and State University

Fred Hounshell (1922–2004) and his wife, Martha June (1926–2018), operated a farm in Black Lick (Wythe County). In addition to organizing storage for root vegetables—such as potatoes—they gathered dozens of jars of preserved vegetables, pickles, jams, and jellies in their cellar to be used throughout the year.

Penny Stilwell, 2004

Morgan Miller / Virginia Humanities

"[C]anning was always just something you did. It was just how we survived. My mother, she canned everything. And she never wrote any of her recipes down. Actually, I don't remember her ever really teaching me about this. I guess I just learned by watching. It was just always around."

Penny Stilwell, Master Canner from Wythe County, 2004

Frances Davis making fried apple pies, 2016

Pat Jarrett / Virginia Humanities

Fried pie is a tradition that arrived in Virginia as Western European immigrants migrated from Pennsylvania in the 1700s and 1800s. The pies look like an empanada or turnover. Filled with apples, peaches, and other fruits, these portable delicacies were easy to transport and eat on-the-go.

"My mother taught us how to cook apples [and] dry the apples on screen doors. [Dried apples] make the best pies. . . . There's a lot of love put into making the pies."

Frances Davis, from Rocky Mount (Franklin County), discussing her famous "fried dried apple pies," 2016

LIVING IN A COMPANY TOWN

The hard-to-reach mountains made it necessary for Southwest families to make their own clothes, blankets, tools, food, and other necessities. The arrival of trains in the late 1800s made importing and exporting items easier, and residents could rely on more store-bought rather than homemade goods.

Railroads also attracted new companies to harness the region's resources. Owners set up towns, jobs, and stores for the local workers. Frequently, an entire community's livelihood revolved around a particular industry or company. Hence, once a mill or mine closed, a whole town suffered.

"[Our town had] just one big company store. Had everything that you needed . . . groceries, farming equipment, shovels, and picks. . . . The biggest thing they had was bibbed overalls. That's what everybody used to wear. . . ."

Kenneth Keys, a former resident of Steinman (Dickenson County), 2016

Laura Lu Scherer Copenhaver, undated

Courtesy of Mr. and Mrs. Tom Copenhaver

In 1916, Laura Lu Scherer Copenhaver (1868–1940) started Rosemont Industries in Marion (Smyth County) to provide economic opportunities for a region underserved by state resources. This craft collective used local materials and artisans to make household items, including coverlets, rugs, and other textiles, in traditional Appalachian designs. The company sold its products worldwide. After she passed away, the business stayed in her family and was later run by her children and grandchildren as Laura Copenhaver Industries, Inc., but ceased operation in 2013.

Lover's Knot coverlet, mid-1900s

Rosemont Industries (manufacturer)

From the collection of Rita and Tim Copenhaver

Woven coverlets (bed coverings) were among Rosemont's best-selling items, and this pattern was in high demand. According to Copenhaver's catalog descriptions, the love knots symbolize "the stability of wedded joy," and the pine tree border suggests the "strength and beauty of the mountains."

"The coverlets are exact reproductions of those woven generations ago. . . . The wool is carded, dyed, spun, and woven in the mountains. From the first wool fiber to the finished coverlet all the work is done in the mountains. Every purchaser is sure of receiving a coverlet direct from the loom."

"Colonial Coverlets," Rosemont catalog, 1927

Woman working at a loom in Southwest Virginia, early 1900s

VMHC Collection, Gift of Robert H. Austin

Southwest Virginia has a long, rich history of textile traditions. Women primarily made home-produced textiles, using locally grown and processed flax and wool. Families passed down techniques and patterns, along with quilts, hand-woven coverlets, and other items made by earlier generations. Despite the rising availability of affordable, commercially manufactured textiles, many Southwest families continued to create their own, preserving the craft tradition and regional designs in the late 1800s and 1900s.

Hettie Roberts, one of the youngest spinners at the Washington Cotton Mills, Fries (Grayson County), Virginia, 1911

Lewis Hine (photographer)

Library of Congress, Prints and Photographs Division, National Child Labor Committee Collection

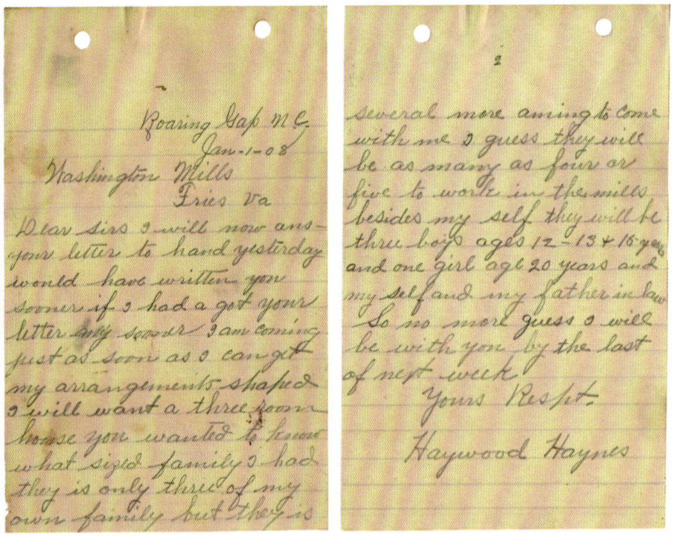

Roaring Gap N C
Jan-1-08
Washington Mills
Fries Va
Dear sirs I will now ans-
your letter to hand yesterday
would have written you
sooner if I had a got your
letter any sooner I am coming
just as soon as I can get
my arrangements shaped
I will want a three room
house you wanted to know
what sized family I had
they is only three of my
own family but they is

2
several more aiming to come
with me I guess they will
be as many as four or
five to work in the mills
besides my self they will be
three boys ages 12-13 + 15 years
and one girl age 20 years and
my self and my father in law
So no more guess I will
be with you by the last
of next week
Yours Resp.
Haywood Haynes

A letter to Washington Cotton Mills about coming to Fries, 1908

Special Collections and University Archives, University Libraries, Virginia Polytechnic Institute and State University

Washington Mills and other companies in Southwest Virginia recruited workers from across the region. In this letter, Haywood Haynes (1885–?) informs mill management that he and his family are coming to work at the mill and that they will need company housing when they arrive from Roaring Gap, North Carolina.

A view of the Washington Cotton Mill (left) and the town of Fries from the New River, 1911

Lewis Hine (photographer)

Library of Congress, Prints and Photographs Division, National Child Labor Committee Collection

The town of Fries—established in 1902—was quickly built to accommodate the families who would work at the nearby Washington Cotton Mill. As with other mill towns, the company owned all the homes and strictly regimented virtually every aspect of daily life. Despite arriving from diverse places, a strong sense of community emerged because the employees shared the experience of working and living in a company town.

"The 'blanket mill,' as it was locally called, was an important industry in the small town of Cedar Bluff and for Tazewell County. Nearly every citizen had a family member who either worked for the mill, did the hand-finish work at home, traded, or sold wool to the mill, or supplied coal to keep the furnaces going."

Kathleen Curtis Wilson, textile historian, 1995

Lap robe or blanket made by the Clinch Valley Blanket Mill, late 1800s to early 1900s

From the collection of the William King Museum of Art, Gift of John Henry and Pat Smith

In 1916, Charles E. Goodwin (1853–1932), who learned the weaving trade from his father, established the Clinch Valley Blanket Mill along the Clinch River. Using water-powered looms and historic patterns, the mill specialized in traditional woven wool coverlets. It also produced lap robes for wagon or buggy travel and supplied blankets to the U.S. Army before ceasing operation in 1950.

Dunbar (Wise County), Virginia, 1930

Westmoreland Coal Company

Hagley Museum and Library

Stonega Coal and Coke Co. opened the Dunbar coal mines in 1919. The company built uniform, two-family-style houses and a Methodist church (left) for the workers. The mine closed in 1952, and many families left in search of other opportunities. In 2020, there were seventy-nine residents living in Dunbar.

Company store of the Raven Red Ash Coal Company, No. 2 Mine (Tazewell County), 1946

National Archives and Records Administration

In communities created by textile and coal mining companies, many workers were paid in "scrip," a company-specific currency that could be used in its general store.

Norton Coal Company $1.00 scrip token, 1940

VMHC Collection

Blue Diamond Coal Co. 5 cent scrip token, 1941

VMHC Collection

St. Charles C. & C. Company 25 cent scrip token, first half 1900s

VMHC Collection, Gift of Robert R. Linkous

FELLING TREES

Birch, hemlock, oak, poplar, gum, and cherry are just a few of the many tree species that populate Southwest's mountainsides and forests. For generations, Virginians have relied on the trees of this region for personal use and for profit. For example, ash trees were made into agricultural tools and pine trees fueled furnaces or were pulped for paper. Logs were hollowed out for canoes, felled for homes and telephone poles, or cut into lumber for boat hulls, house shingles, and fine furniture. Historically, loggers considered Southwest's forests an unlimited resource. Today, harvesters are looking at more sustainable practices.

Logging with horses in Patrick County, 1950s
Earl Palmer (photographer)
Courtesy of Blue Ridge Institute & Museum

"Present lumbering operations . . . due to the depletion of the virgin timber, are carried on exclusively by circular mills, with a capacity of 4,000 to 6,000 board feet daily. The work is done entirely by local labor, and often a mill has to stop operating during the harvesting season or when there is other urgent work on the farm to be done."

Fred C. Pederson, State Forester of Virginia, 1923

Sawmill on Mill Creek at Raven (Tazewell County), early 1900s

Courtesy of the Library of Virginia and the Tazewell County Public Library and Historical Society

The availability of steam-powered engines freed mills from being tied to water. Companies set up temporary sawmills and moved them closer to the sources of timber when an area was depleted. Unusable slabs, sawdust, and scrap wood were burned to provide heat for steam generation. Here David Howard Vance (left) and Lorn McGlothlin (right) work at a sawmill along Mill Creek.

Lick Creek logging camp, Dickenson County, about 1927

Courtesy of Dennis Reedy

Laboring as many as 16 hours a day, loggers often lived in temporary camps built by the company near the forests being harvested. For months on end, they bunked together in drafty "shanties" with few comforts. Loggers needed to consume significant calories to sustain their work, and the camps were legendary for the quantity and quality of food produced by the camp cooks.

Paul Lee logging with pair of horses, 1940

Courtesy of Dennis Reedy

For centuries, horses and mules have offered a reliable and efficient means of getting logs out of the depths of the forest—particularly in areas difficult for machines to reach. Loggers, like Paul Lee, use heavy chains and a variety of hooks to fasten the logs to the horse's harness. Some loggers continue to use horses because of their versatility and low impact on the environment.

Virginia Hardwood Lumber Company families at their company-owned mobile housing, about 1928

Courtesy of Georgia Stacy Havens

"[M]y father worked for the Virginia Hardwood Lumber Company . . . and we had a home on wheels [that ran] on a railroad track. . . . It was pretty neat and different. . . . [T]he train would come by and hook [each car] up, and move it on to the next campsite."

Georgia Marie Stacy Havens, recalling living in a railcar home during the 1930s in Bland County, 2000

"You can still see American chestnut trees in the forests of the Southern Appalachians, but most are small, mere echoes of the giants that once fed wildlife and livestock and provided that famous spreading shade for farmhouses and city streets alike. In the first half of the 20th century, nearly 4 billion of these iconic trees were felled by a lethal fungus known as chestnut blight, and southern forests and their inhabitants were transformed by what has been called one of the greatest ecological disasters of all time."

Meghan Jordan, The American Chestnut Foundation, 2008

Tom Saielli (left) and Jack La Monica pollinate a wild-type American chestnut tree with potentially blight-resistant pollen, 2020

Cindy Ingram (photographer)

The American Chestnut Foundation

Established in 1983, The American Chestnut Foundation aims to restore the chestnut to Appalachian forests. It is developing a tree that has all the traits of an American chestnut but is resistant to the deadly fungus. This has been done, in part, by crossing a Chinese chestnut, which is resistant to the blight, with the American variety.

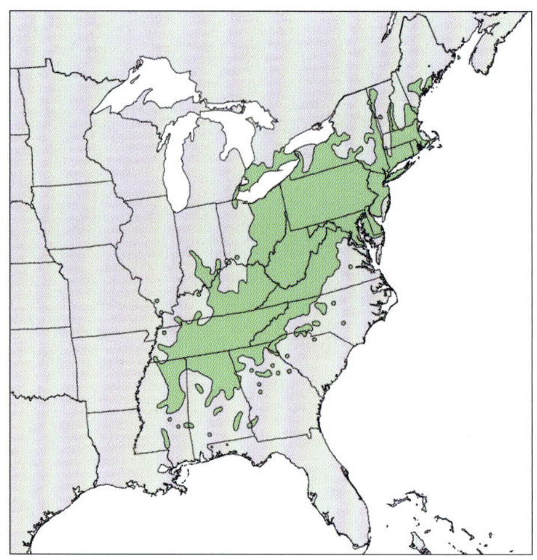

Map showing the natural range of the American chestnut, 1971

From *Atlas of United States Trees* by Elbert L. Little, Jr.

USGS Geosciences and Environmental Change Science Center

MINING FOR COAL

In the 1850s, coal replaced wood as the fuel for America's Industrial Revolution. Its long-burning properties made it particularly effective for manufacturing iron and steel. The demand for coal power skyrocketed with the growth of America's factories, railroads, and cities. Engineers found that Southwest Virginia mountains contained especially deep and high-quality coal deposits.

Coal mining became an important economic driver in the region during the 1900s but removing it from the land was dangerous for workers and the environment. Some companies were indifferent to the health and safety of their employees. Workers in this region made national news in the 1980s when they went on strike to demand better working conditions. Mining continues today but has declined as much of the world seeks cleaner forms of energy. Some abandoned mines have taken on new life as natural resource labs and data storage sites.

I grew up in a coal mining hollow
where the sun is late to shine.
But I'm sure for daddy it grew much darker
as he made his way into the mine.
The days were dark, the nights were darker,
little light did daddy see.
But there in the mines he made a living
For mamma, the rest of the family, and me.

Excerpt from "The Life of a Coal Miner" by Evelyn Cook Davis, who grew up in Coal Bank Hollow (Blacksburg)

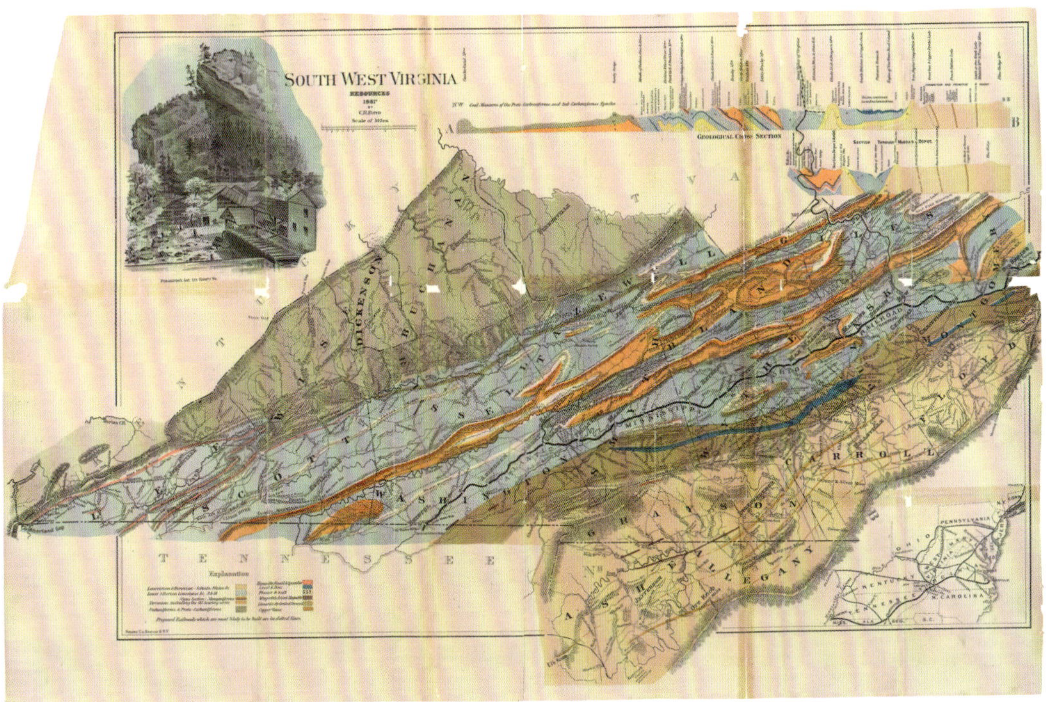

***South West Virginia Resources,* 1881**
Charles Rufus Boyd (publisher)
Courtesy of the Library of Virginia

Most of the coal in Southwest Virginia was created 360–280 million years ago, when the region was much closer to the Equator. Heat, pressure, and the collision of tectonic plates produced Southwest Virginia's seventy-six discrete coal beds. They are remarkable for their low quantities of sulfur and ash. When heated, the carbon-rich product known as coke was ideal for the manufacturing of steel.

Miners at the entrance to No. 8 Mine, Clinchfield Coal Company, 1928

VMHC Collection, Gift of Robert R. Linkous

Organized in 1906, the Clinchfield Coal Company established its headquarters in Dante (Russell County). The railroad and coal industries attracted many immigrants from Central and Southern Europe to the region—particularly people from Hungary, Italy, and Poland—and many settled in the area. Clinchfield was merged into The Pittston Company in 1956.

Mine workers exit Virginia's Pocahontas Mine No. 4 near Richlands, 1974

Jack Corn (photographer)

National Archives and Records Administration

The earliest mine in the Pocahontas Coalfield (Tazewell County) opened in 1883. Coke and coal were transported by train to Norfolk for shipment to other U.S. ports and overseas.

Mining helmet with lamp, 1940s

VMHC Collection, Gift of Robert R. Linkous

Robert "Bob" Linkous (1922–2005) worked in the coal mines for more than thirty-five years. He used this helmet while working for the Linkous Coal Company in Clinchco (Dickenson County). A sticker inside suggests the dangers miners face and provides instructions on what to do when escape from the mine has been cut off.

Kenneth Keys grew up in the Black section of a segregated coal camp in Steinman (Dickenson County) in the 1940s and 1950s. He worked at a conveyor belt sorting excavated slate out of the coal. His father worked in the mine with a team that blasted the coal at night.

"It's so black in there. . . . [Y]ou had big ole lights on your helmet you could see stuff with. . . . [The darkness felt like] something just closing in on you."

Kenneth Keys, recalling working in the mines, 2016

Tazewell County miner drilling a hole in the coal face for explosives, about 1939

Courtesy of the Library of Virginia and the Tazewell County Public Library and Historical Society

Tamping bar, iron needle, and squibs used at Linkous Coal Company, mid-1900s

VMHC Collection, Gift of Robert R. Linkous

Blasting is the process of breaking up coal seams in mine rock walls. First, miners drilled a hole into the wall and stuffed it with explosive powder wrapped in a paper tube. They then used a tamping bar and needle to tamp the powder with incombustible material to limit the blast. Then a "squib" or other type of fuse was inserted and lit to cause the explosion.

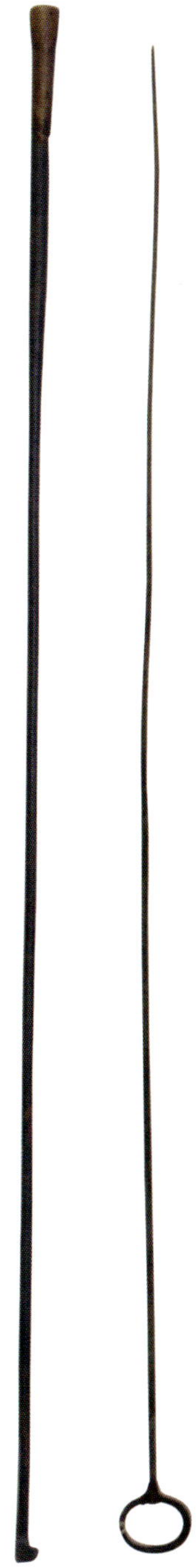

Homemade bird cage, about 1900

VMHC Collection

Among the many hazards of coal mining are suffocation and gas poisoning. From an early date, birds—particularly canaries—were used in coal mines to detect the presence of carbon monoxide. Their rapid breathing rate, small size, and high metabolism made them sensitive to dangerous air quality, and their distress or death was an early warning for miners to evacuate.

Powder can, about 1900

VMHC Collection

Supporters of the Pittston Coal strike bang on pots and pans to gain attention, 1989

Jim West / Alamy Stock Photo

In 1989–90, coal miners went on strike against the Pittston Coal Company after the company announced it was taking away the miners' retirement and health benefits. Their wives ran Camp Solidarity in St. Paul to support the strike. The Pittston Coal strike ended with a restoration of miners' benefits and prompted passage of the Coal Industry Retiree Health Benefit Act of 1992. It is considered one of the most successful labor strikes in the late 1900s.

"[The United Mine Workers of America (UMWA)] have been on strike against the Pittston Coal Group/Clinchfield Coal Company since April 5, 1989. . . . The National Labor Relations Board found Pittston guilty of unfair labor practices, paving the way for the strike. In the first six months, the strike has had 100 percent participation; not a single miner has crossed the picket line to return to work."

Andrew J. Perrin, "Camp Solidarity in Southwest Virginia," *Dissent Magazine*, 1990

"[C]oal country isn't what it used to be. . . . There are not enough jobs to go around, and the jobs we can get pay next to nothing. . . . The good wages that my father and grandfather fought to win are gone. . . . White, black, brown—we're all in this together—fighting for a better life for our families."

Nic Smith, resident of Roanoke, 2016

The Powell River Project, 2020

Justin Perkinson (photographer)

From *Benthos 360*, co-produced with Dr. Matthew Hull

The Powell River Project, established in 1980, is a partnership between Virginia Tech, other educational institutions, environmental organizations, and natural resource industries to improve mine reclamation and environmental management in areas impacted by earlier coal mining.

"Although coal mining dramatically changes the environment, reclaimed mine sites can provide wildlife habitats. . . . Reclaimed mines provide diverse vegetation . . . that may be used by many bird species."

"Enhancing Wildlife Habitat on Reclaimed Mine Lands," a Powell River Project research report on wildlife use of reclaimed mine lands, 2018

Bikers cross Trestle 46 along the Virginia Creeper National Recreation Trail, 2016

Pat & Chuck Blackley / Alamy Stock Photo

Nearly thirty railroad rights-of-way once critical to Southwest Virginia's coal and lumber industries have been converted to recreational areas. Opened in 1989, the Virginia Creeper National Recreation Trail offers 34 miles of scenic hiking and biking between Whitetop (Grayson County) and Abingdon (Washington County).

SCENIC SPLENDOR AND BIODIVERSITY

Southwest Virginia is the Commonwealth's most biodiverse area. The region's varied terrain has created unique habitats and ecosystems that are home to a staggering number of species. One plant—Peters Mountain mallow, discovered in 1927 in Giles County—only grows on the mountain for which it is named! For generations, this biodiversity has attracted hunters, entrepreneurs, harvesters, innovators, and researchers to this region. Today, Southwest's natural areas also draw outdoor adventurers. They hike the rugged terrain, raft the rapids, and run all-terrain vehicles over old train routes.

Cumberland Gap National Historical Park, 2010

Zachary Frank / Alamy Stock Photo

Cumberland Gap is one of the few natural corridors through the Appalachian Mountains and a gateway used by Indigenous people and later settlers moving west into what would become Kentucky and Tennessee. Today, it is part of the stunning 24,000-acre Cumberland Gap National Historical Park.

The Virginia Creeper National Recreation Trail at Green Cove, 2016

Pat & Chuck Blackley / Alamy Stock Photo

The Virginia-Carolina Railroad was completed in 1900 to haul timber between Abingdon, Virginia, and Todd, North Carolina. The steep grade and curves required trains to move slowly, and it became known locally as the "Virginia Creeper." Among its stops was Green Cove station in Damascus (Washington County). Today the abandoned railway is part of a popular rails-to-trails project known as the Virginia Creeper National Recreation Trail.

Wild ponies on Mount Rogers, Virginia, 2021

Cavan Images / Alamy Stock Photo

About 100 wild ponies live along the slopes of Mount Rogers—Virginia's highest peak. Likely the result of local ranchers hoping to breed small horses that could survive atop the Appalachian Mountains, these ponies have been there since the 1940s and regularly delight hikers along the Appalachian Trail. Today, the herds are managed by the Wilburn Ridge Pony Association.

Elk (*Cervus elaphus*), 2021

Mike Roberts (photographer)

Mike Roberts' Outdoors, LLC

Before the arrival of Europeans, herds of native elk could be found grazing in Virginia. By 1855, elk had been driven from the state—the result of over-hunting and the loss of grazing land. Efforts starting in the early 1900s to reintroduce elk across the state met with limited success. Between 2012 and 2014, despite opposition from area farmers, the Virginia Department of Game and Inland Fisheries released 71 elk in Buchanan County with a goal of growing the herd to 400.

"Elk restoration in Virginia is one of the state's most successful restoration projects, with a herd of nearly 200 elk spread across multiple counties in Southwest Virginia, that began with only 71 that were released in 2014. The herd has grown and ventured into other areas in the corner of the state, primarily staying near their original release site in Buchanan County."

Emily George, Virginia Department of Wildlife Resources, 2019

Mountain laurel, 1754
Mark Catesby (artist)
VMHC Collection, Gift of Hartley Graham

English naturalist Mark Catesby (about 1682–1749) traveled to Virginia in 1712 and studied its native plants and animals from the Tidewater region to the Appalachian Mountains. His *Natural History* was the first comprehensive illustrated publication on the flora and fauna of southeastern North America. He noted that the mountain laurel was native to Virginia and how it had an overall "beautiful Appearance."

"The time for the blooming of the azalea and the kalmia (mountain-laurel) was past, but the pink and white rhododendron was in full glory, masses of bloom, not small stalks lurking like underbrush, but on bushes attaining the dignity of trees, and at least twenty-five feet high. The splendor of the forest did not lessen as we turned to the left and followed up Pigeon Creek. . . . Such a wealth of oak, beech, poplar, chestnut, and ash, and, sprinkled in, the pretty cucumber-magnolia in bloom!"

Charles Dudley Warner (1829–1900), writer describing the forests in Wise County, 1889

Green Salamander (*Aneides aeneus*), Lee County, 2017
David Burkart (photographer)
David Burkart

Wise County and the City of Norton are home to more than twenty salamander species—making it one of the planet's most diverse salamander communities. The Green Salamander has a flat body that allows it to squeeze into the crevices of its preferred rocky outcroppings.

"[Usually when] hunting for salamanders you're flipping over logs or rocks on the forest floor or in a stream, and with this thing, you're literally climbing up mountains and getting to a cliff where you're taking a headlamp or flashlight and staring into these tiny crevices and seeing these little eyes staring back out."

Wally Smith, Professor at the University of Virginia College at Wise, 2020

Tom Wieboldt at the Massey Herbarium, 2019

Nancy Sorrells (photographer)

Virginia Native Plant Society

Founded about 1927, the Massey Herbarium at Virginia Tech (Blacksburg) is the largest herbarium in Virginia and includes over 115,000 specimens of vascular plants, fungi, bryophytes, and lichens. Tom Wieboldt curated the collection from 1981 to 2016. He provided plant identification across the Commonwealth and to state and federal agencies and conservation organizations.

"[I started an interest in native plants] early as my father taught me some trees and shrubs. Then as a teen, my neighbor, Peter Mehring, introduced me to birding. . . . We were teenage boys on adjoining farms with access to thousands of acres of field and forest. . . . We divided up plant families to learn so we could teach each other when we were out exploring. We learned from field guides at that time, but then my brother-in-law gave me a copy of Gray's Manual of Botany, 8th edition. I was hooked."

Tom Wieboldt, Former Curator of the Massey Herbarium, 2021

Peters Mountain mallow (*Iliamna corei*), 1989

Discovered in 1927, the small population of surviving *Iliamna corei* is only found in the Narrows, a site on Peters Mountain in Giles County. It is among the rarest native plants in the United States. The Nature Conservancy of Virginia purchased the 398-acre Narrows Preserve specifically to protect Peters Mountain mallow.

AFTERWORD

"What does Virginia mean to you?"

Each day at the Virginia Museum of History & Culture guests are asked to consider that question and share their responses. Most frequently, people mention the beauty and diversity of the landscape and the state's rich, complex, and sometimes painful history. They also joke about traffic and the way Virginians drive, accents, the less-than-obvious pronunciation of place names, and the endless uses Virginians have found for parts of a pig. Some describe their intensely personal relationships with Virginia—being connected to their ancestors, when and how their family came to be here, where they met their partner, and pride in their alma mater. The response we see most often is simply, "Home." The pages of this book feature people, places, and events that not only shape the distinctive character of each region of our Commonwealth, but also our own identity.

Any single volume can only offer an incomplete snapshot of Virginia's ever-evolving stories. This work would be successful if it evoked a sense of place that would be familiar to those who live or have visited here. Our definitions of Virginia's regions could be debated—and should be—because of the diversity that exists within each. Although both can be considered part of Tidewater, the experiences of people in Hampton Roads, for example, are significantly different from those in Accomack County. Likewise, the characteristics featured in each region were informed, in part, by feedback from the people who live there, but are by no means definitive or exclusive. Across the Commonwealth, Virginians honor distinctive features important to their communities, are making art and music, and are developing and adapting both old and new industries.

The Virginia Museum of History & Culture has been the keeper of our Commonwealth's history since 1831. This work is not done simply to be able to know what happened, but because an understanding of the past is critical to shaping our own identity, motivating us to explore and innovate, and to inspire us to make informed decisions for the future. *Our Commonwealth*, both the exhibition and the book, offered opportunities for the VMHC to engage communities from across the state—many of which are not yet well-represented in the museum's 9-million-object collection. In this way the VMHC is better able to fulfill its mission to be able to share the stories of all Virginians for the benefit of future generations.

Virginians have stereotypically been criticized for resisting change, but change is the only constant. Today, a majority of people living in Virginia were born somewhere else. Each lend their unique perspectives, ideas, and traditions to their new communities. As the Commonwealth continues to evolve, so will the Virginia Museum of History & Culture. With each passing year, it will continue to provide the tools that can help people better understand what Virginia means to them.

Young visitors explore the Our Commonwealth exhibition at the VMHC, 2022
Troy Wilkinson (photographer)
Virginia Museum of History & Culture

INDEX